Computer Graphics and Multimedia: Applications, Problems and Solutions

DATE DUE

Demco, Inc. 38-293

IDEA GROUP PUBLISHING
Hershey • London • Melbourne • Singapore

Computer graphics and
multimedia

Acquisitions Editor:	Mehdi Khosrow-Pour
Senior Managing Editor:	Jan Travers
Managing Editor:	Amanda Appicello
Development Editor:	Michele Rossi
Copy Editor:	Sharon Gable
Typesetter:	Jennifer Wetzel
Cover Design:	Lisa Tosheff
Printed at:	Yurchak Printing Inc.

Published in the United States of America by
 Idea Group Publishing (an imprint of Idea Group Inc.)
 701 E. Chocolate Avenue, Suite 200
 Hershey PA 17033
 Tel: 717-533-8845
 Fax: 717-533-8661
 E-mail: cust@idea-group.com
 Web site: http://www.idea-group.com

and in the United Kingdom by
 Idea Group Publishing (an imprint of Idea Group Inc.)
 3 Henrietta Street
 Covent Garden
 London WC2E 8LU
 Tel: 44 20 7240 0856
 Fax: 44 20 7379 3313
 Web site: http://www.eurospan.co.uk

Library of Congress Cataloging-in-Publication Data

Computer graphics and multimedia : applications, problems and
solutions / John DiMarco, editor.
     p. cm.
Includes bibliographical references and index.
  ISBN 1-59140-196-8 (hardcover) -- ISBN 1-59140-266-2 (softcover)--
  ISBN 1-59140-197-6 (ebook)
 1. Computer graphics. 2. Multimedia systems. I. DiMarco, John,
1969-   .
  T385.C5725 2003
006.7--dc22   2003014943

British Cataloguing in Publication Data
A Cataloguing in Publication record for this book is available from the British Library.

All work contributed to this book is new, previously-unpublished material. The views expressed in this book are those of the authors, but not necessarily of the publisher.

Computer Graphics and Multimedia: Applications, Problems and Solutions

Table of Contents

Preface

Making sense of the extensive disciplines and sub-topics within computer graphics and multimedia is a lifelong challenge. No one can be versed in all areas at once due to the vast amounts of information that exists on all the subject areas and due to the dynamic nature of technology. Inevitably, we specialize. Programmers create programs and artists create art. Computer scientists are programmers and artists use computers to paint digitally and perform graphic design. That's the way it is today, is that not accurate? Nothing could be further from the truth. In 1919, Bauhaus pioneer Wassily Kandinsky stated, "And so the arts are encroaching upon one another, and from a proper use of this encroachment will rise the art that is truly monumental" (Packer, xv, 2001). The emergence art that is truly monumental has not yet been seen. The same can be said of technology and science. Of course, time is marked by influential events that shape the history of the discipline, but one monumental event ultimately replaces another. Looking back is essential to growth, but looking forward to "the next big thing" is the prominent response to success. What has emerged on a superficial level is an artistic and technical society that has ingrained disciplinary boundaries that often characterize researchers, scholars, and artists as one-dimensional practitioners that do not stray from their grass roots. This notion has been changed with the growth of digital technology. Technology has promoted interdisciplinary collaboration to become an integral part of mainstream educational practice. Academic programs that institute interdisciplinary projects and exploration have begun to nurture a movement in collaboration that is genuine, exciting, and boundless. This can be seen in distance education trends, interdisciplinary degree programs growth, and the transformation of working individually on a project or being part of a specialized team. In academia, this collaborative approach is born from the need for every scholar to define new applications for development within their specialization. Secondly, the interdisciplinary approach fosters a new multitude of problems that incite exploration of multidimensional and often multidisciplinary solutions.

US VS. THEM

Although collaboration is the goal, often artists and programmers stray from each other's tools, techniques, and processes. Therefore, the debate begins. Here is an example of a typical artist vs. techie debate; What is better to use in web design, HTML hand coding, or WYSIWYG software such as Macromedia Dreamweaver? Is HTML hand coding better than writing the code transparently within an intuitive user interface? Does it truly matter? The result is the same — a web page. Why the debate? Well, we all want to think that our discipline and approach is a better solution. One main cause for tech vs. art is the natural inclination of the masses to view technology as simply a term for computers and peripherals. When in fact, the Greek word *technikos* means **of art**. The word technical is also defined as: *of or relating to technique*. In addition, the word also carries the meaning: *having special knowledge of a mechanical or scientific subject*. Technology is defined by Merriam Webster as: *a manner of accomplishing a task using technical methods or knowledge*. If the word technology is so scientific, where did it find its way into art? Billy Kluver, a Swedish-born engineer in the late 1950s became a chief catalyst for the art and technology movement in the 1960s. Kulver was a pioneering proponent in the marriage between art and technology. Inspired by Aristotle's notion of Techne — in which there was no differentiation between the practice of art and science. Kluver was a crucial conduit in interdisciplinary collaboration between artists and scientists. In a 1996 essay titled, "The Great Northwestern Power Failure," Kluver states, "The artists work is like that of a scientist. It is an investigation which may or may not yield meaningful results; in many cases we only know many years later." Kluver was a visionary who understood the value of technology as a gathering force in collaboration, not a obstacle. The work Kluver accomplished with Robert Rauschenberg in their founded group Experiments in Art and Technology (E.A.T.) was critical to today's interdisciplinary collaborations. E.A.T. encouraged artists and engineers in interdisciplinary technology-based art projects (Packer, 2001).

SHARING WORDS

Highly shared words throughout many disciplines, computer graphics and multimedia have become foundations for scholars to explore within their own contexts. The terms are found universally throughout many disciplines that bear no resemblance to each other in purpose, process, and output. It is appropriate that the digital scholar is to understand, embrace, and explore the countless tributaries of opportunity that exist within computer graphics and multimedia. Within concentration areas, there exists a mountain of terms that has an immeasurable amount of specialization and hybrids. Each one is important in the unique function of a particular problem. Engagement of unknown areas is critical to developing a true meaning for the word technology.

BOOK ORGANIZATION

This book has a diverse authorship that spans several disciplines, countries, and levels. Specifically, three main areas are focused on. Section I is *Digital Design*. Chapters in this section explore topics within digital design education, production, culture, and techniques. Section II is *Computer Science*. Chapters in this section provide extensive insight into computer science research topics including 4d visualization, virtual environments, graph aesthetics, and video indexing. Section III is *Multimedia and New Media*. This section contains chapters that cross boundaries between digital design and computer science. However, because the chapters engage multiple media and integrate interactivity in the discussion, they are classified as multimedia or new media chapters within this text. The topic areas include Macromedia Flash programming, digital asset alignment and management, analysis of digital audio, and machine vision in the arts. This diverse array of art, technology, and science all come together to make up a small piece of the vast subject we know as computer graphics and multimedia. One major goal of this text is to enable the reader to open their minds to the extensive journeys that can be taken exploring merely one specialization in computer graphics and multimedia. This book also hopes to encourage artists to understand and embrace collaboration in science and technology. And to encourage scientists, engineers, and techies to open the doors to collaborative interdisciplinary projects allowing scientists and artists to come together as hybrid technologists who share the same vision and principles towards problem solving, but do not share the same educational, experiential, and technical backgrounds.

There are 12 chapters in this book. They are fairly divided between digital design, computer science, and multimedia/new media. Here is a brief description of each chapter's significance.

Section One: Digital Design

Chapter One, *Teaching Computer Graphics and Multimedia: A Practical Overview*, analyzes and identifies problems and solutions facing the digital teaching professional. The text develops a dialogue for new and existing instructors to understand and utilize in their digital teaching. The principles behind the chapter guide the reader into a practical understanding of rudimentary pitfalls, successful strategies, technology issues, and communication techniques that are imperative to teaching digital subject matter.

Chapter Two, *Digital Prepress: Issues and Solutions for the Preparation of Print Media*, addresses the changes that have occurred in the print design industry as a result of the digital revolution. The text focuses on print media and its preparation in the world of digital technology. This chapter highlights common problems and concerns that are present in the design, production, and output of print media.

Chapter Three, *Screenspace*, the author takes a fascinating journey through Tokyo landscape to uncover the Screenspace and Cellspace that has engulfed the lives of the Japanese. Fully interactive cellphones and jumbo LED displays have become commonplace in urban life. This chapter crosses boundaries into multimedia and ultimately describes the technical, virtual, and digital re-design of a living environment and culture as a result of integrating technology into everyday life. This text also places the screen into the true context it occupies in real life.

Chapter Four, *How to Use Photoshop to Improve the Gestalt of an Image*, develops an understanding of visual communication through images. The chapter discusses the composition of forms within the image having a structure, or Gestalt to carry the content through the end-user's perception process to a state of understanding. Discussions are included on the use of Adobe Photoshop for cleaning up distracting visual trash such as dust, hair, scratches or unwanted objects. Systematic directions and examples explain the entire process.

Section Two: Computer Science

Chapter Five, *Adaptive Narrative Virtual Environments*, will explore the technologies and issues surrounding Adaptive Presentation Management for Narrative Virtual Environments. Discussion will also examine the subject in a broader context, with regards to plans for enhancements and future systems in order to make VE technology more accessible to a wider range of applications in areas such as education and training, visualization, and communication, and even to enable new types of entertainment and games. Some of the burden of managing the presentation should be lifted from the designer and the user, and placed on the computer.

Chapter Six, *Isoluminance Contours: A Fast, Simple Model for 4D Animated Visualization*, presents important background information on 4d visualization. The chapter highlights the Isoluminance Contour Model that not only provides a quick and easy method for generating images, but also dramatically reduces the amount of work required by traditional computer graphics methods. This chapter introduces the ICM for visualization, chronicles successful research findings and presents tangible results.

Chapter Seven, *Content-Based Video Indexing and Retrieval*, presents recent advances in digital video compression and networks. Content based video retrieval systems are reviewed and a new framework called *ClassView* is proposed to make some advancement towards more efficient content-based video retrieval. The chapter highlights several advances in video retrieval. The proposed framework includes efficient video content analysis, a hierarchical representation scheme, and a video database indexing structure.

Chapter Eight, *Evaluating Graph Drawing Aesthetics: Defining and Exploring a New Empirical Research Area*, describes a long-term project to investigate the validity of the design principles on which many automatic graph layout algorithms are based, not from the perspective of computational efficiency, but from the perspective of human comprehension. The chapter summarizes all the empirical work the author has done on the effectiveness of 2D graph drawing aesthetics. It also describes the process of initiating a new experimental research area, and of developing a framework for empirical studies within the area, with specific reference to the experimental methodology and statistical analysis issues involved.

Section Three: Multimedia/New Media

Chapter Nine, *Client and Server Side Programming Concepts Incorporating Macromedia Flash*, explains that the motion graphics and authoring package is more than a graphic arts program. This application allows the designer to create a true and unique graphical user interface (GUI). This GUI can be precisely programmed to support end user interactivity. Flash is not limited to the World Wide Web, however, it has found tremendous treatment in this arena. The general perspective of this chapter is to discuss Macromedia Flash as a tool for the delivery of multimedia content via the World Wide Web. In addition, object oriented programming and server-side scripting will also be addressed within and related to the context of this application. Short tutorials will reinforce the subject matter. These will enhance the reader's understanding in gaining a deeper perspective of Flash. This chapter will also address Flash's place in the many avenues and perplexities of web applications.

Chapter Ten, *Everything That Can Communicate Will: Aspects of Digital Asset Alignment and Management*, deals with the concept of aligning and managing digital assets as a reaction to the evolution of digital production and digital networks. This chapter highlights digital asset management as it relates to value and importance in the roles of digital liquidity, digital continuity, and digital viability.

Chapter Eleven, *Analysis of Musical Content in Digital Audio*, discusses how automatic analysis of digital audio with musical content is a difficult but important task for various applications in computer music, audio compression and music information retrieval. This chapter contains a brief review of audio analysis as it relates to music, followed by three case studies of recently developed systems that analyze specific aspects of music.

Chapter Twelve, *Certain Aspects of Machine Vision in the Arts*, attempts to consider the consequences of machine vision technologies for the role of the image in the visual arts. After a short introduction to the topic, the text gives a practical overview of image processing techniques that are relevant in surveillance, installation and information art practice. Example work by practitioners in the field contextualizes these more technical descriptions and shows how computational approaches to digital imagery can radically expand the use of the image in the arts.

–John DiMarco
Long Island University, USA

REFERENCES

Heller, S. (1998). *The Education of an Graphic Designer*. New York: Allworth Press.

Heller, S. (2001). *The Education of an E-designer*. New York: Allworth Press.

Packer, R., & Jordan, K. (2001) *Multimedia: From Wagner to Virtual Reality* (pp. xv, xvii, 17, 33, 34). W. W. Norton & Company, Inc.

Acknowledgments

I would like to thank several groups of special people who have been inspirational and vital to the success of this project.

To the editorial staff: Initially I must thank the superb staff at Idea Group Inc. for their invaluable support throughout this process. Mehdi Khosrow-Pour, Jan Travers, Michele Rossi, Amanda Appicello and Jennifer Sundstrom were tremendous at helping to develop and deliver this project.

To the reviewers: I would like to sincerely thank the following reviewers for their valuable time, expertise, and constructive solutions during the review process: Dr. Eun Jung Holden and Mr. Sam Yeates of the University of Western Australia, Professor John Fekner of Long Island University, Professor Kevin Jones of University of Oregon, Dr. Karl Steiner of the University of North Texas, Dr. Marion Cottingham of the University of Western Australia, Dr. Mark Snyder of Clemson University, Dr. Robert Barone of Buffalo State College, Dr. Fan and Dr. Xiao of the University of North Carolina, Professor Richard Del Rosso of Long Island, and Professor Tom Emmerson of AGS Media Corp. and Nassau Community College.

To my colleagues: My appreciation and gratitude runs deep for the important people who have helped me in my professional career. They are John Fekner, Lynn Croton, Richard Mills, Dr. Najarian, Ali Atieh, Jason Gorman, Kathy Yanatos, Tom Alma and Denise DiGiovanni.

To my family and friends: I would need more space than allowed if I was to thank all the important people close to me. First I want to thank my great friends Steve, Debbie, Joey and Laura, Alex, Joe, Brad, Huck, Dav, Napoli, and Ferrari for giving me the gift of laughter throughout my life.

My parents, John and Frances DiMarco must be gratefully thanked for providing me the opportunities to succeed and to explore my dreams. Mom and Dad, I am sincerely grateful for your love and support. I also need to acknowledge my great family: Roseann, Margaret, Jerry, Joseph, Alexis, Gina, and my godmother Dorothy Flammia. In addition, I would like to acknowledge the Borowski family and Florence Borowski. Also, let me thank Karen, Paul, Paulie, Ginger, Brianna, and Tori Lawrence, my new family: thanks for letting me marry Kimberly.

And lastly, I have to say a very meaningful thank you to my partner, my love, and my life, my incredible wife Kimberly. Thanks for letting me spend countless nights in the office and for giving me help and inspiration in life. To you, I am truly thankful.

John DiMarco
Assistant Professor
Long Island University, C.W. Post

SECTION I

DIGITAL DESIGN

Chapter I

Teaching Computer Graphics and Multimedia:
A Practical Overview

John DiMarco
Long Island University, USA

ABSTRACT

This chapter defines and examines situations, problems, and processes faced by teachers of technology. Based on experience teaching at three colleges with different economic, academic, ethnic, and financial attributes, this chapter provides stable and practical approaches to solving common issues. Each school environment and student population presents different technical and interpersonal challenges. Real experiences involving set up of college laboratories, development of digital curriculum, and creation of accredited programs are highlighted and transferred into tangible strategies. If you are new to teaching digital subjects, this text may help you get started. If you are an experienced teacher, this may bring you a new strategy or perspective. Ultimately, this chapter aims to assist student teachers, experienced teachers, artists, information technologists, and computer scientists in becoming stronger in transferring knowledge and skills in the digital realm. In addition, the chapter hopes to invite scholars and educators to explore teaching computer graphics and multimedia within the context of their own disciplines.

INTRODUCTION

The teaching of technological output requires every student to get value from his or her experiences within the laboratory environment. The coursework and laboratory work that challenges a student should simulate real conditions. Course problems should present both conceptual and technical challenges to students. As a digital design professor, I feel that all "digital teachers" have a great responsibility to students. We must transfer knowledge and skills at the highest levels. We must be thorough in our approaches and precise in our criticisms. We teach what we know and must know what we teach. We must teach using real-world materials and techniques. Although we may have varied control over curriculum directions, we do have control over our success or over that of our students. We must encourage participation, communication, responsiveness, and critical thinking about design and final output. We must always encourage and never insult. We must facilitate practice — and plenty of it. We must be lifetime learners. We must have a personal technology budget. We must be empathetic toward the problems of the individuals we teach. We must take responsibility for the success of the students in our courses. We must care and commit to excellence.

MOTIVATION AND CONFIDENCE
Clear Your Mind and Prepare for Intense Mental Challenges Ahead

Go into the teaching environment with a clear head and focus on the task at hand. It is nearly impossible to communicate effectively when you have worries or problems on your mind. You can use concentrated breathing right before class to free your mind and body of negative energy. Here's how:

1. Sit down (preferably on the floor or on a comfortable chair)
2. Raise your arms and breath deeply with big inhales and exhales for seven to 10 repetitions

3.   Concentrate on only your breathing, repeat raising your arms, and take five deep breaths
4.   Relax your mind and empty it of all thoughts
5.   Get up slowly and focus on the task at hand
6.   Review and talk out your lesson outline before leaving the house
7.   Arrive at class a few minutes early — rushing will raise stress levels

Remember that teaching computer classes is a mental workout. It makes your mind move rapidly through a barrage of material. It requires you to take information and present it in a hierarchical structure. That requires clear thinking! Here are some tips to help build confidence and success.

Walk Around the Class Frequently

If possible, make it a point to stand briefly near each student. Doing this generates attentiveness and immediately revives a bored student. Mobility keeps people awake!

It is essential to engage students freely and often. It induces interactive communication and results in illustrating your teaching style as a "hands-on" approach. Stay in tune with student work to nurture revision and improvement. Take pride in the project's success: the student is a product of your guidance and cultivation.

How do you stay mobile? Wear comfortable shoes — you will be on your feet. And make a 10-minute rule. If you are seated for 10 minutes or more, get up and walk around. It will keep you sharp and the class listening and alert.

Avoid Frustration

Frustration is one of the biggest obstacles for computer teachers. You must be able to reverse negative student attitudes. You must be able to deal with people who, at first, do not get it. No matter how much you repeat, they do not understand and cannot execute. Try to refrain from berating foolish questions. Be critical, but kind. Become the nicest person you can be — then get even nicer. Being friendly results in relaxation and comfort for the student. Be friendly, but firm. Expect results and anticipate initial failure. Be ready to console and control the negative situation. This is extremely important in the arts where creativity must flow freely. Whoever said "patience is a virtue" never taught computer-based coursework. Do not crack under pressure. Being a computer teacher requires the patience of a saint. Why? Because every time you have a class that exceeds one person, you have students who have different levels of knowledge and skills with computers. Unless you are teaching an introductory course in computer basics with a room full of blank slates, you will have some students who are more knowledgeable than others. Students may walk into class who have never have touched a computer. In that same class, there may be students who have used computers at home, at school, at work, or in prior training and coursework. You may have a disruptive student or an extra-experienced one who wants to stump the teacher with outlandish or unrelated personal equipment questions that cause class flow to be halted. In the classroom, your brain will be torn in many directions. Do not give up. Stay with it.

Remember Who Controls the Class — You Do!

You control the class, the class does not control you. Therefore, you should set a pace appropriate for your teaching speed — not appropriate to the levels of one or two students. Do not try to cover an abundance of material to satisfy one advanced student. You will end up losing the rest of the class. Let the student explore advanced techniques on their own time or during individualized help sessions with you. Do not lower the goals of the class to cater to one student. We work in a competitive world where computer art and multimedia may not be for every student. Let students understand the responsibilities involved in learning. Both the teacher and student are responsible for success. Without mutual effort, respect, and extensive communication learning will be retarded. Allow a lagging student to work under less intensive criteria; in an academic setting, however, grade accordingly. Sometimes it is best to allow an advanced student to explore new concepts and techniques. Encourage the right students to accelerate or to slow down while keeping the entire class working on the same project at the same pace. This seems like an impossible equilibrium, but try to achieve it. This helps when demonstrating techniques. It helps eliminate premature and old questions.

STUDENT INTERACTION

Motivate Students by Relating Hard Work to Tangible Reward, Not to Academic Failure

Be a coach. Install a winning attitude in every student! Make your class a win-win situation for all students. Let them know that the efforts they put in during class sessions will reap rewards later in their careers. Equate effort to success. Learning computer graphics and multimedia requires a concerted effort toward success. This must include diligent work inside and outside of the classroom and the computer lab. It requires a commitment to lifelong learning and the expansion of skills that occur regularly throughout one's career. Students have to buy into the fact that you are not just their teacher, but also an expert and a valuable resource for them. They have to trust your abilities and they have to share a common goal with you — their success. I believe that a teacher on the college level should try to avoid threatening students with bad grades; rather, make students aware that their grades rely upon success in the course and the projects assigned. Students' success is directly related to effort inside and outside the classroom. Here is my philosophy — I share these thoughts with my students on the first day of each new course:

> *To learn our craft, we must practice. Practice takes the form of projects. Projects must be completed to succeed in the courses. Completed, well-done projects in our portfolios and backgrounds help us get new projects and jobs. Projects portray our skills, abilities, and experiences. Make your portfolio scream of completed projects and you will succeed in getting the opportunities you want.*

Determine "Can't Do Students" from "Won't Do Students"

Throughout my career, different types of students have challenged me in valuable ways. I have had to learn how to guide them to meeting goals. I categorize notably challenging students in two ways: "can't do students" and "won't do students".

The reasons behind both types of students may be abundant. However, I have found that there are general consistencies between each type. Determining student type and motivation will help you in your goals to help these students succeed in the course, and inevitably to build confidence, skills, knowledge, and work.

"Can't Do Students"
- May have personal problems that are affecting class involvement (missing class for work or illness)
- May not have the time to devote to practice and/or to continued learning
- May not have the resources (lacking a computer at home or the proper software)
- May lack prerequisite skills
- May have a learning disability

"Won't Do Students"
- Put obstacles first and success last
- Always have a list of excuses for not practicing or completing projects
- Battle tooth and nail before joining the pace of the class
- Ask meaningless and obscure questions to help interrupt the flow of the class
- Venture off on their own, not following class procedures and lectures
- May feel they have superior knowledge or experience over the instructor and feel the class is a waste of time for them

Sound familiar? If you have taught computer graphics, you may have encountered these challenging students. We will explore how to make them successful.

Talk to Students and Give Out Initial Assignments to Discover Who is a "Can't Do" or a "Won't Do" Student

A little conversation and some simple questions will go a long way when trying to determine "can't do" students from "won't do" students". I want to learn about my students so I can identify potential highlights and possible problems.

Initially, get to know your student's approaches to his or her own career. What do they plan to do when they graduate? What medium and technology are they most interested in? Ask about prior classes, teachers, outside experience, and determine their genuine interest in the subject. If enthusiasm is low or if the student begins to complain about a former teacher, do not embark on the past obstacles — instead, help become a catalyst for change. Reassure the student that you are committed to their success in this course. Explain that with cooperation, trust, and collaboration, everyone wins. Let the student know that you have the confidence that they will succeed. Always avoid negative comments or confrontation.

An effective method to begin to identify certain student types is to assign a simple homework problem that involves brainstorming on paper. This can be applied to projects including database development, programming, graphic design, multimedia, web design, and video production. I usually make each student begin to write out concepts, metaphors, interaction, messages, and prospective images for the term projects. I require everyone to do it. Those students who do not complete the assignment can be assumed to be possible "won't do" students and will require extra encouragement and more one-on-one time during the learning process. You must continue to work with "won't do" students to help facilitate involvement. Sometimes "won't do" students will require extra attention and extended feedback on projects to continue valid participation.

When you encounter "won't do" students who insist the projects are below their expectations or abilities, allow them to develop their own approaches. However, specify that they are subject to your approval. This will allow you to monitor the situation to insure the proper focus is maintained. Nevertheless, it will also allow the students to explore new and advanced territory. The result could be extraordinary work.

"Can't do" students need extreme focus to succeed in the digital realm. They will be identified during the first or second project. To help them succeed, practice time must be multiplied, hands-on instruction should be increased and, in extreme cases, students may need to be asked to explore prerequisite courses, possibly more than once. Because "can't do" students often require extra time to complete projects, this will inevitably disrupt the flow of the course during the term. Try to keep all of the students on schedule. Encourage and assist slower students to catch up by increasing practice time and simplifying project approaches and, perhaps, possibly criteria.

Develop an Approach for Each Type of Student: New, Experienced, Young, and Older

Embrace the new challenge, understand it, and conquer it. Your student populations will be a collaboration of diverse personalities, backgrounds, skill sets, dispositions, and problems. We have to embrace this fact and figure out how to cater to everyone's uniqueness in the classroom. Sounds daunting, I know. It's one of the hardest challenges to teaching digital curriculum — managing people and personalities to encourage creativity and generate results in the form of projects.

Controlling Unfavorable Situations

You must control the situation, but never become confrontational, regardless of the student's tone. Always be serious, but never angry. Listen first to understand, then explain clearly to be understood. If you feel that you are out of control, take a class break and calm down. Then discuss the incident with the person after class so that other students are not involved. This helps avoid feelings of embarrassment for you and for the student.

Your goal is to make all parties involved happy. Convey the fact that you always want a win-win situation and the student to be ultimately happy and satisfied. Show the student that you are there to help, not hinder. Let the student know that you are a resource for them to utilize. This type of giving approach will help generate trust, admiration, and connection between you and your students. Above all, be empathetic to the student's problems and concerns.

Make Proper Ergonomics a Priority for You and Your Students

Everyone will be happier and healthier when they sit properly. Ask students to sit, put their feet flat and have both hands ready to use the computer. Institute a "two hands at all time rule" because it will keep students alert and working properly. You cannot slouch at a computer and use two hands. It is impossible. Should you request that students use two hands on a computer? I explain to students that in the "real world", (I refer to the "real world" often), creatives are paid by the time they spend on projects. All programs have shortcut keys (such as "apple + z" or "control + z" to undo) and all graphics and layout programs have multi-key combinations that are needed for performing certain functions (for example, to scale an object and keep it's aspect ratio, you must hold shift in most programs). Therefore, using two hands becomes the professional approach that everyone should emulate.

Ergonomics is the study of the human body at work. As a science, it has roots in the industrial revolution. Initially, time and motion studies were used to improve workers' performance. Today, computing and medical societies realize how important it is to health.

Besides efficiency, maintaining sound ergonomics helps to eliminate physical stresses that working on computers can foster. Pain in the wrist, forearm, back, neck, and legs can be lessened or eliminated by employing sound ergonomic components including a drawing tablet, a good chair, proper posture, adequate lighting, and an appropriately-sized workspace. These assets may not be present in your teaching environment. You should try to obtain as many as possible because they make a difference in the quality of work and student success.

TEACHING STRATEGIES FOR BUILDING SUCCESS

Understanding Your Objectives

The first question that must be clarified before you start to teach is, "What are my objectives?" What do I want to accomplish? What goals are to be met? There are certain state standards that must be reached when teaching in a public school setting. In college there are certain standards for each department and there are certain requirements that must be enforced for institutional accreditation. With all of those standards and objectives, why do we need anymore? The objectives discussed here are important to the success of a teacher of computer graphics and multimedia in any discipline. I stress the word success. In my opinion, this list has no particular order.

- *Objective:* Introduce new techniques and technologies to the student.
- *Objective:* Develop style by discussing historical and professional references.
- *Objective:* Adhere to your prescribed "state standards" if they dictate curriculum.
- *Objective:* Teach the student new vocabulary related to the technology and design process.
- *Objective:* Develop student understanding of the design process and its relationship to solving problems and completing projects in their discipline.
- *Objective:* Develop "computer confidence" in the student.
- *Objective:* Motivate the student to cultivate new creative concepts, approaches, and content into their work.
- *Objective:* Transfer practical skills and pass on real world experiences to students.
- *Objective:* Direct the student towards completion of a tangible project that is portfolio-ready.
- *Objective:* Critique student work and offer critical feedback and guidance on design, usability, visual, presentation, and commercial strength.
- *Objective:* Present student work to a broad audience (web portfolios).

Focusing on these objectives will help you and your students succeed. Remember: begin with the end in sight. You want your students to finish the course with a new interest in the subject, exposure to jargon and vocabulary words, confidence that they can use computers effectively, and an understanding of the design process within their discipline. You also want the student to develop a new skill set, portfolio-ready projects, and an understanding of how feedback can improve project strength.

Teach in Outlines

Teaching in outlines presents information in a hierarchical structure. Structure allows students to grasp the information in steps. Each step is a building block to the next step. Without the hierarchical structure, there is confusion on appropriate direction and process.

For example, students in a digital imaging class are using Adobe PhotoShop. What tools or techniques are taught first? What project will be issued to reinforce the use of those tools and techniques? Should digital painting techniques or image manipulation be taught first? What about production using layers and paths? What do we lecture about on the first day? Development of a hierarchical structure is vital to teaching computers, graphic design, and multimedia.

Here's how to teach in outlines. First, perform research. Acquire books, articles, and web content on the technology and curriculum samples or cases. Go to publishers' and booksellers' websites to get abstracts and table of content samples. Read them to discover and learn about the things that are unfamiliar to you. Create a simple list of five major areas that seem important to the technology. Create an outline of these five topics. Write down important information regarding the technology and the applications. Specifically, understand what tools and applications are used to execute projects to completion. Remember to look for hierarchical structure. See how the various books and articles describe use of the technology. Take note of chapters and content. Does the book seem to move from beginner techniques to advanced? Examine other digital curriculums related to your discipline to expand your thoughts on subject hierarchy. Once you feel comfortable understanding the flow of information and the design process needed to complete a project, document it in a lesson plan. Then follow the steps in the plan to completing the process and complete the project. Alternatively, jump around through the table of contents of books to scrutinize the proper hierarchy to fit your lesson plans. Keep it simple. Don't overload your students or yourself with too many concepts too fast. Stick with the hierarchy and the outline. Your major topic outline will help you to figure out what to teach without overwhelming you with too much information. This is crucial to learning in small steps. Small steps in learning will ultimately develop a complete understanding of the subject.

Use a Topic Outline

The topic outline should include this information:

1. *Provide an overview of the technology to the class.* Explain what medium the technology is used for (TV, computer kiosk, video, gaming, print, etc.). Provide the names of the companies who make the applications. Give an overview of the class projects that will be created using these tools and technologies.

2. *Present some new, vital vocabulary words.* These will come up so you need to clarify them early. Explain resolution to a digital imaging class or vector graphics to a digital illustration class on the first day.

3. *Describe the tools, palettes, and menus in overview form.* Use metaphors to relate the fine art world with the digital art world. For example, talk about Adobe PhotoShop having a canvas, a palette, and brushes all for painting — digital, of course.
4. *Describe the creative design process* that the class will go through to develop concepts, source materials, and content for the projects. Plant seeds in students' minds so that they will have creative control and consistently generate new approaches to their art, design, programming, multimedia, and communication pieces.

Talk About it First to Get Feedback and Levels of Experience

Always discuss the subject before everyone jumps to use the computers. Make your discussion interactive. Don't just lecture — question. Make a strong appeal to have the entire class give answers. What are you asking? Questions that you have devised from your outline. These questions will help you gain an understanding of the experience levels of your students. It will also help generate some background information on the students that may come in helpful later. Shy students, talkative ones, highly experienced, inexperienced, and exceptional students will all coexist within your learning environment.

Have a general discussion that involves the class. Begin with a question directly related to the name of the course. WHAT IS DIGITAL VIDEO? What does digital mean? Does our VCR play Digital Video? These are the questions I ask eager students. Who has heard of Adobe Premiere or Apple Final Cut Pro? What do they do? Who in the class has used them?

When you ask with enthusiasm and you demand involvement, students respond. You will notice that everyone is thinking. There is no better gratification for a student in class then presenting the right answer in a class discussion. Students strive for it. They may give all the wrong answers, but that's fine at this point. The chance to give the right one is worth it. The main thing is that we have succeeded in making them think about the processes, technologies, and applications they will use shortly.

Factor in Practice Time at the Start

Good design work takes a good amount of time. Conceptualization is crucial and changes are constantly upgrading the design. Thus, it is necessary to increase our time for the project. At some point, there is a deadline. Let students know immediately that they should expect to spend time outside of class to work on projects. If the context of the class is not a serious commercial-level audience, make sure practice time is factored into class time. Students learn computer graphics and multimedia in steps. Each step leads to the completion of a technique. The techniques help build the project to completion. The techniques require practice for the ability to execute and also to remember after the class is over. Maybe the person has to go back to work on Monday and use the new skills immediately. Practice must be factored in! If students can't make a commitment to practice they will never learn to complete projects and reach class goals.

Talk About It, Show It, Do It, and Do It Again: Answer Questions and Do It One More Time

This is a process that I use constantly to achieve retention. Retention is the key to student development. If students can't remember the technique, how can they implement it? If you look at students and they give the impression that you are going too slowly, you've hit the mark: retention. There is no such thing as over-teaching a topic. Be sure everyone understands before you move on to the next topic.

Review should be part of everyday lectures. Techniques lead into other techniques. Therefore you can always lead into a discussion on a new topic by reviewing the last topic and it's relationship to the next one (remember the hierarchy of information).

Don't Overload Students with Useless Information

We should not be teaching every single palette, menu, and piece of a software package or technology. Why? Information overload and time. The student needs to learn the material following the hierarchical structure that produces project results. There are things that will be left out simply because they do not rate high in the hierarchy. The information has less value. Therefore, it does not need to be covered formally. Books and student discovery can help teach the less important features and save brain space for the most topical information and techniques.

Projects are Mandatory and Needed — Assign Them, Critique Them, and Improve Them

The most important indication that learning and growth have occurred in art, design, film, video, computer art, graphic design, multimedia, web design, illustration, motion graphics, 2d design, programming, and 3d design are the projects. Practice should come in the form of project work.

Student projects should be evaluated on an ongoing basis. The critique of the student work should provide a forum for comments that provide constructive criticism. The goal is to get comments, not just compliments. The student must also realize that what is said is opinion only and can be discounted as easily as it can be used for improvement in the art-making process. However, the design process has specifications that need to be followed to complete a project accurately. The designer cannot alter these "specs". Elements such as page size, color usage, typography treatments, media, and message are all dictated in the design process and instructions must be followed. After critique, adequate time should be given for students to refine their work and then submit it for a grade.

Critique for design projects in any discipline may include criticism on:
- *Concept:* original idea that facilitates and supports a design solution
- *Development:* research and design aimed at defining project goals and strategies
- *Technique:* skills and processes used to execute design production
- *Style:* specific approach to creating unique identity and definitive cohesion within the project design
- *Usability:* functionality and effectiveness within the media which is related to stated goals or specs
- *Output:* adoption into final deliverable (print, web, CD-ROM, Digital Video, DVD, executable application)
- *Presentation:* visual and verbal summary of the value and success of the project

Stifle Disruptive Students Early

Teaching is difficult enough without having a disruptive student. Usually disruptive students come in pairs of two. The word RUDE is non-existent in their vocabularies. However, you must be polite and provide verbal and nonverbal signals that you want quiet when speaking and during in class work periods.

Typically, talking between two students is common. Simply and politely, ask everyone to listen to you now. That will stop talking sometimes. If it is persistent, stand near the talkers and ask them directly to wait until break to talk. Explain to them that the class is going to start and that everyone needs to work in a quiet environment. If it gets bad, speak to the student after class and explain that there are others who cannot learn with the constant disruptions. Explain that everyone is paying for this class and that talking is slowing the pace and the success of the class. This should help curb or solve the problem. The last resort: speak to your supervisor about possible solutions.

Always remember to require headphones for students working on multi-media projects containing audio.

Don't Do the Work for the Student

You have heard the proverb many times. Give a man a fish and feed him today. Teach him how to fish and feed him forever. It's the same with teaching digital coursework. The student must perform the techniques over and over again to learn. If we try to help students by sitting at their computers and doing the work, we are actually hurting them. Students will expect the teacher to fix problems by clicking a few buttons. That's not the case. The teacher should rarely touch students' computers. The exception is in extreme situations or when students have gone way beyond where they should be and now need to have their screens reset.

I tell students that it's easier for me to fix a problem than for them try to figure out the solution based on what they know. Sometimes, I encourage students to think about what the problem is and try to find a solution on their own — then we will discuss how the outcome was derived. Thinking through a problem is part of the learning process and design process. It is also important to help students become problem solvers.

Save Early, Save Often

Institute a blatant policy on saving. Too many times I have heard horror stories and consoled distraught students after they have had digital tragedies. I've seen it all. Zip disks going into CLICK DEATH, where the Zip drive is clicking your disk and corrupting your data (Iomega was sued for this), a meltdown of media due to being left on the car seat in hot sunlight, lost files and disks, and crashed hard drives. It happens. We should be prepared with backups. The student should be saving constantly. Computers crash frequently, regardless of platform, brand, or operating system. If we have created something that is important, we should be saving it in two places. By the second or third class meeting, you should have a formal lesson on saving. You want students to understand how to save, why it is so important, and where it is done.

All students should have external storage media with them by the second class. A zip or writable CD-ROM if applicable to your workstations. Also, students can use plug-and-play Firewire hard drives that provide hundreds of gigabytes of storage space. Show the student how to access external media.

production, and new media. Windows 98/2000/XP is dominant in business applications, information sciences, and computer science. Running graphical software and producing multimedia on the Windows platform is now as seamless as on the Macintosh. The real question is, again, what does the staff feel most comfortable with? Moreover, what is the industry standard? There are some distinctions that bring the old folklore that Mac and Windows PC's were mainstream competitors and they did not work well together exchanging files. That has changed dramatically since about Mac OS 6 (1993). That's when Apple bundled the application PC exchange with the OS. The extension allows Windows media to be read on Macintosh systems — right out of the box. Windows does not have that ability yet. Therefore, Macintosh has been touted as the friendlier platform in some circles. Throughout the publishing industry, Macintosh has been a standard platform since the inception of desktop systems.

Three-dimensional modeling, motion graphics, and multimedia applications gave way to the need for workstations that employed multiple processors and huge storage drives. Workstations are used in television production, film effects, video, DVD and CDR authoring. The workstation allows a massive amount of processing power to output gigantic files. Macintosh systems cannot provide the muscle that some workstations can. However, Macintosh is competing in the desktop arena by providing innovative hardware and software solutions for DV and DVD production. Apple computers allow users to capture, develop, and edit full-length digital video using a Digital Video camera. The digitized video can then be output to multiple media including web, broadcast, video, CD-ROM, and DVD.

Here are the main differences between Mac and Windows from a user's point of view:

- Windows systems on a base price level can be purchased at a lower cost than Macintosh. The reason is that there are so many manufacturers of windows-based computers in the United States that prices fluctuate and there are constant price wars in the PC market. Macintosh is a brand that owns its platform. No other company manufactures products running the MAC OS. Apple products are sold at a fair market price and are very competitive with comparably matched Windows Systems. However, a few operational differences make Macintosh more desirable for the print, multimedia, and content creation arenas.
- Macintosh accepts and reads files on the Mac platform and will open Windows files created with the same application. Windows will do the same, but will only read Windows media.

- Macintosh allows digital video input and output right out of the box. Previously, many Windows computers could not say that. If you want Firewire (ieee1394 or Ilink) technology for digital video use on the Windows platform, you must buy an aftermarket video board. You must install it and hope it is compatible with your computer and digital video editing software. Most PC manufacturers are adding Firewire cards bundled with their systems to avoid incompatibility issues. Macs also typically come with digital video editing software when purchased. It's not the high desktop applications we use in the professional industry, but is enough to create, edit, and output digital video—right out of the box. It's great for educational settings where content and basic knowledge are more important than teaching high-end applications.
- Macintosh computers have network capability directly out of the box. All that is needed is an Ethernet hub and Cat 5 cables and the AppleTalk takes care of the rest. For Windows machines, an Ethernet card would have to be purchased for each computer on the network as well as a hub. The Macs come with Ethernet built right in.

Bottom line, it does not really matter. Windows computers may lack some simple features that we have come to adore on Macintosh, but when it comes to sheer horsepower, Windows XP multiprocessor workstations are the choice for the professional film and TV editing, three- and four-dimensional modeling, and animation developers. The price factor makes Windows a bit more desirable, but Macs give added features out of the box that provide networking and multimedia capabilities to students. In a digital design lab environment, Macintosh may provide some functional advantages. In a computer science environment, Windows machines are typically more desirable. Ask your colleagues and staff what they prefer. Then ask them why. Collect the information and make a majority decision based on budget and priority.

Prioritize Your Purchase Regardless of the Platform and Put First Things First!

You must have your priorities in order when you are developing a computer lab. The decisions you make when the lab is delivered are the same decisions that come back to haunt you when you need more resources or things do not meet expectations.

- *First priority:* Make sure that you have enough computers for every student. If the class size exceeds the number of computers due to enrollment, cut class size. If class size is too large, you will need to make shifts of student to work on stations. Your teaching load will double per class because you will be shuffling around students to get everyone working on something. Inevitably, student work will suffer. There is a better way. Demand there are enough computers for each student.

- *Second priority:* Get as much ram as you can afford. Load up. You'll be happy when software versions change and your hardware budget is on hold until further notice.
- *Third priority:* Removable storage drives such as Iomega ZIP drives. Students need to back-up and transport their work. These drives allow them to do that. Having one drive becomes chaos. Saving and archiving become afterthoughts and hassles to the students. Also a good choice, but a bit more expensive for the student compared to a ZIP disk are removable Firewire hard drives. Eliminate the fear of losing files by making student backup an important priority. Also needed are archival media and drives, including CDR and DVD. These drives should not be used for primary, daily storage, but for final project output and archiving.

If You Develop Any Computer Lab Learning Environment, Try to Make the Following Items Part of Your Proposal

These will make teaching much more manageable. I'm sorry if these items are considered luxuries due to budget constraints. However, I cannot stress the importance of these items on what I call "quality of lab teaching life".

- *Hardware security system* including cables and padlocks for systems, monitors, and peripherals to keep the lab safe from theft.
- *Software security system* to lockout vital folders like the System Folder. These are now the duty of the lab manager. The needed functions can be found in the latest network operating systems for each platform.
- *A presentation panel for display on a screen or wall.* Although expensive, these technology learning tools are extremely helpful in the digital (smart) classroom. A decent one will cost you $3,000 to $4,000 dollars. Make sure you consider this item seriously when distributing your budget.
- *Pneumatic adjustable chairs.* This should be nonnegotiable. Bad chairs breed bad work habits. To help ensure an ergonomic lab environment, you should insist on the best chairs you can afford.

- *A file server and an Ethernet network.* This will help you transfer files and applications between stations and will allow maintenance to be easier with all machines connected. You will need this for internet access throughout your lab and to institute a software security system. Add a tape backup to the configuration for complete backup of the server.
- *Removable, rewritable, cross platform storage device* such as a Zip drive. Students need these to backup and transport files.
- *Internet accesses via a high-speed line or backbone,* especially if you are teaching a web centered course. A T1, T3, or cable connection is the minimum.
- *Server space and FTP access for web classes.* You should demand this if you are teaching a web design course.
- *A scanner for image acquisition.* One is the bare minimum you will need. This is a necessity. Without it, content will be virtually nonexistent in digital imaging and layout courses. Also include a digital camera for shooting stills and small video clips and a digital video camera for capturing full-length digital video and audio.
- *Enough computers for all students to have their own workstations during class time.* Without this, you are really challenged. It is not an impossible situation, but it requires some compromise to your teaching schedule. Inevitably, students will suffer. You can't watch and learn computer graphics and multimedia. You have to be hands in and knee deep, practicing constantly.
- *Lab hours outside of class.* This will allow students to practice and work on projects outside class time. Even if they are limited to small increments, lab hours are necessary for student abilities and confidence to grow. There has to be someone in charge during lab hours, so think about work-study students or graduate assistants to help with lab management.

CONCLUSION

Building student confidence, developing project-based skills, presenting vocabulary, and working towards project-based goals are crucial components in helping students succeed in digital coursework. But before you can do it, you must become comfortable with not knowing everything and understanding that you will be growing perpetually. Becoming an expert at teaching digital subjects presents very demanding challenges. Understanding, adapting to, and conquering those challenges will be realized through perpetual research and raw experience.

The future will undoubtedly present more and more interdisciplinary scenarios for programmers, designers, artists, production professional, writers, and musicians. This surge towards collaboration will be reflected in digital education. In the past decade, multitudes of schools have instituted new programs in multimedia, interactive multimedia, new media, educational technology, information technology, instructional technology, and many more multi-discipline disciplines. The convergence of media, process, skills, and deliverables makes teaching computer graphics and multimedia an extremely challenging, dynamic responsibility that requires artists to learn more programming and programmers to learn more about visual communication.

REFERENCES

Heller, S. (1998). *The Education of a Graphic Designer*. New York: Allworth Press.

Heller, S. (2001). *The Education of an E-designer*. New York: Allworth Press.

Michalak, D. F., & Yager, E.G. (1979). *Making the Training Process Work* (7-72). New York: Harper & Row Publishers.

Tieger, P. & Barron-Tieger, B. (1988). *The Art of Speedreading People*. Boston, MA: Little, Brown & Company.

Chapter II

Digital Prepress:
Issues and Solutions for the
Preparation of Print Media

Mark Snyder
Clemson University, USA

ABSTRACT

This chapter identifies changes that the printing industry has undergone during the past 25 years as a result of the digital revolution. It also provides a brief historical perspective of the printing industry and how it has evolved. It is undeniable that the computer has had an impact on the development of print media and today it is rare to find any prepress work done without the use of some digital technology. The workflow of a traditional printed piece is described from start to finish and is compared to a more modern digital workflow to familiarize readers with the processes and contrast the old with the new techniques. This chapter will identify common problems that occur in the preparation of print media using digital technologies. In particular, it will explore a variety of problems and solutions related to the use of digital prepress as well as identifying new innovations intended to improve prepress operations in the future.

INTRODUCTION

The printing industry has undergone major changes during the past 25 years as a result of the digital revolution. It is undeniable that the computer has had an impact on the development of print media and today it is rare to find any prepress work done without the use of some digital technology.

This chapter will provide a brief historical perspective of the printing industry and how it has evolved. The workflow of a traditional printed piece will be described from start to finish and will be compared to a more current digital workflow to familiarize readers with the processes and contrast the old with the new techniques. It will also identify common problems that occur in the preparation of print media using digital technologies. In particular, this chapter will explore a variety of problems and solutions related to the use of digital prepress as well as identifying new innovations intended to improve prepress operations in the future.

Traditionally, the central purpose of printing was to generate reproductions in quantity. Before printing existed, scribes reproduced manuscripts by hand — a slow and arduous task. Frank Romano, in the foreword of his book, *Pocket Guide to Digital Prepress*, tells the story of a German monk who, shortly after Gutenberg's development of cast-metal movable type sparked the advent of printing, authored an essay titled "In Praise of Scribes". The essay advocated the continuation of copying manuscripts by hand because of the character-building values it instilled in the scribes. The ironic part of the story is that the monk decided to have his manuscript printed. The moral that Romano teaches us is that the monk "was caught in the paradox of transitioning technologies" (1996, iv) and that a similar situation is certainly taking place as digital technology revolutionizes the printing industry.

BACKGROUND

Movable type, as a matter of fact, existed long before the time of Gutenberg. Clay letterforms have been traced back to China where they were used during the Sung dynasty as early 960 A.D. Wooden movable type were also used in the Southern Sung (1127-1276), tin movable type in the Yuan (1271-1368), and bronze movable type were widely used in the Ming Dynasty (1368-1644).

However, the concept of mass-reproduction of graphic images was not realized in Europe until Gutenberg, through his knowledge of metallurgy and entrepreneurial spirit, created metal type and adapted a wooden screw-type olive press to invent printing. This invention, which occurred around 1450 A.D., was the key that unlocked and opened a door enabling the western world to move from the Dark Ages and into the Enlightenment. In 2000, based on a survey of prominent scientists, Gutenberg was recognized by the London Times, as the "Man of the Millennium" for this technological achievement that revolutionized graphic communication.

Typesetting, in one form or another, remained the primary form of "prepress" work for about the next 500 years. The industrial revolution brought several technological advancements to the printing industry such as mechanical press systems, offset lithographic printing, and photographic processes. In the middle of the 20th century, phototypesetting became the norm for generating type and artwork was assembled into paste-ups to be "shot" on a camera. Films were stripped into flats (often as large signatures) and then used to make printing plates. Many people were involved in the process of getting a job ready to go to press. Designers, photographers, copywriters, proofreaders, editors, typographers, paste-up artists, camera operators, color separators, strippers, and platemakers all were occupations supported by this process.

An "imagesetter" sounds like yet another person involved in the prepress process but actually it is a device developed around 1980. It represents a transitional technology that uses digital information and a laser to create an analog product-film. At about the same time, page-layout software was developed that allowed the merging of text, line art, and digital photographic images into a layout. Output the page layout from a computer to an imagesetter, add the ability to electronically separate colors, and we have process-color films that are already positioned, thus eliminating the need for several workers.

More recently, platesetters and other direct-to-plate technologies have eliminated film, and its associated costs, from the process. Now, even offset lithographic presses are available with platemaking systems right on the press. A file can be sent from the computer directly to the press. Apparently, the invention of the silicon chip, and associated digital technologies, has virtually (pun intended) eliminated the majority of the occupations listed earlier.

In fact, "desktop publishing," enabled by the Postscript page description language, makes it possible for one person to be all of the above and also the printer. As computers become more affordable for a larger number of people, many are attempting to make the most of their investment by generating their own newsletters, flyers, etc. Many of these do-it-your-selfers proceed to create printed matter regardless of the fact that they have little or no experience with typography or formal layout and design principles. The result is typically less than pleasing to the graphics professional's eye.

Today, the vast majority of professionally printed jobs are created using computers. Often they include a mix of text, line art and photographic images. All of these types of "copy" are typically created using different software applications that have evolved to become very powerful each in their own way. Word processing software is great for generating text copy. Copywriters use this type of software and send their text files to a designer or prepress professional. Vector-based software allows designers to create digital line art referred to as object-oriented art. Graphic designers are often very talented with this type of software that uses complex mathematical functions to generate postscript files. Scanner operators are skilled professionals who know just how to scan a photo, and other art, to make it look its best. Also, many professional photographers are now using digital cameras and generating digital "photo" files directly. Photo editing software makes it possible to change these bitmapped images pixel by pixel and apply various functions so that beautiful full-color halftone pictures can be reproduced as effectively as possible on printing presses.

Once all of this various copy is generated it can be merged together using an electronic page layout application. This is the heart of professional digital prepress. Assembling all of these elements into an aesthetically pleasing design that is capable of being printed is the specialty of a good graphic designer and/or in-house prepress professional.

Digital technology, along with highly-skilled personnel, has made it easy to do tasks that were once challenging. The rapidly increasing processing power of computers coupled with ingenious software tools, and tremendously useful peripheral devices, has enabled the printing industry to make significant improvements in speed and quality. But, it has also increased the likelihood of mistakes and poor design. Overall, the new technology has created an entirely new set of circumstances within which different challenges exist. The technology continues to advance, but so do the problems that need to be solved.

ISSUES, CONTROVERSIES, PROBLEMS

Because the technology is readily accessible to non-professional designers, a lot of unprofessional design work is being created and submitted to printing companies these days. For example, a large company may outfit an employee who has little or no training in prepress design, with a computer and software that enables him to create page layouts for a company brochure that a printer could not possibly print without a lot of rework.

In some cases, customers set up jobs for printers with word processing software. This can be very problematic. Word processing software is capable of displaying digital photos and clip art but it really was not designed for the purpose of creating technical layouts. As a result, it does not have the capability of handling some of the sophisticated operations that are required for true publishing operations such as generating page impositions when multiple pages are printed together in signatures. Word processing software also is not able to perform color separations and properly output to high resolution output devices. High-end page layout programs directly produce postscript page descriptions and word processors do not. The use of word processing applications is a fairly common problem when dealing with non-professionals who walk in "off the street".

While graphic designers and printers don't always see things the same way, they do know that they need each other — and their ability to communicate will have to continually improve as digital prepress technology advances. Since the traditional occupations held by craftsperson's such as typesetters, paste-up artists, color separators, and strippers are virtually obsolete, "designers are taking on more and more of the prepress process themselves" (Agfa, 1994, p. 1).

Most professional graphic designers have enough experience working with printing firms that they are familiar with the common issues related to preparing art and text for printing. However, sometimes they actually go beyond the limits of what can be achieved. Occasionally, like a builder who may realize the impracticalities of an architect's radical design, the printer can face very challenging, if not downright impossible, tasks simply based on the design concepts proposed. Just as a student of architecture might benefit from working a brief time in construction, a designer who is not familiar with the printing process may be wise to seek more education in graphic communications, or to intern in a printing firm for a short time.

Unfortunately, many printers are locked into doing specific types of work based on the equipment that they own — but others relish the challenge of helping designers see new and exciting design ideas spring to life. In the realm of packaging, especially, designers and printers often work together to solve unique packaging solutions that will protect products and promote sales.

While the majority of people who submit a job to a printer will claim that it is "ready to go" (to film, plate, or press), unfortunately, this is usually not the case. Since the vast majority of jobs come to printing companies as electronic files, the printer will typically have prepress personnel "preflight" (named to relate to pilots' preflight check of their aircraft before flying) computer files to make sure that they will work when sent to film, plates, and/or press. A preflight technician (one new job description that evolved since the digital revolution) reviews all data sent to a printer to make sure that all artwork, fonts, file formats, etc., are included and will work with the systems in place at that printing firm. Other technical concerns that a preflight technician might delve into would include checking whether a job meets size limitations, whether trapping issues are resolved, imposition, and if finishing and bindery requirements are met.

Most jobs, even jobs submitted by professional designers, rarely make it through a preflight check successfully the first time. Bob Atkinson, an electronic prepress consultant, claims that, "only about 15% of clientele-supplied files are actually ready to output without problems. The other 85% have one or more problems — some are minor and hardly noticeable in the final piece; others have more serious problems that will jam your imagesetter or other output device or, worse, produce an unacceptable print job that the client won't pay for" (2001, p. 1).

The most common mistakes in jobs that are submitted to printers are typically problems that relate to fonts. Because fonts are not metal anymore, we can put a lot more of them into our computers. (Count the number of fonts on your system and imagine the mass equivalent in lead type of those font families in your laptop!) As a result, we tend to go wild and use a lot of different fonts. Although the appropriate number of fonts to use in a printed piece is open to artistic interpretation, the ability to output them is not. If designers do not provide printers with the fonts they used in a design, the printer cannot output that job without the missing fonts being replaced with other fonts.

Like fonts, any graphics files that are placed into a page layout file must also be included with a job. Most layout applications will show a low-resolution thumbnail version of an image on screen but when the file is output it tries to link to the high-resolution resource file that will provide a high-quality printed image. If the resource file is not included, the output will be a low-resolution image that will appear pixelized. Also, if a bitmap file is placed into a vector-based application and saved as a file and then that file is placed into a page layout program, we have created a "nested" file. Nested files can also create a lot of problems when trying to output a job to films or plates.

File formats are another puzzle needing to be figured out. In its educational brochure titled *An Introduction to Digital Color Prepress*, Agfa Corporation stated, "bitmapped images may be saved improperly and print poorly when placed into page-layout…applications." The company continued, "to overcome these problems, a variety of graphics file formats have been devised which link text, graphics and separation capabilities among different programs and computer platforms" (1997, p. 24). Understanding which file formats are appropriate for the planned end-use is important. For bitmapped images, the most common file formats used for digital prepress are TIFF, EPS, and JPEG. Most other formats are typically converted to one of these three if printing the images is the end goal. Most object-oriented artwork is simply saved in EPS format for transfer into page layout applications. Text files are usually the easiest files to place into layouts if they are saved as ASCII files. ASCII is such a simple code that it is a basic function of most computers.

Obviously, the creation of graphics files can be very tricky. Photos scanned on desktop scanners have also proven to be a common problem area for printers. Not many people can answer the question "at what resolution should I scan this picture?" — and that is because it depends on a few different variables. Digital cameras are becoming very popular and, like most new technologies, they have more features than we know what to do with. However, if we plan to use the images in printed media, we need to know what resolution we are capturing with that new camera.

One of the keys to the resolution issue is understanding halftones and the line screens that are being used for printing halftone images. A halftone converts a regular photographic image (referred to as continuous tone) into dots of various sizes. When printed on white paper, this provides the illusion of tones (grays or various colors). The line screen specifies the number and frequency of these dots. Even if a client submits a file at the right resolution, they may set screen frequency, angle and dot shapes incorrectly which will cause problems with halftone images.

Trapping is actually an old concept that is just handled differently with digital technology. What used to be referred to as "spreads" and "chokes" is now typically handled by "overprinting stroke" or can be done automatically with some software applications. The concept of trapping is one that can be, unless you get your hands on it, difficult to appreciate. The general concept is that we want two adjacent colors to overlap just slightly when printing so it does not leave a white space if it is printed slightly out of register. Presses and press operators are not perfect yet so it is good to plan for this possibility by trapping your colors. (See Figure 1.)

Ah yes, color. Color management is perhaps the most vexing and perplexing problem facing design and printing professionals today. The problem with color management in prepress is that it extends beyond just the prepress area. The issue of color begins with the original art or image that is captured and continues all the way through the process of creating the printed piece. Sam Ingram, a professor of graphic communications, stated, "a color management

Figure 1.

Off register —   *Trapped —*
White shows through   *Colors overlap slightly*

system is a set of tools that permits consistent and predictable color reproduction. This includes all equipment in the production workflow having an impact on the color files as they move from one device to another" (2001, p. 26). The people involved in this process, and using these systems, must have an understanding of color theory and how to make different devices generate color the same way.

In many cases, designers and digital prepress departments do not use color management and simply rely on experience and/or guesswork to approximate color matching. When showing customers color proofs of a job, graphics professionals often apologize in advance for their inability to match specified colors. Sometimes clients view "soft proofs" from a monitor (one that is not color managed) and when the colors end up completely different from what they saw, they reject the job. Proofing itself is a significant issue to digital prepress today because there is such a wide range of proofing devices available that produce color using many different methods.

Despite all of these relatively technical problems, one the most significant, and yet simplest, problems that is recurring with jobs today are typographical errors that seem to slip by and get printed on the final product. Traditionally, jobs went through the hands of many people in the process of getting printed. Now, the chain of human workers that touch a job has become so short that many minor errors go unnoticed (and sometimes the errors are not so minor or can be very embarrassing). Direct-to-press technology, which will be discussed in more detail, now makes it possible for jobs to go right from a designer's computer to a press. While this is incredibly more efficient than in the past, it also enables us to make mistakes much faster than ever before!

SOLUTIONS AND RECOMMENDATIONS

Starting from the design stage, perhaps the most important concept for a designer to remember is that printing is primarily all about the reproduction of large quantities of media. Designing something that requires handwork, for example, makes mass reproduction very difficult, or at least very costly. In most cases, this is the type of issue that causes a design concept never to be realized.

Generally, if we design with the fewest number of fonts possible — without compromising the design itself — and use more common fonts, we will save a lot of wasted time. Otherwise, designers need to be organized and include all fonts and linked graphics files into a folder that contains everything needed for that job. Preflighting will likely turn up some problems and it is the designer's, and/or client's, responsibility to either provide missing resources, correct any errors, or approve charges for correction by the printer.

Capturing images with a digital camera, or scanning them, at the proper resolution is essential to generating quality bitmapped images. Following the Nyquist Theorem for digital sampling of analog information, we typically try to sample at 1.5 to 2 times the screen frequency, or lines per inch (lpi), at which we intend to print the image. This should then be multiplied by the scaling factor (sf) for the job (see Figure 2). Using images captured at lower resolutions will impair the quality of the reproduction and image files with higher resolutions than necessary will be too big and require excessive processing time that will, again, incur charges.

Printing companies of all sizes are beginning to see value in offering training to their regular customers, and designers, that send them problem files. Many are also providing websites that explain how to capture images at the proper resolution, upload files, use preferred file formats, prepare graphics files, etc. These specifications are typically customized to meet the requirements of the particular equipment owned by the printing company.

Outputting files with stochastic (or frequency modulated) screening is an alternative to conventional halftones. In traditional screening, halftone dots vary in size and are spaced equally from one another. Stochastic dots are placed irregularly and are all the same very small size — much like a stippling effect. This technique eliminates the possibility of moiré, an optical phenomenon that occurs when screens overlap at close angles, and provides excellent reproduc-

Figure 2.

$$\text{Resolution} = 1.5 \times \text{lpi} \times \text{sf}$$

tion of details in a printed image. Stochastic screening is available for postscript output devices. "The film separations can be proofed using conventional methods and plates can be printed on standard web and sheetfed offset presses" (Agfa, 1997, p. 17).

Digital data transmission has improved the way that customers can transport jobs to printers. Telephony makes it possible for jobs to be sent via phone lines instead of through couriers. Some printers installed dedicated phone lines for connecting with big clients who send a lot of work. Others have used File Transfer Protocol (FTP) sites, but these were not very popular because customers had a difficult time using FTP software. In the past few years, companies that use the internet to provide private network services for the printing industry have emerged. A user-friendly browser makes it simple for a client to drop job folders into a transfer folder and send their files to the printer almost instantly. File transfer services are big time savers but they still don't eliminate the fact that all needed files, fonts, and links must be included in a job folder.

Digital workflows for the printing industry in general have improved a lot during the past five years. Sean Riley stated in *Package Printing* magazine:

"One often overlooked stage that printers have begun to explore in an effort to improve workflow, and therefore costs, is the prepress facet of the industry. Improvements in prepress workflow and/or data transmission have been available for quite a while now but [printers] have been slow to take advantage of these opportunities" (2002, p. 14).

Proprietary systems that automate much of the digital prepress workflow are offered as complete packages by vendors who also manufacture peripheral equipment such as platesetters. Trapping, color management and raster image processing (RIPing) can all be quickly and easily accomplished via seamless solutions running on powerful workstations. These systems are typically programmed for very specific prepress production methods and are fast, accurate, and capable of making complex changes without completely rebuild-ing files.

Open Prepress Interface (OPI) is another digital workflow solution that improves digital prepress performance by minimizing the amount of data that is handled while generating page layouts. Typically, graphic files can consume very large chunks of system memory as well as file space. OPI servers employ an extension to Postscript "that automatically replaces low-resolution place-holder images with high-resolution images" (International Paper, 2000, p. 224). Basically, the OPI server reduces the amount of information traveling over a local area network until it is needed for output.

Color management is another process that has improved digital prepress in recent years. Tools such as spectrophotometers have become affordable and make it possible to consistently measure color and make it look the same the whole way through the printing cycle from concept, design, prepress and proofing, to the finished product off the press. "At this point it is apparent that moving to a color managed workflow is not a simple process handled by a single individual. A color managed workflow includes everyone in the color repro-duction food chain" (Ingram, 2002, p. 29). It is a scientific approach to what is commonly thought of as the domain of an artist — color. It does not achieve perfect results, but it is amazing to see how much of an improvement there is over a non-color managed environment. Color management is an advancement that offers a definite solution to a very real digital prepress issue.

Proofing is an area that directly benefits from color management. First, it is rarely advisable to use soft proofs (viewing from a monitor) for contractual color approval. It is far better to choose a proven proofing system that utilizes media similar to the finished product and is definitely known to match output from given press systems through a color managed workflow. Still, soft proofing is being done a lot more often these days because of the expediency of sending a page independent file and viewing it on screen. Soft proofing is acceptable to check for positioning and layout but even when monitors are color corrected, the color gamut it can reproduce with RGB additive primary colors is much different than what printing presses can produce with CMYK subtractive primary colors. Many printers favor proofing systems that produce colors using a subtractive colorant system that produces some type of dots to approximate halftone systems.

TRENDS

One continuing trend in the printing industry is that technology is enabling a shorter route from design to press. More and more, digital prepress peripheral systems, such as scanners and imagesetters, are being bypassed by digital cameras, direct-to-plate and, now, direct to press systems. As these systems become more and more automated, and direct-to-press technology evolves, it seems possible that the printing press will soon be under control of the prepress department of printing companies and viewed as just another output device.

Digital printing is a new category in the hierarchy of printing processes. Although most printing processes today employ digital prepress solutions, at some point a printing plate or some other type of master is produced and the final act of printing becomes an analog, mechanical process. One way to identify digital printing processes "is to refer to any printing device that inputs a digital data stream and outputs printed pages as a *digital printer,* and then further distinguish between printers that first build a physical master from which multiple copies are printed and those that do not" (Cost, 1997, p. 79).

Digital printing devices typically fall into one of the following five categories: photographic, thermal, ink jet, dye sublimation, and electrostatic. The primary advantage of digital printing is that it is commonly used for reproducing smaller numbers of reproductions more cost-effectively. Although the cost per sheet of a color offset job may be less than a single color copy, that is only possible because thousands of reproductions must be produced. If we only need two hundred reproductions, it is more cost-effective to make color copies than to go to the trouble of producing plates and getting a press ready to print. "Virtually every market analyst places flexographic printing growth second only to that of digital printing" (Hogenson, 2002, p. 1). The rapid development of high-quality color digital printing devices has made digital printing the fastest growing printing market segment today.

Digital printing brings the realization of a completely digital workflow. Another technology that is simplifying digital workflows is Portable Document Format (PDF).

Huff and West report that, "the goal of a PDF workflow system is to deliver electronic files to a film or plate recorder, or to a digital press or printer, with a minimum amount of operator intervention" (2000, p. 42).

PDF files are independent of authoring software, such as layout programs, and system software, so they can be opened on any platform. The format is derived from Postscript and enables files to be created that are page independent and device independent. "PDF files serve as a digital master throughout the entire continuum of communication — from posting on the Web to outputting on a press" (Agfa, 1998, p. 1). This incredibly versatile format is equally useful as an interactive media tool or as a tool for commercial printing.

Printers especially like what PDF has to offer them. "For print-on-demand service providers, PDF erases many of the current variables introduced by the variety of platforms, application programs and printers involved in any corporate system" (Young, 1998, p. 57). Perhaps the biggest advantage of using PDF for prepress is embedded fonts and graphics; prepress operators will no longer need to spend time spent searching for missing image files (Snyder, 1999, p. 35). If your document can be "distilled" into a PDF file, it is very likely to be output with no problems.

Variable data printing is another trend that is taking full advantage of the speed of digital processing. This type of printing produces products that can be individually customized. Yes, that is right, every subsequent printed piece is different. Does that not defy the whole notion that printing is essentially geared towards mass reproduction of the same image? Again, yes, it forces printers to accept a whole new paradigm.

Currently, variable data printing is used primarily for rapid identification of manufactured goods, and direct-mail applications. It is also being used creatively for numbering printed tags. Most variable data printing is fast, low-quality ink-jet marking but higher-quality systems that can print bitmap images do exist — although they are significantly slower and are targeted for short-run markets. In many cases, such as direct mailing, the variable address data can be simply added on to preprinted forms and then shipped. Customized labels are another popular example of this technology.

What is required from prepress for variable data printing? It means that database management may become part of the responsibilities of digital prepress personnel. Also, for high-quality work, the variable data needs to be placed into an actual page layout. Once the layout is developed, a fixed page is created — yet another way that PDF can be utilized. Specialized applications exist that enable pictures to be placed as variable data into a PDF document and then printed individually. As digital printing technology advances, variable data processing will become faster and more commonplace. This will open a plethora of new design capabilities and applications.

CONCLUSION

In 1978, F.W. Lancaster, a noted library futurist, authored a book titled *Toward Paperless Information Systems* in which he raised, and answered, the question, "Will paper be as important in the information systems of the year 2000 as it is today? Almost certainly not" (p. 1). This has proven to be true in most library systems — paper is not as important as it used to be — but it is still there. Further into his book Lancaster generalizes his vision to ponder a broader perspective. He stated, "the paperless society is rapidly approaching, whether we like it or not" (p. 166).

Lancaster was correct about technology reducing the necessity of paper as the basis for our information systems, however, it would seem that the same technology has also made it possible for us to produce more printed media and packaging than ever before. According to the University of Tennessee Department of Forestry, Wildlife and Fisheries, "the so-called paperless society that was projected to evolve with the computer age has actually led to a 40% increase in office printing in the United States." They also estimate that paper production will have to increase by 30% to keep up with global demands (Mercker, 1999, p. 1).

Look around, as computers become commonplace in our homes, does it seem as though we are moving toward a paperless society? If not, then why? In many ways, the computer has actually helped to generate more printed media. Printing spans a wide realm of applications that include business forms, catalogs, envelopes, labels, high-quality art reproductions, screen printing (on anything from textiles to CDs) — and the (preprinted) list goes on.

Packaging is the second-fastest growing print market today. (The next time you go shopping, consider all of the items that are packaged in some sort of printed media.)

Fruscione reported that growth in the flexographic printing industry in the United States and Mexico has been tremendous primarily because of digital prepress and computer-to-plate advancements. "Flexographic printing held 22% of all printing volume last year and 70% of the packaging industry" (2000, p. 2).

Publishing is another area that has improved considerably with the use of computers. In the 1960's and 1970's magazines were typically published with a colorful cover and mostly black text inside. Process-color images were difficult and time-consuming to reproduce in a magazine. They were considered something special. That has gradually changed to the point where, today, most of the magazines we pick up are printed in full color from front to back. Full process-color printing is expected. Realistic color images are now taken for granted. Commercial offset lithography, the largest segment of the printing industry, also continues to grow — and will never be the same.

A quick review of the history of printing should point out that a very gradual evolution in printing processes occurred during the course of about 500 years until, in the late 20th century, digital technology revolutionized the industry.

Since then, the process of creating print media has undergone rapid changes and tremendous technological advancements that have brought new problems, and new solutions, to the forefront. Ultimately, it seems that we have arrived, as Gutenberg did, at another very significant technological crossroad. Much of what is done in digital prepress today can be repurposed for use in a variety of media forms. Although printing was the primary form of graphic communication for hundreds of years it is now simply one of a number of ways to output digital information.

REFERENCES

Agfa (1998). *Agfa Digital Roadmaps, No. 3*. USA: Bayer Corp.

Agfa-Gavaert, N.V., & Bayer Corp. (1994). *Working with Prepress and Printing Suppliers*. Randolph, MA: Agfa Educational Publishing.

Agfa-Gavaert, N.V., & Bayer Corp. (1997). *An Introduction to Digital Color Prepress*. Randolph, MA: Agfa Educational Publishing.

Atkinson, B. (2001). 10 prepress troubleshooting tips. *Graphic Monthly*. Retrieved October 5, 2002 from: http://www.graphicmonthly.ca/DigitalReports/novdec01/10ppt.htm.

Cost, F. (1997). *Pocket Guide to Digital Printing*. Albany, NY: Delmar.

Fruscione, E. (May, 2000). FFTA Forum tackles flexo's future head-on. *Converting, 18*(5), 10.

Hogenson, B. (2001). Analysis of Digital Flexo Opportunities for Trade Shops. Retrieved September 25, 2002 from: http://unix.barco.com/graphics/packaging/analysis_digital_flexo.htm.

Huff, R. & West, K. (April, 2000). PDF workflow systems. *High Volume Printing, 18*(2), 42-46.

Ingram, S. T. (2001). Color management: A system for improved color reproduction. *SGIA Journal*, Second Quarter.

International Paper (2000). *Pocket Pal: Graphic Arts Production Handbook*. International Paper Co.

Lancaster, F. W. (1978). *Toward Paperless Information Systems*. New York: Academic Press.

Mercker, D. C. (1999). *Landowners dare to say "P" Word*. University of Tennessee Agricultural Extension Service. Retrieved September 15, 2002 from: http://www.utextension.utk.edu/greenTN/2001/026.htm

Riley, S. (August, 2002). *Old habits die hard*. Package Printing.

Romano, F. J. (1996). *Pocket Guide to Digital Prepress.* Albany, NY: Delmar.

Snyder, M. (1999). Portable Document Format: A versatile communications tool. *Visual Communications Journal.* Sewickley, PA: International Graphic Arts Education Association.

Young, A. (1998, May). PDF: It's not just for publishing anymore. *Print on Demand Business, 4*(4), 57-60.

Chapter III

Screenspace

Kevin H. Jones
University of Oregon, USA

ABSTRACT

From tiny interactive cellphone screens (keitai) to supersized jumbo LED displays, Tokyo's urban landscape is changing drastically. A corner that once displayed billboards that occasionally flipped has now become lit-up and is in constant motion. Keitai, with their built-in cameras, now allow images to be sent from one to another and have become essential to urban life. As these screens become architectural and fashion statements, Tokyo's nomadic high-tech culture is commuting even greater distances, living in more compact housing, and allowing for "cellspace" and "screenspace" to merge.

> *Today we live in the imaginary world of the screen, of the interface...and networks. All our machines are screens, we too have become screens, and the interactivity of men has become the interactivity of screens.*
> –Jean Baudrillard

INTRODUCTION

Since the mid-1970s, with the development of the personal computer, interactive screens have slowly become part of our daily lives. The first interactive screens introduced were monochromatic, very much text-driven, and still referred to the structure of the printed page. Rudimentary images had to be cleverly created with the characters presented on the computer's keyboard.

Today, we find ourselves surrounded by vast wireless networks that we interface with through the use of electronic devices ranging from simple text messaging to high-resolution graphics on laptop computers. Various sized screens with rich GUI's (graphical user interface) are portals that allow us to interact with software on these devices. This invisible electromagnetic, hertzian space[1] has been growing rapidly since the mid-20th century. Urban landscapes are not only changing because of the mobility and interactivity of these screens, but also because of the proliferation of large-screen LED displays that are at every corner vying for our attention.

From Times Square in New York City to Shibuya Crossing in Tokyo, urban space is changing drastically. A corner that once displayed billboards that occasionally flipped has now become lit up and is in constant motion. Even though these screens are neither mobile nor interactive, the graphics that are displayed upon their surfaces light up the streets and mirror the motion of the city.

With this chapter, I will be looking at the proliferation of screens found in Tokyo and how they have transformed public and personal space. I will look closely at the "keitai"[2] with its tiny screens that dot Tokyo's landscape, all the way up to the "supersized" LED displays found in major entertainment and shopping areas in Tokyo. I will examine various screens' mobility, interactivity, social effects, and how graphics and typography are displayed on these devices.

CELLSPACE

Tokyo is a city in flux; it is in constant motion. With the daily influx of millions of commuters all with "keitai", cellspace is a dominant structure upon its urban fabric. The term "cellspace" was first coined by David S. Bennahum while using his Palm Pilot with a wireless modem to access the web and send e-mail while waiting for a NYC subway train in 1998. Cellspace surrounds us with its tangible and virtual interfaces, as well as the invisible wireless network that it has created. Today, it is everywhere and is a communication space for the nomad, allowing unparalleled movement and convenience.

Japan is a country with limited space, and Tokyo is one of the most crowded and expensive cities in the world. With high rents and one-third of living spaces averaging 400 square feet, urban apartments average approximately one room in size. Space is at a premium. Because of this lack of affordable and large housing in Tokyo, many Japanese commute up to four hours round trip from their homes in the surrounding suburbs to their places of employment. This distance from their offices makes for a very long commute on Tokyo's extensive rail system — perfect for the use of the popular keitai.

During my first residence in Japan in 1998, my daily one-way commute was one hour and 30 minutes from my front door to the Musashanita train station, then a train to the Megro station where I changed to the JR Yamanote line, which brought me to the Shinjuku train station, where again, I switched to another train that took me to the Hatsudai train station. After a 10-minute walk from there, I would finally arrive at the front door of the graphic design studio where I worked. I quickly discovered that this commute is not unusual for the Tokyo worker, as I was commuting with millions of others five days a week. During my daily commute, I would often read, just as all of the other passengers did to pass the time away and to avoid eye contact. But this has now changed: the majority of passengers are not reading the static text of a book or newspaper, but clicking away with their thumbs at their keitai keys. These commuters are not talking, (that would be impolite), but writing e-mails and entering into their individual cellspace.

The keitai that the Japanese use are extremely sophisticated: all current models are able to send and receive e-mail and have access to a limited amount of official webpages (with a subscription to one of the most popular service providers: I-mode or J-sky). Along with access to an already familiar interface, many phones allow low to medium resolution images to be captured with the keitai built-in camera and sent to another keitai or computer. Called sha-mail[3], these camera-enabled keitai have become extremely popular. Their screens allow thousands of colors of resolution and have built in 3D polygon engines. Streaming video from one keitai to another is on the horizon. With the rapid development of technologies related to the keitai, one can only imagine what the next generation will bring. How wonderful would it be to conduct a videoconference with my associates at Sony as I finish my cup of coffee at the local coffee shop. Or, even better, play network games, watch bootlegged movies, or use it as a spy-camera. What this next generation of keitai will present is not only a hyper-cellspace: it will add to what I will refer to as screenspace.

SCREENSPACE

Tokyo is a city of not only cellspace, but of screenspace. Electronic displays are everywhere, from the tiny keitai screens to the monolithic LED screens found on the buildings in Shibuya, Shinjuku, and other major entertainment areas. The largest concentration of these large-scale displays can be found in Shibuya, a popular shopping district in Tokyo. Standing outside of the Shibuya JR (Japan Railroad) train station waiting to cross a busy intersection, one is assaulted by a total, at last count, of three large LED displays[4], one at least six stories tall and meshed into a building. All attempt to gain your attention. Here, screens become architecture, screens overtake the physical space, dwarf pedestrians, and launch you into screenspace.

All at once, you find yourself surrounded by things in motion, people with and without keitai, automobiles, images, and type. This experience of screenspace is one that is on a grand scale, but there are countless other examples of screenspace to be experienced in Tokyo. JR Trains now have large

Figure 1.

hi-definition screens throughout the cars updating us on the weather forecast, news, and latest canned coffee drink as we commute. Plasma screens are also all the rage in Tokyo; having one mounted — hung like a painting — in your apartment makes any image on it a work of art.

Also on the streets of Tokyo, one finds the flickering video arcade. Inside, there is the martial-arts superhero game with its familiar joystick controller along with games having much more developed physical interfaces. One involves a dance floor where users interact with a virtual character and try to keep up with dance beats. Another requires a user to beat on taiko drums as digital images on a screen key you when to do so. These hyper-interactive tangible interfaces mesh screenspace to a physical presence. Like the keitai with its individual interaction, these video games are changing the physical and virtual landscape of contemporary Tokyo.

As the video arcades in Tokyo exhibit tangible interfaces fused with screens, the even more common Pachinko parlors now have small-embedded LCDs. The Pachinko parlor itself is a spectacle. Upon entering, the sound of thousands of cascading silver balls all at the control of gravity release a pulsating wave of metal. These machines also play computerized jingles. With the addition of movement from computer graphics on the built-in LCD screens and the drive to gamble, an electrifying effect is created.

As the physical world meshes with the virtual in Tokyo, the screens are friendly and unintimidating. For example, at the JR Shinjuku station, I interface

Figure 2.

with the ticket machine through its extremely clear GUI as I choose my fare. A 180-yen ticket is presented, a virtual ticket agent bows with a "thank you," and I am on my way. Throughout Tokyo, this interaction with various electronic devices and their screens is polite, apologetic, and clear. Warning beeps or alarms tend to be pleasant and instructive, rather than loud and embarrassing. Cute characters along with strategically placed blinking LEDs explain instructions and directions. It seems that the Japanese are at a much greater ease with technology and its integration into daily life.

This acceptance of technology into daily life in Japan permits screenspace to exist. Major electronic companies such as Sony, Panasonic and Hitachi, to name a few, all release their products for consumer testing on the streets of the Akihabara district in Tokyo. Akihabara — "electric city" in Japanese — is very befitting. On its streets, one finds everything from the latest electronic goods to the raw components that make up these high-tech devices. Here in this bazaar of capacitors, transistors, and micro-controllers, various screens can be found — from simple LED displays to compact high-resolution screens. These raw

Figure 3.

components found in Akihabara fuel the ingenuity and creativity of Japanese electrical engineers, designers, and artist.

With all of these screens in Tokyo, the keitai, with its mobility and personal space, is the most powerful. The mobility that the keitai exhibits is drastically changing daily life in contemporary Japan and can be compared to some of Tokyo's compact architecture. The keitai is small, functional, and mobile. It is necessary for anyone traversing Tokyo's urban landscape. (In fact during my last visit, I found myself feeling awkward having to use the vulnerable payphone.) The ubiquitous capsule hotel also exhibits the same characteristics: functional and necessary in contemporary Tokyo. Positioned near major intersections of travel and entertainment, the capsule hotel allows the businessman[5] who has missed the last train home a sleeping birth one meter by one meter by two meters, sleek yet brutally functional. This functionality and compactness to support all forms of mobility is exemplified in Kisho Kurakabo's Nakagin Capsule Tower found in Ginza. Built in 1970, its 74 capsules are all equipped with a single bed, unit-bath, and entertainment center, initially intended to be purchased by companies to allow temporary stay for the mobile businessman. This compactness and mobility that the Japanese have become accustomed to is essential to the keitai popularity. With the amount of commuting and time spent away from home, the keitai presents itself as a necessary interface for contemporary Japan.

DIGITAL TYPOGRAPHY: AESTHETIC OF THE PIXEL

With the multitude of screens found in Tokyo, viewing graphics or reading their type can be tiring on the eyes. Type, in particular, can be troublesome: it is often in Japanese and in a vertical format. All images and characters must adhere to various screen resolutions creating, at times, very coarse graphics and jagged type.

On the keitai, one will often find Hiragana, Katakana, and Kanji[6] with little English. Much typography on the keitai is comparable to type on an early Macintosh SE. It is typically black on white, static, and read in the body of an e-mail or a simple interface. It is meant to be personal and clear. This treatment aligns itself with the printed page and Tschichold's New Typography: simple, clear, and clean. But upon closer look, the type is coarse and blocky, adhering to the screen's matrix of pixels.

Figure 4.

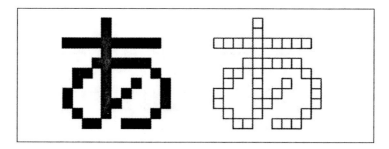

This coarse and blocky type is not new to typography. Wim Crouwel's 1966 Vomgevers poster for the Stedelijk Museum in Amsterdam used a typeface that adheres to a rigorous grid. Called Stedelijk, this typeface has a very similar look to many "pixel fonts" that are being designed for screens today. Later, in 1967, Crouwel designed New (Neue) Alphabet, a result of his using the first electronic typesetting machines. New Alphabet was a radical design: it removed all diagonal strokes and curves in its individual characters. New Alphabet reduced characters to their essential elements, creating a font that is strictly vertical and horizontal, again adhering to the grid.

More recently, in 1985, Émigré released the Oakland typeface. Designed by Zuzana Licko, it is a coarse bit-mapped family that was a response to graphic design's shift from tangible to computer screen-based production. This digitally influenced typeface announced the beginnings of the shift in typography from "hands-on" to digital layout.

Today, we find ourselves in what I call the aesthetic of the pixel, which in turn is part of screenspace. Currently, there are countless fonts that are specifically designed to be read on the screen. These pixel fonts — with clever names such as Silkscreen, Seven-Net and Superpoint — are designed to be

Figure 5.

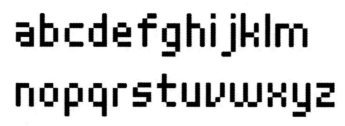

Stedelijk typeface

Figure 6.

New Alphabet typeface

read on very small scales. Their geometry responds to the screen's matrix and, compared to the typeface Oakland, seems much more refined.

This then brings me back to the keitai screen's resolution and pixel dimensions. Most current keitai screen resolutions are around 132x176 pixels, with a few at 360x480 pixels. Color keitai screens range from the basic 256 colors to a crisp 266k colors. The various keitai built-in cameras can capture still images from 176x144 to an astonishing 640x480 pixels and some with even a few seconds of video.

With these achievements in high screen resolutions, KDDI Corp. and Okinawa Cellular released four keitai in August 2002 with built-in cameras that are able to capture up to 15 seconds of smooth running video and audio. Captured video can then be viewed, subtitles and voiceovers can be added, video can be attached to an e-mail and easily sent to another "Movie Keitai" or computer. These keitai take advantage of the third-generation CDMA2000 wireless network which has data transmission speeds of up to 144 kbps allowing captured images to be sent and downloaded smoothly.

There are hundreds of paid subscription services for the keitai that provide everything from astrological information to financial transactions. All of these

Figure 7.

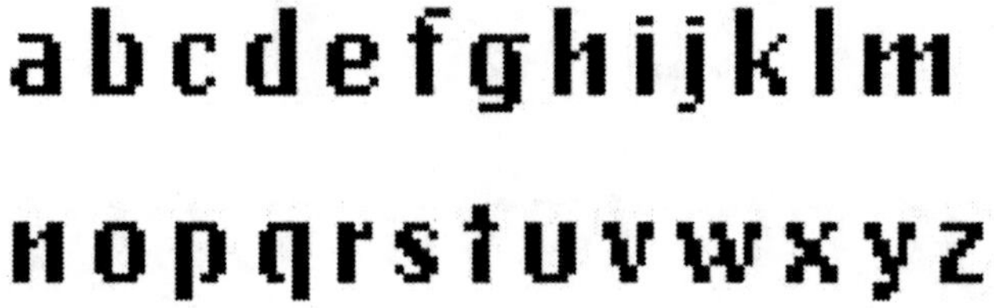

Oakland typeface

services have rich GUI's and some are animated. But probably one of the most interesting uses of graphics and interaction is the map service simply called "Keitai Map" provided by Zenrin. Enter a simple search query on your screen and up comes a vector map image that zooms in and out smoothly. The maps are clear and if used in tandem with one's built-in GPS you will never be lost in Tokyo's labyrinth of streets again.

Along with captured images, subscription services, and Japanese characters, an iconic graphic language has emerged for quick messaging on the keitai. Called "emoji," (a shorthand) it evolved from the use of text to make images that would represent a user's emotions. Examples: ^_^ represents the user is happy; ($_$) represents the user is greedy; and (olo) represents the Japanese superhero Ultra man. There are now hundreds of little emoji 16x16 pixel icons, mostly static, some animated. Emoji has become hugely popular. A typical message — "Meet me for a beer at 7 p.m." — could consist of the emoji for a frosty beer mug and a clock showing 7 p.m. Emoji has become a new typography developed for the keitai.

In contrast to the personal graphics and text created on the keitai, graphics and type on the large LED screens are much more robust and often in full motion with sound, creating the ultimate experience of screenspace. Most screens are typically only a few meters across, but the huge screen called Q Eye, found in Shibuya, is a least six stories tall. Located on the Q Front[7] building in Shibuya, it is an example of architecture becoming a screen or a screen becoming architecture. On its front surface there is a large display made up of three separate screens containing more than 121,600 LED clusters broken into red, green and blue. Q Eye towers over pedestrians as they navigate the intersections around the JR Shibuya station. It is composed of three separate screens: two "banner" screens on the top and bottom and one main screen in the center. Since the screens are synchronized, they create the illusion of one large screen towering six stories tall. Q Eye seems to be always on and in constant motion, displaying videos of Japan's hottest pop stars to advertisements for Sony's new cameras. At night, the glow from its screens, along with the two other small screens in its vicinity, light up the streets, giving Shibuya an eerie feel as colors and images shift and move.

FUTURE TRENDS

As Tokyo's streets shine and flicker from the ever-popular keitai and newly constructed jumbo LED displays, major companies are developing the next generation of screens. Of particular interest for these researchers: improvement of screen resolution, energy usage, thinness, and flexibility. The focus on flexibility and thinness is evident in current research on organic electroluminescence (OEL) and E-ink's screens.

Electronic ink's (E-Ink's) main components consist of thousands of tiny microcapsules that have the diameter of 100 microns (about the width of a human hair). These microcapsules contain both positively and negatively charged particles of white and black color. When a positive electric field is applied to the microcapsule, the white particles become visible; when a negative charge is applied, the black particles become visible. With these microcapsules turning on and off, thousands are necessary to create an image. Arranged in a grid, they function in a similar fashion as a pixel on a computer screen.

These microcapsules are suspended in a liquid, allowing E-Ink to be printed on virtually any surface from plastic to metal. The main advantages that E-Ink demonstrates over current display technologies include low power usage, flexibility, durability, and readability. First introduced in 1999, E-Ink displays draw only 0.1 watts of power and only when changing its display; an E-Ink sign with static information draws no power.

Electronic paper, which is very similar to E-Ink, is being simultaneously developed by Xerox. First developed in the 1970s it functions in a similar manner to E-Ink, but has microscopic balls that are black on one side and white on the other. These balls rotate when an electrical charge is applied, showing either black or white.

E-Ink is currently more desirable because of its simplicity and cost compared to electronic paper, which also requires complicated wiring. The main drawback with current E-Ink and electronic paper technology is that their screens are only monochromatic (multicolored screens are in development).

Organic electroluminescence displays (OEL) contain thin organic layers made of a carbon-based compound that illuminates brightly when an electric charge is applied. This allows for thin, flexible, cool (temperature), brightly glowing screens that operate on very low power. Monochromatic passive-matrix OEL screens are currently found everywhere from car stereos to keitai. Currently, full color active-matrix OEL displays, driven by thin film transistors (TFT), are limited in size due to production cost.

The future market potential for large OEL screens is tremendous. Major companies (e.g., Pioneer, Sony, Sanyo, Kodak, NEC, and Samsung) have been pouring millions of research dollars into perfecting the production and performance of large full color OEL active-matrix displays. From this research, Sanyo has developed and put into production a 260,000-color OEL screen for use with third-generation multimedia keitai currently found in Japan. This commitment by Sanyo indicates the future direction of keitai screen technology.

The real breakthrough will occur when full color OEL displays reach 10" (diagonal measurement) or more with screen resolutions of 800x600 pixels and greater. In 2001, Sony was the first to produce a prototype screen measuring 13" with a screen resolution of 800x600 pixels and measuring just 1.4 millimeters in thickness. Mass production of these large OEL screens will replace the cathode ray tube and current LCD monitors, bringing us one step closer to jumbo OEL screens.

Pioneer began mass production of monochromatic passive-matrix OEL displays in 1997. Used on Motorola cellphones, these passive-matrix screens do not need integrated circuits or a glass base, allowing the screen to be built on plastic. From this research, Pioneer has prototyped wearable plastic OEL screens attached to winter coats and has begun the mass production of small passive-matrix screens for PDAs.

The cutting edge research that is being done is essential for the future of screenspace. With E-Ink and electronic paper, screens will be more flexible and will require little maintenance and energy consumption. But the real future of screenspace relies upon the research in OEL display technology. With the possibilities of screens being incorporated into clothing and jumbo OEL screens (as well as meshing into newly constructed buildings) every surface has the potential to become a screen.

Along with this vast research being conducted by R&D labs of major companies, two artists — Ryota Kuwakubo and Sugihara Yuki — are expanding our ideas of screens and how we interact with them. Ryota Kuwakubo's work uses low-powered LED screens that are part of highly interactive devices. As users interact with the objects, elegantly designed circuits transmit signals to small clusters of LEDs creating patterns, symbols, and simple smiling faces. Bit-Man, designed to be worn around the neck while dancing, has an LED display of a man that responds to various sensors. The electronic man consists of a grid of red LEDs; the more Bit-Man is shaken, the longer and faster the electronic man dances. If Bit-Man is rotated in any direction, the LED man positions himself upright.

In contemporary Japan, Yuki Sugihara steps away from the traditional use and understanding of screens. She utilizes water as a "screen" to project light and images upon. Sugihara's work, titled "Head-Mounted Water Display," recently exhibited at NTT's Intercommunication Center in Tokyo. It invites viewers to step into a dark room. Inside, a cascading dome of water has been placed in the room's center and users step under the water dome one at a time to view colors and patterns projected upon the fluid surface of the dome. Sugihara brings the natural and the technological together in an elegant display of water, color, and image.

CONCLUSION

As of this writing, Japan leads the world in the development of the small personal keitai screens along with the jumbo LED displays. Times Square in New York City seems to be the only other location that rivals Shibuya with its saturation of screens. Major cellular phone companies in America are now realizing the popularity of wireless web access and have developed limited web access applications[8]. Movies such as *Minority Report* (2002), *The Time Machine* (2002), and *Brazil* (1985) present us with glimpses of what the future could hold for us and how we might interact with screenspace. Screens are becoming more affordable and sleek LCD flat screen monitors are more common, replacing the bulky CRT (cathode ray tube). Also, with research on OEL displays (E-Ink and the next generation of keitai) screenspace and cellspace will eventually become one.

As these technologies mature and new technologies are discovered, displays will not only get clearer, but will have the ability to be anywhere and everywhere. Screenspace and cellspace will become one, and urban land-scapes will flicker brightly in the night sky.

ENDNOTES

[1]   Hertzian Space is used by Anthony Dunne and Fiona Raby to described the invisible spectrum of electromagnetic waves that are emitted from various devices.

[2]   Japanese for cellphone and translates to "portable".

[3]   Sha is short for photograph in Japanese.

[4]   As of July 2002, there were three large LED displays at Shibuya crossing.

[5]   Capsule hotels are typically for men only.

[6]   Hirigana and Katakana are phonetic characters where Kanji is more complex and each character represents various words depending on context.

[7]   Q eye is a LED screen located on the front of the Q front building at Shibuya crossing in Tokyo, Japan.

[8] mMode from AT&T Wireless and PCS Vision from Sprint are bringing high-speed access to their cellular phone users. These services allow web access, gaming, instant messaging, custom ring tones and images to be sent from on phone to the other.

REFERENCES

Barlow, J., & Resnic, D. (June 6, 2002). *E Ink unveils world's thinnest active matrix display.* Retrieved from: http://www.eink.com/news/releases/pr60.html.

Bennahum, D S. (n.d.). *CellSpace.* Retrieved from: http://www.memex.org/meme4-03.html; http://whatis.techtarget.com/definition/0,,sid9_gci211762,00.html.

Grotz, V. (1998). *Color & type for the screen crans.* RotoVision SA.

Miyake, K. (October 7, 2001). *Organic EL displays make many appearances.* Retrieved from: http://www.cnn.com/2001/TECH/ptech/10/07/organic.el.idg/.

Nelson, T. & Revie, J. (1996). *Thin-film transistor LCD displays.* Retrieved from: http://www.cs.ndsu.nodak.edu/~revie/amlcd/.

Ross, M.F. (1978). *Beyond Metabolism: The New Japanese Architecture.* New York: Architectural Record.

Suzuki, A. (2001). *Do Android Crows Fly Over the Skies of an Electronic Tokyo?* (Trans. J. Keith Vincent). London: Architectural Association.

Wurster, C. (2002). *Computers: An Illustrated History.* Koln, Taschen.

Chapter IV

How to Use Photoshop to Improve the Gestalt of an Image

Linda Emme
Art Center College of Design, USA

ABSTRACT

Visual communication through images depends upon the composition of forms within the image having a structure, or Gestalt, to carry the content through the end-user's perception process to a state of understanding. Looking at an image while squinting the eyes and thus suppressing color information and detail can easily identify composition problems. Visually disruptive problem areas can be selected in Photoshop, and the value and color corrected using Adjustment Layers. Directions are included for cleaning up of distracting visual trash such as dust, hair, scratches or unwanted objects. Step-by-step directions and examples explain the entire process.

INTRODUCTION

Form is the visible shape of content.

- Ben Shahn

These step-by-step directions constitute a pragmatic approach to looking at an image, analyzing the composition, identifying compositional disruptions, and correcting them using Photoshop 7. First, the Gestalt (the German word for shape or form) theory of visual psychology and perception will be discussed as it is decidedly helpful in understanding how an image is received by the end-user. Then, a value (lights and darks) analysis will be made of the image to identify disruptions to the composition and focal point. In Photoshop 7, the problem areas will be selected and corrected, thus achieving a greater simplicity of forms and a greater chance that the image is perceived as intended. Also included is a brief description of basic color correction and basic image clean up.

Photoshop 7 offers sophisticated tools for controlling composition, value and color correction, mask making, compositing, special effects, and more. It is heavily used for precise image control in industries such as advertising, offset printing, industrial design, film and video postproduction. It is also an essential tool for professionals in many other fields such as multimedia, website design, computer graphics, and photography.

THE GESTALT THEORY
OF VISUAL PERCEPTION

The Gestalt theory of psychology, a major influence at the Bauhaus, was first developed by Dr. Max Wertheimer in Germany in 1912. Through experimentation in visual perception, Wertheimer found that the end-user's perception of an image is influenced by the physical attributes of color cones and rods in the eye, the complex pattern of dendrites in the abstract shape reading area of the brain and, further, by the individual's already established framework of knowledge and culture. Every person sees and analyzes the same image in his or her own particularly individual way. "All perceiving is also thinking, all reasoning is also intuition, all observation is also invention," states Arnheim (1974, p. 5). The viewer of an image seeks simplicity in visual organization, just as computer programmers seek elegance in code. When a

Figure 1.

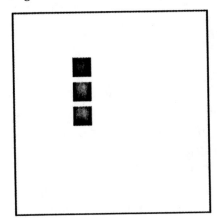

Figure 2.

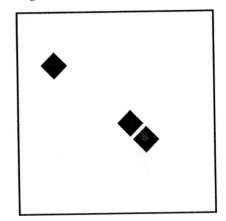

Figure 3.

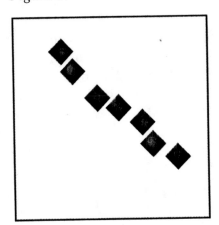

Figure 4.

"coherent pattern and unity … cannot be found, it seems the viewer will turn away and simply ignore the image" (Lauer & Pentak, 1995, p. 23).

The Gestalt Laws include grouping (creating holistic structures) through:

- *Proximity:* Nearness in location produces grouping. (See Figure 1.)
- *Similarity:* Elements that are similar in shape, size, color, spatial orientation, repetition, or movement will be related and grouped. (See Figure 2.) "A shape needs a friend," painter Vern Wilson said while teaching at Art Center College of Design.

- *Continuity:* Shapes that are placed side-to-side will be seen as a continuous line. (See Figure 3.)
- *Closure:* Through a similarity of shape, orientation, and location, an incomplete shape is seen as complete or closed. (See Figure 4.)

Other Gestalt concepts include visual balance, Notan (the Japanese word for dark-light), figure and ground, line and contour, space created through light, perspective, interaction of color, dynamics, tension, leveling, sharpening, and motion. Developing the knowledge and skills to fully control composition may indeed become a lifetime's work. Hokusai created his woodcut *The Great Wave at Kanawaga* (Forrer, 2002, pp. 43-45) as one of 36 views of Mt. Fuji, each with a different composition. The Gestalt Laws deserve an image-maker's thoughtful study, and there are many excellent books that present a thorough explanation (such as those listed in the References).

HOW DOES THE END-USER'S VISUAL PERCEPTION INFLUENCE OUR IMAGE MAKING?

The image's composition is the framework that carries the image's content through the end-users process of perception. Within the perception process, there are many opportunities for misinterpretation of an image. As the creator of an image with the hope of communicating specific content to the end-user, it is wise to make the content as visually clear as possible. An irrelevant bright spot in a corner will distract or even disrupt the end-user's perception process. It may distract from the intended focal point and the intended content.

LOOK AND SEE WHAT IS REALLY THERE

The center of the retina is covered with about five million cones that perceive color and detail. The cones receive color information — the hue, or color itself, such as red; the saturation, or how much of the hue is included; and the brightness, or how light or dark the color is. The larger, surrounding area — 95% of the retina — is covered with rods. Perceiving only lights and darks, or *values*, in low light situations and movement, the rods ignore color and detail (Zakia, 1997, pp. 201-202). In low light, the eye sees only the essentials — light and dark forms and movement.

We can use the rods in our eyes to quickly assess how an image "reads". Is our intended primary focal point—also called the first read—really the first read? Here's the test. First look away and clear your mind of your image. Look at natural light if possible because that resets the body's internal clock and will help relax the body. Then, squint to set up a low light situation where only the cones in your eyes are functioning. Look at your image and pay close attention to your initial response. Where does your eye go first? Where does it move to after that? If your eye did not first go to the intended focal point, but instead to some irrelevant bright spot, you have identified a problem in the composition of the image that can easily be corrected in Photoshop.

BEFORE YOU BEGIN

Before you begin, remove visual distractions (such as a desktop pattern) from your monitor. It is easier for you to see your image clearly if your desktop is 50% gray. (In OSX, go to the Apple Menu > System Preferences > Personal > Desktop > Solid Color Collection > Solid Gray Medium.)

Open Your image in Photoshop

*   Go to Image > Mode > 8 Bits/Channel (Photoshop 7 does not function in 16 Bits/Channel, but Photoshop CS does).
*   Save it as a Photoshop file format (.psd).
*   If the rulers are on, turn them off (Control/Command R).
*   To remove the lock on the Background layer, Control/Option double click on the layer name in the Layers Palette.
*   Make the image window active and press the F on the keyboard to see your image in Full Screen Mode. Press F again to see it with a black background. Then, press the Tab key to hide the toolbox and menu bar. When you are finished, press Tab to show the Toolbox and F to return to Standard Screen Mode.

TARGETING DISRUPTIVE AREAS IN THE IMAGE'S GESTALT

As discussed above, the end-user's eye tries to create understandable forms and structure out of the chaos in an image. The eye moves first to the area that is lightest, has high contrast and detail, and is the focal point of the Gestalt of the composition. This should be the primary focal point. It then searches for the second highest level, then the third highest, thus moving the eye around the image. Any bright, high contrast areas that are unintentional, lie on the outer edge, or are irrelevant information, will be highly disruptive for the viewer and lessen the impact of the image and its content. Identify problem areas, select them, and change them by following these steps:

Step 1: Squint Your Eyes and Look at the Image — Be Aware of Where Your Eyes Go First

Look away from your image, clear your mind, then squint and look directly at your image. Be aware of your first impression — the first read — and monitor your reaction carefully. What do you see first? Is that what you want to be seen first? Is an area disruptive or distracting to the eye? If the answer is yes, then you have found an area that needs to be isolated and adjusted in Photoshop.

In this image, the composition problem lies in the top right corner. The light area distracts from the play of light through the leaves and makes it difficult to see the leaves. Also, the rest of the background is a little too dark to silhouette the leaves.

Figure 5. Original Scan of 'Fall Leaves'

Figure 6. 'Fall Leaves' (seen with squinting the eyes)

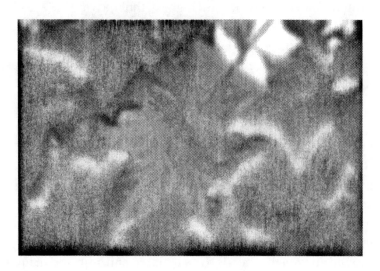

Step 2: Select the Area to be Adjusted

Making Selections

When you make a selection, it is really a selection mask. It protects the image outside the selection (the marching ants) while allowing the area inside to be altered — lightened, darkened, desaturated, the color adjusted or changed completely, etc. Selections can be made with any combination of selections tools — the Marquee, Lasso, Magnetic Lasso, Magic Wand (feathering must be set in the Select Menu after the selection is made), the Pen Tool, Magnetic Pen or Color Range (under the Select Menu). Just hold down the Shift key and use another selection tool.

My preference for making selections is a combination of the Lasso Tool, the Pen Tool, and the Magic Wand. In many situations, making a selection includes defining the shape when one shape blends into another. In such cases, the selection process can begin with the Magic Wand or Color Range, but must be more carefully defined with the Lasso.

The Pen Tool is used for anything with large, smooth curves, such as a body or fruit, an airplane or product packaging. Also, the Background Eraser does an excellent job of erasing a background color from around hair. Once the background is completely erased, Control/Command clicking on the layer can load the layer transparency as a selection.

To select with the Magic Wand, first click on the tool, then go to the Options bar and choose:

- Tolerance 32 (Range 0-255) — the number of values and colors you will select. A higher number selects more values and colors.
- Anti-alias
- Contiguous — to select values and colors next to each other only.

Click on an area in the image. Hold down the Shift key and add another and another area. To feather (soften the edge), go to the Select Menu > Feather …

- 0 gives you a hard, jagged edge
- 1 pixel gives you a sharp photographic edge
- 2 pixels give you a soft photographic edge
- 5 to 8 pixels give you a blurred edge

To save this selection as an Alpha Channel that you can access later, go to the Select Menu > Save Selection > New Channel. To load the selection, > Load Selection. You can load the selection later, work on it, and save it again with Replace Channel. Save the file to save the Channel.

Figure 7. The Light Area Selected with the Magic Wand and Lasso Tools

To define areas of the selection first load it, then click on the Lasso Tool and look at the Options bar. Always have Anti-aliasing clicked on. In the Feather box, type the appropriate number to match the focus, soft or hard, of the area you are selecting.

- 0 gives you a hard, jagged edge
- 1 pixel gives you a sharp photographic edge
- 2 pixels give you a soft photographic edge

To add to another selection with the Lasso, first hold down the Shift key and draw right on the edge of your object. End by coming back to the place you began. If you don't like the selection, click Control/Command D to deselect. You can also click outside of the selection to get rid of it.

Since the selection is probably a bit rough, you may want to add areas to it. To add to the selection, hold down the Shift key, click *inside* the selection and circle the area you want to add. Come back inside the selection to finish it. Release the mouse. You can also add areas that are not connected by using the Shift key and circling those areas.

To subtract from the selection, hold down the Alt/Option key. Start *outside* the selection, circle the area you want to get rid of and come back to where you started. Release the mouse.

Zoom in and keep adjusting your selection until it is correct. If you forgot to feather, or need to change the amount of feathering, go to the Select Menu > Feather and type in the appropriate number.

Step 3: Turn Your Selection into an Adjustment Layer

Open the Layers Palette by going to the Window Menu > Layers.

With your selection active, go to the Adjustment Layers icon at the bottom of the Layers Palette (the split circle, third icon from the right). Pull down on the menu and choose Solid Color or Levels. This will make a new layer that contains only the area you selected. When you fill the selection with a color, it fills only that area. (I then went to the Layers Palette > Mode > Linear Burn > Opacity 50%.) When you change the settings in Levels, it will affect only your selected area; and you can return to the Adjustment Layer to modify your settings. Adjustment Layers give you a great amount of flexibility!

Figure 8.   Selection Turned into an Adjustment Layer for Solid Color (Using the Pre-Selected Foreground Color)

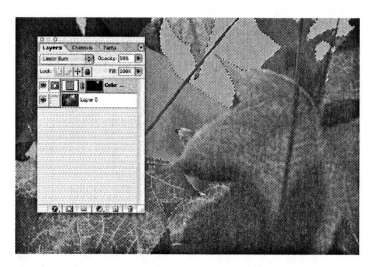

Step 4: Use Levels to Lighten or Darken the Area within the Selection

To adjust the value and contrast in your Adjustment Layer, double click the layer thumbnail — the icon with the graph and slider. The histogram shows how the pixels' values are distributed in the area you selected. The triangular-shaped sliders represent:

- Black point on the left
- Mid-tone (gamma) in the center
- White point on the right

Begin by adjusting the mid-tones in your selection. Move the center slider to the left to lighten them or to the right to darken them.

To increase the contrast, move both the black and white sliders toward the center.

To decrease the contrast, go to Output Levels at the bottom of the dialogue box and move the sliders toward the center.

Figure 9. A Second Selection is Made of the Rest of the Background; Then an Adjustment Layer for Levels is Made; The Background Darkened to Contrast with the Leaves

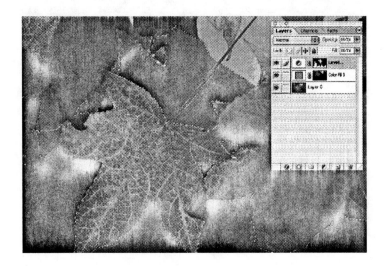

Step 5: Make an Adjustment Layer to Lighten or Darken the Whole Image

Press Control/Command D to deselect any selections.

In the Layers Palette, click on the Adjustment Layer icon (split circle) and pull down to Levels. This will make a new Adjustment Layer above the last one. Since it is on top in the stacking order, it will affect the entire image and all layers below it.

Look at the histogram (graph) of your image. It represents the number of pixels in each value from black to white. In an image with a full range of values (from black to white) that has been scanned, it is common to find a little empty space to the right or left of the "mountains" of pixel values. The contrast needs to be corrected.

Before you begin, be aware that every image will have a different histogram — a seascape on a foggy day will have very little contrast and if the contrast were increased, it would no longer look foggy. A photograph shot outside at high noon will have very high contrast and may need a decrease in overall contrast. Many images may only need adjustments made in specific areas to correct the composition: the "read" — not overall adjustment.

If your image needs an overall adjustment to value and contrast:

- Move the white point slider to the left to where the pixels of the image begin (to set the white point).
- Move the black point slider to the right to where the pixels of the image begin (to set the black point).
- Move the gamma (mid-tones) slider — the center slider — to the left to lighten or to the right to darken them.
- To increase the contrast, move the black and white sliders toward the center.

All of these settings are adjustable by double clicking on the layer thumbnail icon for Levels.

This may be all that some images require, but I recommend that you return to Step 1, squint, and look at your image anew. Make a new selection and Levels Adjustment layer for each problem area. Adjust and readjust them as needed.

Step 6: In Addition, You May Need to Adjust the Overall Color

Before you begin color correction, your monitor should be calibrated to your desktop printer or offset printer so that what you see is what you get. If you also have a scanner, the scanner-monitor-desktop printer should all be calibrated together. On the Mac, this can be done using hardware and software: the Pantone Spyder Color Calibrator; visually with the Adobe Gamma utility (Mac OS 9) or Displays control panel (Mac OS X) and Display Calibrator Assistant-plus ColorSync and ICC profiles. For more information see Weinmann and Lourekas' (2003) *Photoshop for Windows and Macintosh* (pp. 37-50).

To adjust the overall color, look at the top of the Levels dialogue box for the Channel pull-down menu. When adjusting values, choose the RGB channel. To adjust color, choose the R or G or B channel. Adjust each as needed. Do this with caution and small adjustments!

- Move the sliders to add or subtract that color from the mid-tones, shadows, or highlights.
- To add red to the mid-tones, move the middle slider to the left.
- To reduce the amount of red in the mid-tones, move the middle slider to the right (to de-saturate the red).
- Continue adjusting with each of the red, green, and blue channels as needed.

The same adjustment can be made in the Color Balance. To adjust the overall image, make a new Adjustment layer and choose Color Balance from the pull-down menu.

- Click on the Mid-tones radio button in the Tone Balance section, then proceed to the upper section to adjust the colors. If the image has an overall magenta tone, push the slider toward green. Play with the slider first to see that big adjustments will colorize the image (and add contrast), while small adjustments will neutralize and balance the color.
- Next, click on the Shadows radio button and adjust the colors. In general, shadows are cool colors such as cyan, green, and blue.
- Click on the Highlights radio button and adjust the colors. The highlight tone should reflect the colors around it.

Tip: When you made a selection and then an Adjustment layer, you were also saving that selection. You can access that selection in the Layers Palette by Control/Command clicking the layer mask thumbnail (the small black and white picture of your selection.) This will activate your selection.

Step 7: Adjust the Color in Your Already Selected Areas if Needed

To adjust the color in a selected area that is already an Adjustment layer, double click on the Layer Thumbnail icon for Levels. Choose the Channel you want to work with, such as red. Follow the directions in Step 6 to increase or decrease the amount of red in that area. Push the mid-tone slider to the left to increase the amount of red, and push it to the right to decrease the amount of red.

Step 8: Removing Dust, Hair, Scratches, or Unwanted Objects From the Scanned Image

The Clone Stamp Tool and Healing Brush Tool

Before you begin, go to the Photoshop Menu > Preferences > Display and Cursors > Painting Cursors > Brush Size to see the real size of the brush on your file. When using these tools, always choose a brush size that is appropriate to the job. If the object to be replaced is small, choose a small, fairly hard-edged brush. Using a very soft edged brush with the Clone Stamp Tool creates an out of focus ring around the brush.

The Clone Stamp Tool is used to copy and move the pixels selected by the brush to another part of the image or another layer. It is used to remove dust, hair, scratches, or unwanted object, such as a telephone pole, by covering the unwanted pixels with pixels from another part of the image, such as a tree or sky.

- Mode — Normal
- Opacity — 100% to begin, down to 50% to blend areas
- Flow — 100%
- Check Aligned
- Leave Use All Layers unchecked if you want to work on just one layer
- Check Use All Layers if you want to use pixels and change pixels from all layers

Alt/Option click on your file to define the area you want to copy.

Release the Alt/Option key and click somewhere else on your image to copy to. You can keep painting with the brush to cover a larger area. The Clone Stamp Tool will not work on Adjustment Layers. When you first Alt/Option click to define the place you want to copy, you must be on the layer that contains those pixels. Then you can copy those pixels to another area of the same layer or to a different layer (Use All Layers checked).

Figure 10. Clone Stamp Tool is Used to Cover White Pixels in a Very Small Area of a Stem (a five pixel, hard-edged brush was chosen to replicate the crisp line and subtle shading of the stem)

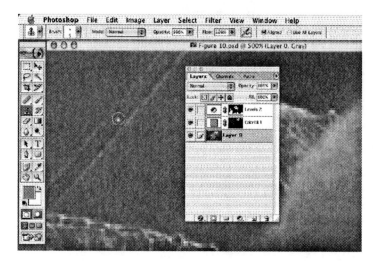

The Healing Brush Tool also copies pixels from the sampled area and pastes them onto another chosen location; but it blends the color, value, and texture of the two samples together. In most situations, this greatly speeds up the process of retouching. However, if you need to get rid of a piece of red pepper on a white tablecloth, the Healing Brush will create a pink spot because it is blending the two. To totally get rid of any traces of red or pink, first use the Clone Stamp Tool and cover the red. Then, use the Healing Brush to blend the gradations from light falling across the tablecloth.

To use the Healing Brush, click on the tool and then go to the options bar. Choose the:
- Brush Size — pick the right size brush for the task
- Mode — Normal
- Source — Sampled
- Check Aligned

Alt/Option click on your file to define the area you want to copy.

Release the Alt/Option key, and click somewhere else on your image to copy the sample taken.

Step 9: Once the Image is Complete ...

You will know when the image is complete when it "reads" with a Gestalt, or structure, that is clear. The primary and secondary focal points will appear without disruption, moving the eye around the image.

When you are finished, save a version of your file with the Adjustment Layers so that you can adjust it in the future if needed. If you are printing to an inkjet desktop printer, keep the color Mode in RGB for brighter colors. Epson printers do not require that you Flatten the file.

If you are printing on an inkjet desktop printer, but making a match print for an offset printer, change the color Mode to CMYK. Go to the Image Menu > Mode > CMYK. If you are preparing a file for offset printing, consult the Photoshop manual or Photoshop 7 for Windows and Macintosh, by Weinmann and Lourekas, for further information on converting to CMYK.

To make a smaller, flattened file for printing, go to the drop-down menu in the top right corner of the Layers palette. Pull down to Flatten Image. All visible layers (with the Eyes on) will be combined into the background layer. Depending on its projected use, the file can now be saved as a .psd, .tif, .jpeg, or .pict file format.

CONCLUSION

Visual communication of content through images will be improved by paying attention to the underlying Gestalt, or composition (structure), of the image. Disruptions and distractions in the composition make it difficult for the end-user to "read" the image and to understand the content. For an image to "read" correctly, the end-user must be able to see the primary and secondary focal points and to move through the image with them. However, the image-maker is often too close to the image to see it as the end-user will. Using the method of evaluating an image by looking at it while squinting allows the image-maker to see what the end-user sees and to identify composition problems.

Once a composition problem has been found, the image-maker can use Photoshop and follow the step-by-step process to change that area. Since most focal point problems are caused by values in an area being too light or too dark, the image-maker first selects the area and then uses a Levels Adjustment Layer to change the values. In addition, once values are changed, colors in the area may also need adjustment, using a Levels or Color Balance Adjustment Layer. Depending upon the individual image, the overall contrast and color may also need adjustment. Finally, scanned images usually need removal of dust, hair, scratches, or unwanted objects, which are also visually distracting. In Photoshop, the Clone Stamp Tool and the Healing Brush provide excellent tools for this clean up.

Once the visual problems have been taken care of, it is wise to return to the first step and look at the image while squinting. Some secondary problems can be seen only after major problems have been eliminated. When the image "reads" easily and clearly, and the content is accessible without visual disruption, the image is complete and ready for the end-user.

REFERENCES

Arnheim, R. (1974). *Art and Visual Perception.* New Version. Berkeley, CA: University of California Press.

Forrer, M. (2002). *Hokusai.* New York: Barnes & Noble.

Itten, J. (1975). *Design and Form.* (Rev. ed.) New York: Van Nostrand Reinhold.

Lauer, D., & Pentak, S. (1995). *Design Basics.* 4th ed. Fort Worth: Harcourt.

Newberg, A., M.D. (2001). *Why God Won't Go Away: Brain Science & the Biology of Belief.* New York: Ballantine.

Shahn, B. (1972). *The Shape of Content*. Cambridge, MA: Harvard University Press.

Weinmann, E., & Lourekas, P. (2003). *Photoshop 7 for Windows & Macintosh*. Berkeley, CA: Peachpit Press.

Wilson, V. (personal communication).

Zakia, R. (1997). *Perception and Imaging*. Boston, MA: Focal Press.

SECTION II

COMPUTER SCIENCE

Chapter V

Adaptive Narrative Virtual Environments

Karl Steiner
University of North Texas, USA

ABSTRACT

Narratives are an important method of human-to-human communication. Combining the power of narrative with the flexibility of virtual environments (VEs) can create new and innovative opportunities in education, in entertainment, and in visualization. In this chapter, we explore the topic of narrative VEs. We describe the characteristics and benefits of narrative VEs, review related work in VEs and in computer-generated narrative, and outline components of an architecture for managing narrative VEs. We present the current status of our work developing such an architecture and conclude by discussing what the future of narrative VEs may hold.

INTRODUCTION

Storytelling is a significant method of human-to-human communication. We tell stories to share ideas, to convey emotions, and to educate. As new communication technologies have become available we have employed them in our storytelling, allowing us to reach wider audiences or to tell stories in new ways. Narratives were among the initial and most popular content types as books, radio, movies, and television were introduced to the public. VEs may provide the next technological advancement for presenting narratives. Consider the following examples.

Illustration 1

An inexperienced army specialist enters an immersive simulator in order to practice skills such as identifying and overcoming threats in an urban environment. The specialist encounters a hostile unit on Main Street, but chooses to retreat to a safe location. No longer sure of her ability to handle the hostile unit, the officer continues to explore the environment, but avoids Main Street. Aware that the specialist is no longer able to interact with the hostile unit on Main Street, the environment attempts to surprise the officer with a new hostile unit near her current location. This time she is better prepared. Rather than retreat, she engages and subdues the hostile unit.

Illustration 2

A child, nervous about an upcoming surgery, is given an opportunity to explore a virtual hospital. The child follows a patient about to undergo similar surgery, sees all the preparations that take place, and becomes familiar with the various people who are involved in the procedure. While he does not see the actual surgery take place, the environment makes sure the child notices that there are other children waiting for surgery and that they are all experiencing many of the same emotions that he is. He is reassured after his exploration — not just with his knowledge of the procedure, but that his fears and concerns are normal.

Illustration 3

A young adult begins interacting with a new mystery game set in a virtual environment. In the initial interactions, the player continually chooses to explore the environment and look for clues, rather than chase and subdue suspects. Noting the players interests, the game adjusts the plotline to emphasize puzzles rather than conflicts.

These examples illustrate three powerful, yet underutilized, potentials of VEs. The first attribute is that events occur not randomly, but according to a plan based on scenario or narrative goals. The second attribute is that the system may recognize and respond to user goals and interests in addition to the given scenario goals. And the third attribute is that the system chooses when, where, and how to present events in order to best meet the user and scenario goals.

In this chapter, we will explore the topic of narrative VEs. We begin by describing the characteristics and benefits of narrative VE. We review related work that has influenced the current state of both VE and computer-generated narrative and outline components of an architecture for managing narrative VE. We describe the current status of our work developing such an architecture and conclude by discussing what the future of narrative VE may hold.

BACKGROUND

Narrative VE

Narrative VEs are an emerging multimedia technology, integrating storytelling techniques into VEs. VEs and virtual reality have been defined in different ways. For this chapter, we will define a VE as a computer-generated 3D space with which a user can interact. The concept of narrative also has different meanings in different contexts. In our work, we consider a narrative to be a sequence of events with a conflict and resolution structure (a story). So, for us, a narrative VE is an immersive, computer-generated 3D world in which sequences of events are presented in order to tell a story.

Not all VEs are narrative, nor are VEs the only way of presenting computer-based narratives. Most VEs do not have an explicitly narrative structure. While most VEs include events of some sort, they do not provide the plot-driven selection and ordering of events that separates stories from simulation. For example, a driving simulator might model the roadways of a city, complete with cars, pedestrians, and traffic signals. Events in this simulation-oriented VE might include a traffic light changing from green to red, a pedestrian successfully crossing an intersection, or a collision between two cars.

In a simulation, the rules that govern when and how events occur are based primarily on attributes of the world and the object within it. In our driving VE, the stoplight may cycle from green to yellow to red every 30 seconds. Pedestrians cross roads successfully when there is no traffic. A collision may occur whenever the paths of two objects intersect at the same point in space and time. While simulation rules are adequate to describe object-object interactions and can even be used to model very complex environments (such as flying a 747 or driving through city traffic), they do not typically address broader goals or plans of the users or authors of the environment. The rules and random probabilities of a simulator do not take into account how an event will impact the environment or the user.

In a narrative VE, however, the occurrences of at least some key events are based on storytelling goals. For example, in a narrative VE designed to illustrate the dangers of jaywalking, the stoplight may turn green as soon as the user's car approaches the intersection. The pedestrian may wait to start crossing the intersection until the user's car enters the intersection. While these events may be similar to those in a simulator (traffic signal changes color, pedestrian crosses the street), the timing, placement, and representation of these events is done in such a manner as to communicate a particular story. This is what differentiates a simulation from a narrative.

Benefits of Narrative VE

Combining the power of narrative with the power of VEs creates a number of potential benefits. New ways of experiencing narratives as well as new types of VE applications may become possible. Existing VE applications may become more effective to run or more efficient to construct.

Narrative VE can extend our traditional ideas of narrative. Unlike traditional narrative media, narrative VE can be dynamic, nonlinear, and interactive. The events in a narrative VE would be ultimately malleable, adapting themselves according to a user's needs and desires, the author's goals, or context and user interaction. A narrative VE might present a story in different ways based on a user profile that indicates whether the user prefers adventure or romance. A user could choose to view the same event from the viewpoint of different characters or reverse the flow of time and change decisions made by a character. A narrative VE might adapt events in order to enhance the entertainment, the education, or the communication provided by the environment. And a narrative VE might adapt events in order to maintain logical continuity and to preserve the suspension of disbelief (Murray, 1998).

These narrative capabilities could also open up new application areas for VE. Training scenarios that engage the participant, provide incrementally greater challenges, and encourage new forms of collaboration could become possible (Steiner, 2002). Interactive, immersive dramas could be created where the user becomes a participant in the story (Laurel, 1991). Presentations of temporal or spatial data could be self-organizing, arranging and rearranging the data based on different perspectives or emphases (Gershon, 2002).

While it is possible to add narrative elements to an otherwise simulation-oriented VE, the process can be difficult for designers, and the results less than satisfying for users. The most common application area for simulation-oriented VEs with narrative elements is computer games. A review of the current state of the art in 3D narrative games is instructive in considering the challenges VE designers face.

Many computer games now include narrative elements, though the quality and integration of the narratives vary widely. One of the most common narrative elements is a Full Screen Video (FSV) cut-scene that advances the storyline. These typically take place after a player has completed a level or accomplished some other goal. Other devices include conversations with non-player characters (NPCs) that are communicated as actual speech, as text, or as a FSV. These conversations are typically scripted in advance, with the only interactivity coming from allowing the user to choose from prepared responses.

Even with the best-produced narrative games, the narratives are generally tightly scripted and linear, providing little or no opportunity for influencing the plot of the story. Since the environment remains unaware of narrative goals, the designer must take measures to force users into viewing narrative events. This usually means either eliminating interactivity and forcing users to watch FSVs; or keeping interactivity, but eliminating choices so that the user must ultimately proceed down a particular path or choose a particular interaction. These solutions are unsatisfying for many users and time consuming for designers to construct.

A fundamental issue behind the limited interactivity is the tension between the user's desire to freely explore and interact with the environment and the designer's goals of having users experience particular educational, entertaining, or emotional events. Advances in visualization technology have exacerbated the issue. VEs are now capable of modeling more objects, behaviors, and relationships than a user can readily view or comprehend. Techniques for automatically selecting which events or information to present and how to present it are not available, so VE designers must explicitly specify the time, location, and conditions under which events may occur. As a result, most VEs support mainly linear narratives or scenarios (if they support them at all).

Related Work

While there has been substantial research on the application of certain intelligent techniques to VEs, there has been little attention to adaptive interfaces for narrative VE. Still, in realizing an architecture for adaptive narrative VE, many lessons can be drawn from work in related areas. These include adaptive interfaces, intelligent agents in VE, automated cinematography in VE, narrative multimedia, and narrative presentation in VE.

Adaptive interfaces are those that change based on the task, work context, or the needs of the user. Often, the successful application of an adaptive interface requires simultaneous development of a user modeling component. A user modeling system allows the computer to maintain knowledge about the user and to make inferences regarding their activities or goals.

Adaptive interfaces allow computer applications to be more flexible, to deal with task and navigation complexity, and to deal with divers user characteristics and goals. Adaptive interfaces can be applied to almost any human/computer interaction. For example, the immense popularity of the WWW has lead to a corresponding amount of research on adaptive hypermedia. Similarly, adaptive techniques based on user models can also be employed in VEs.

Automated cinematography is a form of adaptivity particularly for VEs. Camera controllers or automated cinematographers are designed to free users and designers from explicitly specifying views. Simple camera controllers may follow a character at a fixed distance and angle, repositioning in order to avoid occluding objects or to compensate for user actions such as running. More complex controllers seek to model cinematography convention (He, 1996), to dynamically generate optimal camera angles to support explicitly stated user viewing or task goals (Bares, 1999), or to link camera control to a model of the ongoing narrative (Amerson, 2001).

Over the years, researchers have created various systems for dynamically generating textual narratives. One of the earliest systems, Talespin, created fable-like stories (Meehan, 1980). These narratives exhibited a conflict-resolution structure driven by characters seeking to achieve their goals; but the text was frequently repetitive, and the stories were not particularly engaging. Universe (Lebowitz, 1984) created a dynamic textual narrative based on a simulation of characters in a soap opera. While such a setting provides rich dramatic content, the narrative was again dictated by characters pursuing goals, rather than being dictated by a plot. In more recent work (Calloway, 2001) researchers have created the Author Architecture and the Storybook application, a narrative generation system capable of creating real-time fairy tale text almost on a par with human generated text.

A natural extension of the character driven textual narratives are character-driven VEs. Several VE systems have been built which allow users to interact with lifelike, believable, or emotional agents (Hayes-Roth, 1996). As with the character-driven textual systems, the results of interacting with these agents may be interesting or believable; but they may not exhibit an overall narrative coherence.

There has also been work on VE environments that seek to provide such coherence. In the OZ Architecture for Dramatic Guidance (Weyhrauch, 1997) a director gives instructions to actors in a VE, seeking to maximize the dramatic potential of a situation. Mimesis (Young, 2001) includes a director that works to detect and prevent potential plot conflicts due to user activities. The Dogmatics project (Galyean, 1995) attempts to direct user attention by manipulating the environment.

AN ARCHITECTURE FOR NARRATIVE VE INTELLIGENT INTERFACE

Building on this prior work, we are developing an architecture for adaptive narrative in VEs. This architecture combines components common to adaptive systems and VE systems and adds data and control structures capable of representing and reasoning about narratives. The architecture includes the following components: Adaptation Manager, Narrative Manager, User Modeler, and a 3D Engine. While other VE systems devoted to narrative presentation have addressed elements of VE architecture, we believe that our approach to adapting events represents a unique contribution to the field. Our narrative VE architecture is illustrated in Figure 1.

3D Engine and World State

Graphic VEs of the type we have been describing (as opposed to textual VEs such as MUDs and MOOs) rely on a 3D Engine to render the real-time images that make up the visual presentation of the environment. While there are many relevant research topics related to presentation of 3D images, our research focuses primarily upon technologies related to interaction, adaptivity, and narrative. Accordingly, rather than develop our own 3D engine, we have taken advantage of the many powerful VE environments that are now available to researchers and commercial developers. Like a growing number of academic researchers, we have found that the ease of development and flexibility of the current suite of game engines meets our development needs (Lewis, 2002). In particular, we are using the A5 3D game engine from Conitec.

Figure 1. Adaptive Narrative VE Architecture

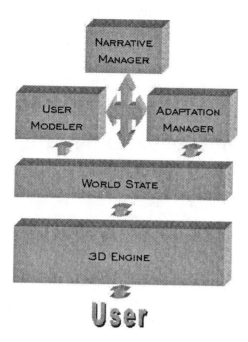

The world state contains information about the object within the world, such as its location and its current status. This information may be maintained within the 3D engine or may be managed by an external data store.

User Modeler

User Modeling describes the ability of a system to make observations about a user and to use these observations to adapt the experience to better meet the user's wants or needs. For a narrative VE system, the User Model could receive information such as a user profile, a history of user activities within the VE, and information about the activities of others with the VE. Using this information, the User Modeler could provide information regarding the user beliefs about the current story or which aspects of the story appear interesting to the user.

In order to develop reliable inferences, the User Modeler would require a variety of input. This input could include information regarding user information and attributes (e.g., age, occupation, computer experience, hobbies and interests, etc.). The user model would also receive a record of activities performed by the user within the environment. This activity log would be more than just a list of specific interactions (e.g., movement to coordinates X, Y, Z, interaction with object Q, etc.), but would also provide contextual information used to establish the significance of interactions (e.g., moved farther away the threatening dog, interacted with the door to unlock the secret room, etc.). Using this information, the system could generate various "beliefs" about the user, such as the user's goals (the user seeks recreation and intellectual stimulation), the users interests within the narrative VE (the user is seeking treasure and wealth), what the user believes about the narrative or the VE (the user believes there is a treasure in the hidden room or the user believes that the dog is hostile and will attack), and whether the user falls into a recognized "type" (the user is an "explorer" rather than a "fighter").

Narrative Manager

In order to present a story, a VE requires some control mechanism for scheduling and presenting the events that make up the narrative. While simulation-oriented VE have rules for triggering or scheduling events, they do not take into account the narrative purpose of the events, instead focusing on some other guiding structure such as game physics. In the simplest narrative VEs (such as many recent computer games), narrative events are "canned" FSV pieces that occur when certain conditions are met, such as completion of a level, or the solution of a puzzle. In a more robust narrative VE, there would be more variety in the type of events, in the scheduling of events, and in the presentation of events. For example, in addition to or instead of FSV, events might be more contextually inserted into the environment itself. Instead of a pre-recorded FSV showing one character talking to another at a particular location, a real-time animation of the characters can be dynamically created showing their conversation at any location. Instead of narrative events occurring only between levels, narrative events might occur anytime or anywhere within the environment, with the timing, placement, and form of the event being dictated by the storytelling goals of the system (see Adaptation Manager). The basic outline of the narrative (or the plot of the story) could be predefined by a human author or could be generated dynamically by the computer.

In our current implementation, the outline of the story is expressed through narrative events (see Figure 2). Other interactions may take place in the system, but the narrative events are those that have significance to the story, have corresponding triggers, and have their presentation controlled by the Adaptation Manager.

Figure 2. Event Data Structures

NARRATIVE EVENT	
SLOT	**DESCRIPTION**
Name	Name of Event
Location	Location where event should occur
Time	When event should occur
Participants	Actors who are involved in event
Actions	Set of actions that make up the event
Presentation	The preferred form of communicating the actions, e.g. direct observation, indirect observation, hearing, intermediated, etc.
Side Effect	Facts or flags that should be set as a result of this event

NARRATIVE EVENT TRIGGER		
CRITERIA	**DESCRIPTION**	**EXAMPLES**
Time	Events may need to occur at a specific or relative time or in a specific sequence.	`Session-ends` should occur 20 minutes after `session begins;` `Car-breaks-on-ice` should occur immediately after `car-accelerates-past-user`
Location	Events may need to occur when actors (human or computer) arrive at or leave certain locations	`Stoplight-turns-red` should occur when user arrives at corner of main and center
Other	Events may need to occur when other conditions (indicated by flags, often set as a result of a side-effect associated with an event)	`Car-stops` should occur when `car-out-of-gas` is true

ACTION	
SLOT	**DESCRIPTION**
Actor	Actor or object who is to perform the action
Action	Specific primitive action that the actor performs (e.g. animation, movement, function, etc.)
Object (optional)	Actors or object to or on whom the actor performs the action
Other Parameters (optional)	Any other parameters necessary to specify the Action

Adaptation Manager

Given an event and contextual information, the system should be capable of modifying the event to maintain plot and logical continuity and to help the user and author achieve their narrative goals. For the author, these goals may include communicating an idea, teaching a lesson, or conveying an emotion. For the user, goals might include entertainment, education, relaxation, or excitement. As input, the Adaptation Manager would use information from the Narrative Manager (narrative events), the User Modeler (user goals or beliefs), and the world state (object locations). Given a particular event suggested by the Narrative Manager, the Adaptation Manager will select time, place, and representation based on event constraints, narrative goals, and the state of the world.

CURRENT STATUS

Development is proceeding in phases. We have completed a pilot adaptive narrative VE that includes a limited set of events, a scripted narrative, and an active Presentation Manager. We are in the process of conducting user studies comparing user comprehension and satisfaction both with and without Presentation Management. This feedback will guide us in extending the supported set of events and the types of adaptation supported by the Adaptation Manager. We have also begun work on the User Modeler and plan to turn our attention next to dynamic narrative generation. The following sample interaction provides an example of some of the current types of adaptation supported by our system.

Sample Interaction

In order to test the Adaptation Manager, our event representation scheme, and our overall framework, we have created a sample narrative. The narrative was constructed to include enough events and complexity to exercise a variety of adaptation techniques. The narrative includes multiple characters, a plot consisting of multiple events (including several events that may occur simultaneously), and the events take place at multiple locations in a 3D VE.

Event: A hungry rabbit eats the last of his carrots and goes looking for something else to eat.

Actions: Animation of rabbit eating carrots. Sounds of rabbit eating carrots.

Adaptations: Amplify sound of rabbit eating carrots (to draw attention to rabbit and convey idea that someone is eating something). (Figure 3)

Event: The rabbit notices a snowman's carrot nose and steals it.

Actions: Animation and sounds of rabbit stealing carrot nose.

Adaptations: Delay actions until user is present at the characters' location (so that user may view and hear this key event). (Figure 4)

Event: The snowman follows the rabbit to the lake, but the rabbit has already eaten the carrot. The only item he can find is a dead fish, so he uses that as a temporary replacement.

Actions: Sounds of snowman and rabbit discussing options. Animation of snowman picking up fish and using it as nose.

Adaptations: If the user was not present to see the event, the rabbit talks to himself and recounts the event within the hearing distance of the user. (Figure 5)

Figure 3.

Figure 4.

Figure 5.

FUTURE TRENDS

If the public's past and current appetite for narrative and interactive technology are any guides, then continued development and use of new narrative technologies such as adaptive VEs is likely to be rapid. This development could usher in a generation of more sophisticated and personalized computer training, communication, and entertainment applications, providing more opportunities for people to interact with multimedia technologies. While some may have concerns that such systems could isolate users by providing them with replacements for human interaction, we feel that some of the greatest opportunities for such technologies would be in creating novel and powerful new ways for people to interact with each other. Collaborative narrative VEs could bring users together to explore stories and situations, even if the users were in physically remote locations. In addition to experiencing narratives in new ways, advances in input and output technologies may also allow us to experience narrative in new places. Using augmented or mixed reality technology, a VE could be overlaid on top of the real world, allowing virtual characters and objects to appear side-by-side with real objects. Such technologies would allow us to experience stories anywhere and to incorporate any location into part of an ongoing personal narrative.

CONCLUSION

The application of AI techniques in narrative generation and adaptation to multimedia technologies such as VEs can create new types of experiences for users and authors. We have explored an architecture that supports not only the presentation of a single narrative, but an adaptive capability that would allow narratives to be customized for different users, different goals, and different situations. The development of this pilot application has demonstrated the feasibility of this architecture, and we plan to continue to extend and enhance the capabilities of our system.

REFERENCES

Amerson, D., & Kime, S. (2001). Real-time cinematic camera control for interactive narratives. In *The Working Notes of the AAAI Spring Symposium on Artificial Intelligence and Interactive Entertainment*. AAAI.

Bares, W. H., & Lester, J. C. (1999). Intelligent multi-shot visualization interfaces for dynamic 3d worlds. *Proceedings of the 1999 International Conference on Intelligent User Interfaces* (pp. 119-126). New York: ACM Press.

Callaway, C. B., & Lester, J. C. (2001). Narrative prose generation. *Proceedings of the 17th International Joint Conference on Artificial Intelligence* (pp. 241-248). Morgan Kaufmann.

Galyean, T. (1995). *Narrative guidance of interactivity.* Doctoral dissertation, Massachusetts Institute of Technology.

Gershon, N., & Page, W. (2002). What storytelling can do for information visualization. *Communications of the ACM, 44*(8), 31-37.

Hayes-Roth, B. & van Gent, R. (1996). Story-making with improvisational puppets and actors. *Stanford Knowledge Systems Laboratory Report KSL-96-05.*

He, L., Cohen, M. F., & Salesin, D. H. (1996). The virtual cinematographer. *Proceedings of the 23rd Annual Conference on Computer Graphics and Interactive Techniques.* New York: ACM Press.

Laurel, B. (1991). *Computers as Theatre.* NY: Addison-Wesley.

Lebowitz, M. (1984). Creating characters in a story-telling universe. *Poetics, 13,* 171-194.

Lewis, M., & Jacobson, J. (2002). Introduction to the special issue on game engines in scientific research. *Communications of the ACM, 45*(1), 27-31.

Meehan, J. (1980). *The Metanovel: Writing Stories by Computer.* New York: Garland Publishing.

Murray, J. (1998). *Hamlet on the Holodeck.* Cambridge, MA: MIT Press.

Steiner, K. E., & Moher, T. G. (2002). Encouraging task-related dialog in 2d and 3d shared narrative workspaces. *Proceedings of the 4th International Conference on Collaborative Virtual Environments.* New York: ACM Press.

Weyhrauch, P. (1997). *Guiding interactive drama.* Doctoral dissertation, Carnegie Mellon University. Technical Report CMU-CS-97-109.

Young, M. R. (2001). An overview of the mimesis architecture: Integrating intelligent narrative control into an existing gaming environment. *The Working Notes of the AAAI Spring Symposium on Artificial Intelligence and Interactive Entertainment.*

Chapter VI

Isoluminance Contours:
A Fast, Simple Model for 4D Animated Visualization

Marion Cottingham
University of Western Australia, Australia

ABSTRACT

This chapter introduces the Isoluminance Contour Model, which not only provides a quick and easy method for generating images, but also dramatically reduces the amount of work required by traditional computer graphics methods. It starts with the history of the model from its conception in 1981: it was used to generate flat-shaded greyscale, simple, primitive objects such as cubes, cylinders, cones, and spheres, by generating full-color smooth-shaded images for animated sequences. The model compares the degree of realism and the speed of production it generates with that achieved by using smooth shading and ray-tracing methods. It ultimately describes how the amount of data used by the Isoluminance Contour Model can be adapted dynamically to suit the screen size of the primitive object being generated, making real-time 4-dimensional animated visualization feasible on a Pentium 400 (or equivalent) or faster PC.

HISTORY

In the 1970s and 1980s numerical simulation applications were churning out thousands — even millions — of numerical data values. Because of the sheer volume of data it became impossible to manually interpret all the hidden patterns, trends, and relationships. Software applications were introduced to enable this data to be viewed graphically. The term *visualization* was introduced to describe the transformation of data into visual images. The first wave of these applications typically generated simple two-dimensional line graphs, bar charts, and pie charts on expensive graphics workstations.

The next generation of visualization software enabled three-dimensional images with single data points typically denoted by dots or crosses as shown in Figure 1. The data points formed a data cloud that would often be accompanied by axes lines or enclosed in a wire frame cube that could be rotated with the cloud, giving some indication of its orientation to the viewing position somewhere along the z-axis. Since all the dots and crosses were the same screen size, however, there was no visual depth cue. As the majority of computers were not fast enough to perform the rotation in real-time, there could still be some confusion in visual interpretation.

Cottingham (1981) first introduced the Isoluminance Contour Model (ICM) as an experimental approach to replacing the dots and crosses with simple primitive solids available in CAD applications at that time. This had the advantage of enabling perspective projection to define depth cue.

Throughout the 1990s PCs became widely available as costs plummeted and processing power increased. In addition the color capability jumped from 16 colors to more than a million, which is more colors than the human eye can actually distinguish. There was an ever-increasing demand from researchers in science, engineering, medicine, and commerce for interpreting the large data sets being produced by this growing number of computers. With the reduction in cost, the increases in speed, and the new wealth of colors visualization grew in popularity: it is now common practice to develop visualization packages for tailor-made for individual data sets where there is some correlation between the visual image and the characteristics of the data.

If the visualization provides the ability to fly around the data in real-time, then hidden relationships in the data may become apparent (even if they are not obvious when viewed as a series of still images).

Most of the researchers generating data, however, tended to be experts in their own fields, lacking the high level programming skills required to develop code for complex, traditional computer graphics techniques. They could turn to the functions available in software applications (such as OpenGL or

Figure 1. Data Cloud with Crosses Used to Denote the Positions of Data Points

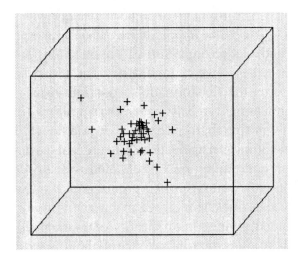

DirectX). These applications contain functions for generating the same simple, primitive objects and only need to be called with a few parameters to define the type, size, and position of a primitive. These applications use polyhedral representation and rely upon smooth shading techniques to provide particular degrees of realism.

A major advantage of the ICM is that it is simple to implement, needing only the knowledge of a programming language capable of drawing lines and filling polygons. The method provides realistic results that are far superior to those produced by traditional methods and that compare favorably with ray casting when the same illumination model is applied to the planes. The ICM produces images in a fraction of the time needed by traditional methods, even though the surface definitions are calculated and stored by the model. This makes it possible to dynamically change the amount of data used to generate a primitive as its screen size changes. Graphics applications do not provide access to the list of vertices that define a primitive, so the ability to easily adapt the number of polygons representing a primitive as it changes its size on the screen during an animated sequence is lost. This is important for efficiency: drawing all the polygons requires more CPU time, which in turn determines whether or not animation is feasible.

The next section takes you through the steps involved in generating the image of a sphere using various traditional computer graphics techniques, including the steps required by the ICM. A comparison is then made between the times taken to generate an image using both approaches.

GENERATING A SPHERE USING TRADITIONAL GRAPHICS TECHNIQUES

A traditional way of simplifying the task of rendering a shaded image of a solid object is to subdivide its surface into a collection of planar polygons that can be dealt with individually. The challenge is to produce realistic images of primitives, such as spheres, cones and cylinders, which have curved surfaces. Surface polygons can be rendered in different ways depending upon how quickly an image needs to be generated and the degree of realism it requires. These are conflicting demands, and one often has to be balanced against the other. A wire-frame showing only the edges of the polygons, with all edges drawn or with hidden edges removed, is often used for quick previewing. Flat-shading or smooth- shading techniques may be applied to the polygons to restore the appearance of the surface's curvature.

The Sphere Template

The sphere is represented by a collection of surface polygons, each defined by four vertices and four edges. Each edge is a straight-line segment defined by two vertices. Calculating a vertex requires a call to the sine function and a call to the cosine function. Rather than creating a sphere from scratch for each visualization item, then, it is common to create one template sphere and derive all the other spheres from it. This template has its center positioned at the origin and a radius of one. All the spheres representing visualization points are created from the template by storing their position coordinates in a translation matrix and their sizes in a scaling matrix. Both matrices are incorporated into the final matrix that is used to convert each vertex from the local template coordinate space to the world coordinate system and onto the screen coordinate system.

Storage Considerations

Each vertex is specified in the Cartesian coordinate system with the x-, y- and z-coordinates representing three-dimensional positions in space. Topological information defines how polygons, edges, and vertices are connected and how they relate to other polygons, edges, and vertices. Baumgart's (1975) Winged-Edge data structure was commonly used by CAD applications to explicitly store this information. This is, however, a fairly complex structure: rings of nodes contain faces, edges, and vertices data, which are inter-connected using pointers and capable of representing any solids. Because the surface polygons from the simple primitives form complete rows and columns, the topology can be implied by the order of storage using CDS (Cottingham, 1985, 1987). This was originally a two-dimensional array, each element containing four vertices that defined a surface polygon — (polygons adjacent on the surface were adjacent in the CDS). CDS can be made simpler to code by storing one vertex at each element (the version adopted in this chapter). The next section provides the pseudo-code, showing how the sphere template is defined.

Creating the Sphere Template

For efficiency's sake, the sphere template is centered at the origin and has a radius of one (see Figure 2). This allows it to be scaled to any size by multiplying it by a single array containing the scale factor at diagonal elements of a unit matrix. The coordinates of the sphere's poles $(0, 1, 0)$ and $(0, -1, 0)$ can be duplicated in all the elements along the first and last rows to force the polygons at the poles to become quadrilateral and having two identical vertices; thus, all polygons may be processed uniformly. The following pseudo-code creates the vertices for the other circles that lie on x-z planes:

> *For every circle **I***
>   *Calculate radius and center*
>   *For every vertex **J** defining a circle on the x-z plane*
>   *CDS(**I**, **J**).Vertex x = radius * cosine theta*
>   *CDS(**I**, **J**).Vertex y = center's y-coordinate*
>   *CDS(**I**, **J**).Vertex z = radius * sine theta*
>   *End For*
> *End For*

The following example shows how to calculate the radius and center for circles defining the sphere template. Because the sphere is centered at the origin, only the y-axis coordinate is required to define the centre of a circle.

> *For every circle **I***
>   *radius = cos (90 – (180/NumberOfCircles + 1))*
>   *centerX = 0*

$centerY = sin(90 - (180/NumberOfCircles + 1))$
$centerZ = 0$
End For

Figure 2. One of the x-z Planar Circles Used to Define the Sphere Template

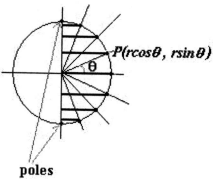

Figure 3 shows a sphere template represented by 40 planes. Each plane is defined by 16 vertices and rendered by drawing lines to connect vertices stored at adjacent columns and rows in the array created by the pseudo-code given above. This is a *wire frame drawing*.

Because of ambiguity, it is normal to cull back-facing polygons and to use the simplified wire-frame image as a quick previewing tool. The next level of quick previewing is achieved by rendering the sphere with culled hidden surfaces and with surface flat-shaded polygons. In general, however, only triangular surface polygons are guaranteed to be planar; it is therefore common

Figure 3. Wire-Frame Sphere

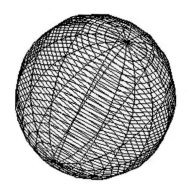

Figure 4. Flat Shaded Sphere Represented by Triangulated Polygons

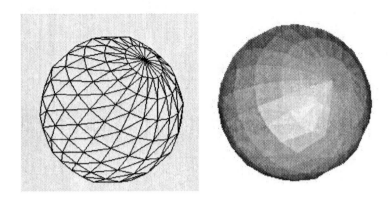

practice to triangulate surface polygons in an attempt to improve the degree of realism. In the case of the CDS sphere, all the surface polygons are quadrilateral: it is thus not difficult to render polygons as two distinct triangles by using three adjacent array elements instead of four. Figure 4 shows a sphere defined by 11 rows and 21 columns of vertices that specify 462 triangular surface polygons and 231 quadrilateral polygons.

The following steps demonstrate how the flat-shaded image of a sphere is generated:

1. Compute the unit normal direction vector for each vertex, which is simply:

$$N_x = (V_x - C_x)/r$$
$$N_y = (V_y - C_y)/r$$
$$N_z = (V_z - C_z)/r$$

where N is the unit direction vector representing the normal to the surface at vertex V, C is the sphere's center, and r is the sphere's radius.

2. The normal at the center of a polygon is calculated as the average of the normals at the vertices defining that polygon.

3. Cull back-facing polygons by calculating the angles between surface polygon normals and the view direction vector using the dot product.

4. Calculate chromaticity values (color) for each polygon by applying an illumination model. This measurement typically includes three components —ambient light, diffuse illumination, and specular reflection. These are

given in the following equation that must be applied three times to compute the red, green and blue contributions to the chromaticity value:

$$I = I_p k_d (N \cdot L) + I_a k_a + I_p k_s (N \cdot H)^n$$

The first component consists of I_p (the intensity of the point light source); k_d is the constant diffuse reflection coefficient representing the level of dullness of the surface (in the range 0 to 1); and the dot product $N \cdot L$ is used as an approximation for the value of the cosine of the angle between the normal to surface and light direction vectors. In the second component, I_a is the intensity of the ambient light present in the environment and k_a is the constant ambient reflection coefficient representing the amount of ambient light reflected off all the objects. In the third component, k_s is a constant specular reflection coefficient; and $N \cdot H$ is the dot product used to replace the value of the cosine of the angle between the normal to the surface and the direction vector that is halfway between the light direction vector and the view direction vector. The n is called the specular reflection parameter, ranging from 1 for dull surfaces to more than 100 for shiny surfaces. This illumination model depends upon using a point light source that is positioned far enough away from the collection of objects so that its direction is the same throughout the scene of primitives.

5.   A polygon fill algorithm is called to flat shade each polygon with its chromatic value.

Smooth Shading Techniques

A higher level of realism is gained by eliminating the apparent edges and restoring the smooth appearance of the curved surface. This requires replacing the call to the polygon fill algorithm at Step 5 (in the previous section) by a call to a smooth- shading algorithm. The two most common smooth shading techniques are Gouraud's (1971) and Phong's (1975). They are described in the next two subsections.

Gouraud's Smooth-Shading Technique

Gouraud's smooth-shading technique renders a polyhedron one polygon at a time by calculating the chromaticity values for each vertex and linearly interpolating these values to get the chromaticity value for every pixel lying within the polygon. Because of the gradual change in chromaticity over the whole polygon, the surface appears much smoother and the appearance of edges is diminished. Gouraud's algorithm requires the following steps:

1. Calculate the normals for all the surface polygons and determine the normal at each vertex by averaging the normals of adjoining polygons as follows:

$$N_v = \frac{\sum\limits_{k=1}^{n} N_k}{\left| \sum\limits_{k=1}^{n} N_k \right|}$$

2. Apply an illumination model using the normal at each vertex to compute the red, green, and blue chromaticity values for that vertex.
3. Linearly interpolate the chromaticity value at each pixel inside the polygon and along its edges based on the chromaticity values at its vertices (see Figure 5).
4. The values of the three-color components are interpolated separately. The value at point P_1 is determined by the values at vertices A and B and the distance of P_1 from A (or B) along the edge. Here is AB's interpolation equation:

$$I_1 = \frac{y_1 - y_B}{y_A - y_B} I_A + \frac{y_A - y_1}{y_A - y_B} I_B$$

Figure 5. Linearly Interpolating the Chromaticity Values for Pixels Lying within a Polygon

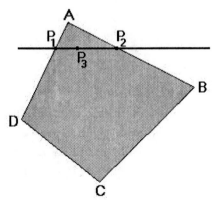

Similarly, the value at point P_2 is determined by the values at A and D and the distance of P_2 from A (or D) along the edge. Here is AD's interpolation equation:

$$I_2 = \frac{y_2 - y_D}{y_A - y_D} I_A + \frac{y_A - y_2}{y_A - y_D} I_D$$

For efficiency, incremental values may be calculated to specify the difference between start and finish intensity values for adjacent scan lines. The following equation shows how the increment for edge AB is calculated:

$$Inc_{AB} = \frac{I_B - I_A}{y_B - y_A}$$

The increment for any other edge is calculated in the same way. The value at point P_3 is determined by the values at P_1 and P_2 and the distance of P_3 from P_1 (or P_2) along the scan line. Use the interpolation equation for calculating the intensity values at a specific pixel:

$$I_3 = \frac{x_2 - x_3}{x_2 - x_1} I_1 + \frac{x_3 - x_1}{x_2 - x_1} I_2$$

For efficiency, an incremental value for the intensity difference between adjacent pixels along a scan line can be calculated as follows:

$$Inc_{1,2} = \frac{I_2 - I_1}{x_2 - x_1}$$

Figure 6 shows the result of applying Gouraud's smooth-shading technique to the surface of a sphere. Gouraud's method does not accurately define the shape of the area highlighted by specular reflection; for this reason, is often used without the specular reflection component included in the illumination model.

Figure 6. Sphere Rendered Using Gouraud's Smooth-Shading Method

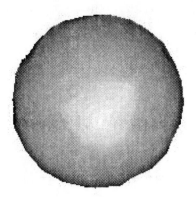

Phong's Smooth-Shading Technique

The technique developed by Phong dramatically reduces the highlight shape problem experienced when using Gouraud's smooth-shading method. Figure 7 shows a polyhedral sphere shaded using Phong's technique. Phong's method linearly interpolates the surface normal vectors rather than the chromaticity values. The CPU time taken to interpolate the three direction components of the normal vectors is equivalent to the time for interpolating the three red, green, and blue intensity values.

After the normals have been interpolated, however, the illumination model still needs to be called for each pixel lying inside the polygon — images generated using Phong's technique take much longer to render. Table 1 at the end of the chapter gives a comparison of the time taken by each method.

To achieve the next degree of realism requires a completely different approach called *ray-tracing*. Researchers who are mathematically adept may find this approach easier to implement: it requires less coding, but it does have the disadvantage of consuming lots of CPU time to produce a single image, making flying around the data space in real time out of reach for most researchers. Ray casting is described in the following section.

RAY CASTING

Ray casting does not create a polyhedral representation of the primitives, but instead uses the mathematical definition of the sphere. It renders a primitive by creating rays that emanate from some viewing position and pass through each pixel on the screen. Each ray is tested for intersection with all the primitives

Figure 7. Shape of Phong's Highlighted Area Reflects the Contour of the Surface

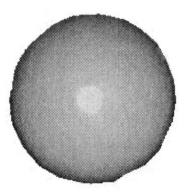

(in this case spheres) in the scene. After the nearest intersection to the viewing position is found, an illumination model is called to calculate the color and intensity at that intersection point.

Because of the number of rays required, ray casting is extremely CPU intensive for rendering even single images and is completely unsuitable for real-time animation (a speed of approximately 20 images per second must be maintained to avoid flicker).

Ray casting provides the highest degree of realism amongst the rendering techniques discussed so far. The ICM described in the next section, however, presents another approach that is extremely simple to implement and yet provides the same degree of realism as ray casting without any time penalty, making it suitable for animation.

THE ISOLUMINANCE
CONTOUR METHOD (ICM)

ICM takes an entirely different approach from others by representing primitive solids as a set of planar contours that are defined by a collection of perimeter points. These points are chosen because they share the same orientation to the light source — they maintain constant chromaticity. This means that the illumination model is called once per contour, after which a polygon fill algorithm (or hardware) is called to render the contours in depth order.

ICM uses the same techniques as traditional graphics to define the contours representing the sphere template. The contours are a collection of

Figure 8. Isoluminance Contour Represents a Sphere by a Collection of Planar Contours

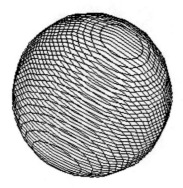

circular planar polygons (Figure 8) that have constant chromatic and brightness values, which are defined by a single row of vertices from the array. In other words, there is no longer any need to connect vertices from adjoining rows: this almost halves the time required for drawing a wire-frame image.

Rendering a shaded sphere simply requires generating planes in depth order using polygon fill. Figure 9 shows the result of filling these planar polygons.

ICM eliminates the need to cull back-facing polygons or perform any other hidden surface elimination, providing enormous savings. The illumination model adopted can be as simple as deciding upon a range of chromaticity values and calling a polygon fill algorithm for each contour, with its color based on its distance from the light source. One can, of course, still apply the full illumination model to achieve the same results as those produced by ray casting.

ICM uses the same sphere template created earlier; and, as previously, its vertices are multiplied by a transformation matrix that scales and positions the

Figure 9. Polygon-Filled Isoluminance Contours

sphere. In order that all the points on the contour have the same color, a rotation matrix is added to this transformation, positioning the sphere's axis parallel to the light direction.

The contours are generated in depth order starting with the one farthest away. No sorting is required because they are already stored in the correct order. One must only decide whether to start with the first or the last row. If the light source and the viewing position lie on the same side of the sphere, then start with the first row in the array; if the light source and the viewing position lie on different sides of the sphere, then start from the last row.

The pseudo-code for rendering an ICM sphere is:

Procedure RenderSphere
    Transform Sphere Template to required position, size and orientation
    For each contour
        For each vertex defining current contour
            Perform 3d to 2d perspective transformation
        End For
    End For
End Sub

The other primitive solids are represented in a similar way. Cylinders are represented as a collection of planar quadrilaterals (see Figure 10) having their ends shaded as a single plane.

Cones are represented as triangular planes that have a parallel edges along the base but have the same respective top vertices in common (see Figure 11).

Figure 10. ICM Cylinders

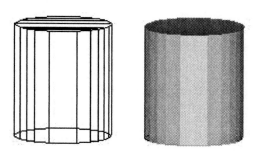

Figure 11. ICM Cones

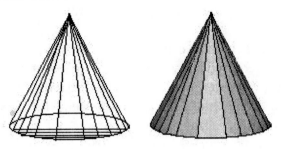

PROBLEMS WITH ICM

A problem occurs whenever the contour planes get close to becoming parallel with the view direction. Because the contours are viewed from the side, they visually deteriorate into parallel lines. This is easily overcome by the following steps:

1.   Find the minimum and maximum x values of the screen coordinates that are on the first two planes stored in the array. These will give you the first and last vertices that are visible from the viewing position. The vertices lying in between are either all visible or all invisible.

2.   If the minimum and maximum x values are equal, then the sphere's axis is vertical — use the minimum and maximum y values.

3.   Construct a temporary contour using the visible vertices from two adjacent rows in the array.

4.   Generate the polygon using a polygon fill algorithm available on your computer.

To handle this glitch, just add the following pseudo-code to the end of the RenderSphere procedure given above.

If 2D contours have degenerated to lines then
    Build polygons from adjacent array rows (contours) and polyfill
Else
    *Polyfill contours in depth order, i.e., process array from first to
        last row or vice versa*
End If

RENDERING TIMES

The time required to create an image depends upon the computing power you have and the complexity of the scene. For real-time animation you must be able to achieve a minimum of 20 frames per second to eliminate any flickering. A Pentium 400 can cope with processing around 800 visualization points, each represented by an ICM sphere. A sphere solid is used for examples in our comparisons: these require more surface polygons than other primitives do, so the timing differences are greater.

Generating a fully-shaded image of a sphere using the ICM requires even fewer CPU cycles than rendering a sphere as a wire frame polyhedra. *Table 1* shows the amount of CPU seconds spent in the creation and drawing stages to render a thousand spheres, each defined by 25 circular planes that are defined by 50 vertices. The table compares the traditional approach with the ICM running on a Pentium 400 computer. Different hardware configurations will yield different results, but the relative proportions of times will remain constant.

The wire frame section of the table shows the timings for generating images containing all the edges defining the spheres and timings for displaying only the visible edges. Drawing all the edges from the polyhedral representation was swift: no back-face culling was undertaken; but when generating only visible edges, normals (as well as the angle between them and the viewing angle) had to be calculated to perform the back-face culling.

The various timings for the shaded images of the polyhedral representation were achieved by applying different methods that produced varying degrees of realism. ICM used in the timings included the specular reflection calculation, which is an add-on rather than part of the illumination model. The specular area shown in Figure 12 is circular because the light source is at almost the same angle as the viewing direction, which becomes more elliptical as the relative light position changes.

ICM always produced the sphere in the fastest time — even faster than the simplest wire frame timing. In the shaded images the main saving was achieved because only one normal and one illumination calculation was required per contour plane. In comparison, flat shading using the polyhedral method required normals and illumination values to be calculated for each of the 25x50 surface polygons. Using Gouraud's method, these illumination values not only have to be calculated for each vertex, but also interpolated at pixels lying inside each polygon. The slowest time was taken using Phong's method, which needed normals for each vertex to be interpolated and the illumination value calculated for each pixel lying inside each polygon.

*Table 1.   Time Taken to Render a Thousand Spheres Defined by 25
Circular Planes Each Represented by 50 Vertices*

		Full Wire frame	Wire Frame Hidden lines removed	Shaded			
				Flat	Triang-ulated	Gouraud	Phong
Polyhedra	Pentium 400	9.33	222	238	262	313	1388
	Pentium IV 2GHz	1.4	32.25	34.5	37	78	1223
ICM	Pentium 400	5.08	5.13	8.07	-	-	-
	Pentium IV 2GHz	.78	.92	1.92	-	-	-

Figure 12 shows all the images produce during the timing. The top three
spheres from left to right were rendered as a full wire frame, a wire frame with
hidden lines removed, and a flat shaded sphere. The bottom three spheres from
left to right were rendered using Gouraud's method, Phong's method, and ICM
with specular reflection. For ICM to have the same degree of realism as the
smooth-shaded spheres more contours would have to be applied. Although this
would increase generation time, massive savings would still be possible.

Figure 12.   Spheres Generated During the Timing Stage

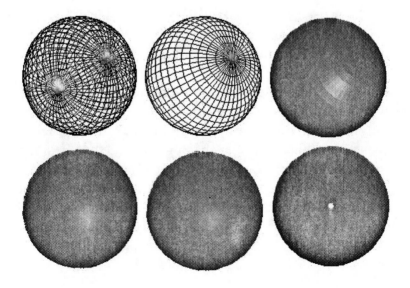

Figure 13. Visualization of the Proportional Sizes of the Major Brain Divisions for a Wide Range of Mammals

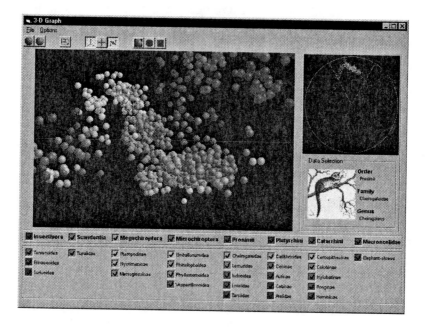

USING IC FOR ANIMATED VISUALIZATION OF DATA SETS

Figure 13 shows the visualization of the same data points shown in Figure 1 that represent the evolution of mammals' brains in terms of changes in overall brain size. The data set was supplied courtesy of Professor Heinz Stephan, Max-Planck Institut fur Hirmforschung, Frankfurt. Exploratory univariate and multivariate analyses were applied by Mr. Willem De Winter and Professor Charles Oxnard, both of the Department of Anatomy and Human Biology at The University of Western Australia. They considered volumes of 11 non-overlapping brain parts from 921 specimens representing 363 species of various taxonomic groups consisting of primates, insectivores, bats, tree-shrews, and elephant shrews. The data was then visualized using software developed by Paul Merendah. During his undergraduate, third-year Computer Graphics course (Department of Computer Science and Software Engineering, The University of Western Australia), the project was specified and supervised by the author.

Uniform-sized spheres represent specimens with the distances between the spheres representing the relative similarities in brain proportions. The screen size of a sphere is determined by a perspective projection transformation that makes spheres in the distance appear smaller than spheres in the foreground — this aspect would have been lost if the original spheres had differed in volume. Each species group was assigned a color derived from the animal group to which it belonged (fourth dimension) and was given a different level of saturation and hue that preserved its relative significance within its animal group (fifth and sixth dimensions).

Although the data set contained 921 data points, using ICM for spheres made it possible to simulate a virtual camera flying around the data cloud in real-time on a Pentium 166 PC. The relative position of the light source to the camera was assumed to be constant; therefore the contours of the spheres did not require reconstruction at any time during the simulation, allowing all the spheres to be created from a single-sphere template that had already been rotated to the correct orientation.

Figure 14 shows the same data set being visualized by Graham Wycherly in the same project.

Figure 14. Visualization of the Major Brain Divisions of Mammals with Different Parameters in the Illumination Model

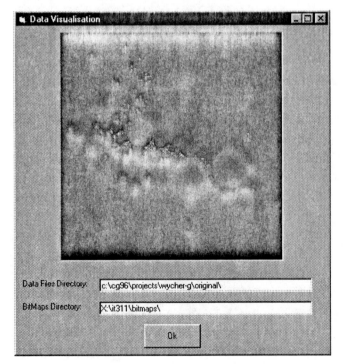

The ability to fly around the data clouds in real-time enables even more information to be retrieved, especially information on the relative distances between data points. Before this data set was visualized dynamically, it was thought that the evolution of the brain in mammals was simply a matter of changes in the overall brain size (Finlay & Darlington, 1995). This visualization demonstrated the existence of different phylogenetic trends in the evolution of the mammalian brain and in that of species sharing a particular lifestyle. The brain had evolved toward a similar proportional organization.

INTRODUCING A
VIRTUAL CAMERA MODEL

Introducing a virtual camera model means that the position of the light source and the camera are independent of each other and that the user is given control over both independently. This means that the light direction vector is no longer constant throughout the scene. The contours defining different spheres are no longer parallel, making it necessary to create each sphere from scratch. This is still achievable, however, in real-time on a Pentium 400 or faster PC.

Figure 15. Light Source Positioned in the Data Cloud in Full View of the Camera

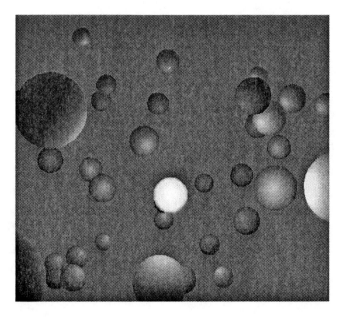

Figure 16. Displaying Bid and Ask Stock Market Data One Day Per Axis

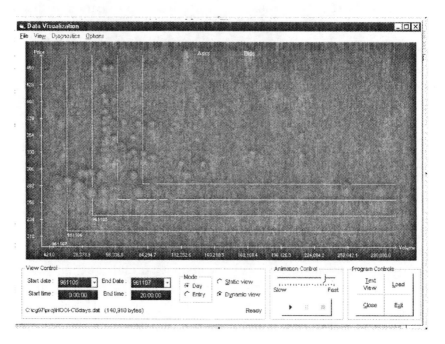

When the light source and camera are independent it is even possible to view the light source itself. Figure 15 shows the light source positioned inside the data cloud in full view of the camera (the light source is the brightest sphere that appears just below the center of the image).

Sometimes it is beneficial to show how data changes over time while maintaining the ability to view all data. The visualization shown in Figure 15 displays a data set containing "bid and ask" stock market items that were supplied by Professor Philip Brown from the Department of Accounting and Finance at The University of Western Australia. The software was developed by Ken Hooi for a third year Computer Graphics course project that was specified and supervised by the author from the Department of Computer Science and Software Engineering at The University of Western Australia.

Asks are shares sold for a particular asking price, and bids are shares bought for a particular bidding price. The asking price is usually more than the bidding price. The bids are displayed as blue spheres and the asks as red spheres. The user specifies a start date and end date for the visualization, and the software creates an x- and y-axis pair for each day requested, displaying them at depths depicting their elapsed times. The x-axis depicts the volume of

Figure 17. Cylinders and Spheres Combined to Form a Chemistry-Like Visualization

the bid (ask parcels of shares), and the y-axis depicts the bid (ask price per share). When an ask parcel and a bid parcel match in price and volume, then a transaction takes place and the relevant spheres disappear off the screen. The dynamic view allows the user to watch transactions that are being processed and to see the unmatched pairs that are left in limbo on a day-to-day basis.

Combining ICM Solids

A popular method of visualizing chemistry data is by using spheres and cylinders. Figure 16 shows a generic data set being visualized.

Two ICM solids are combined quickly: one simply draws contours in their depth order, taking the depths from several arrays into consideration.

Adapting ICM for Real-Time Animation

The sphere template must be created with enough vertices to render a large sphere. It is inefficient to use all these vertices, however, if the sphere has moved off into the distance and appears small on the screen. The number of vertices copied from the sphere template can easily be adapted to reflect the area that the sphere covers in the final image. Suppose the camera position starts close to the sphere and moves away, causing the sphere to diminish in screen size. Initially all the vertices must be used for realism; but as the area taken up by the sphere diminishes, information from rows and columns in the template can be skipped. For our purposes the area can be represented by the sphere's diameter, which can be approximated as (maximum X – minimum X).

Additional information on ICM is available (Conway, 1988; Cottingham, 1989; Conway, 1991; Conway, 1993; Cottingham, 1999).

FUTURE TRENDS

ICM could be generalized by introducing a pre-processing step that takes existing data sets and combines any adjoining polygons that have similar normal direction vectors. This would require a more general data structure such as Baumgart's Winged-Edge Data Structure.

Because of the simplistic nature of ICM, implementing it in hardware should be reasonably straightforward.

CONCLUSION

ICM is a quick and simple model — another way of generating an image using topology implied by the order of storage in a simple two-dimensional array. It eliminates the need for most of the steps required by traditional computer graphics techniques. It is an extremely quick model to use in that it does not require any quick-previewing methods. Its realistic results — indistinguishable from ray-tracing — speak for themselves.

REFERENCES

Baumgart, B.G. (1975). A polyhedron representation for computer vision. *Proceedings AFIPS National Computer Conference*, (589-596).

Conway, D. (1991). Constructive solid geometry using the isoluminance contour model. *Computers and Graphics, 15*(3).

Conway, D. (1993). Fast three-dimensional rendering using isoluminance contours. Doctoral Thesis, Monash University, Australia.

Conway, D., & Cottingham, M.S. (1988). The isoluminance contour model. *AUSGRAPH88 Conference Proceedings, Melbourne, Australia* (43-50).

Cottingham, M.S. (1981). *Movies.* Senior Honours Thesis, The University of Glasgow.

Cottingham, M.S. (1985). A compressed data structure for surface representation. *Computer Graphics Forum, The Netherlands, 4*(3), 217-228.

Cottingham, M.S. (1987). Compressed data structure for rotational sweep method. *Ausgraph87 Conference.*

Cottingham, M.S. (1989). Adaptive data structure for animated (polyhedral) objects. *International Conference on CAD & CG.* China, 10-12.

Cottingham, M.S. (1999). *Computer Graphics with Visual Basic 6.* Australia: Vineyard Publishing.

Gouraud, H. (1971). *Computer display of curved surfaces.* Technical Report, University of Utah, 1971. UTEC-CSC-71-113.

Phong, B.T. (1975). Illumination for computer-generated pictures. *Comm. ACM, US, 18*(6), 311-317.

Chapter VII

Content-Based Video Indexing and Retrieval

Jianping Fan
University of North Carolina–Charlotte, USA

Xingquan Zhu
Purdue University, USA

Jing Xiao
University of North Carolina–Charlotte, USA

ABSTRACT

Recent advances in digital video compression and networks have made videos more accessible than ever. Several content-based video retrieval systems have been proposed in the past. In this chapter, we first review these existing content-based video retrieval systems and then propose a new framework, called ClassView, to make some advances towards more efficient content-based video retrieval. This framework includes: (a) an efficient video content analysis and representation scheme to support high-level visual concept characterization; (b) a hierarchical video classification technique to bridge the semantic gap between low-level visual features and high-level semantic visual concepts; and (c) a hierarchical video database indexing structure to enable video access over large-scale database. Integrating video access with efficient database indexing tree structures has provided a great opportunity for supporting more powerful video search engines.

INTRODUCTION

As a result of decreasing costs of storage devices, increasing network bandwidth capacities, and improved compression techniques, digital video is more accessible than ever. To help users find and retrieve relevant information effectively and to facilitate new and better ways of entertainment, advanced technologies need to be developed for indexing, browsing, filtering, searching, and updating the vast amount of information available in video databases. The recent development of content-based video retrieval (CBVR) systems has advanced our capabilities for searching videos via color, layout, texture, motion, and shape features (Flickner et al., 1995; Pentland, Picard, & Sclaroff, 1996; Rui, Huang, Ortega, & Mehrotra, 1998; Humrapur et al., 1997; Chang, Chen, Meng, Sundaram, & Zhong, 1998; Satoh & Kanade, 1997; Deng & Manjunath, 1998; Zhang, Wu, Zhong, & Smolier, 1997; Jain, Vailaya, & Wei, 1999; Jiang & Elmagarmid, 1998; Carson, Belongie, Greenspan, & Malick, 1997; Cascia & Ardizzone, 1996; Fan et al., 2001a). In general, a CBVR system should contain three main components:

- *Visual Feature Extraction and Content Representation:* Video analysis and feature extraction are the basic steps for supporting content-based video retrieval. There are two widely accepted approaches to support video content indexing: shot-based and object-based (or region-based). Therefore, the objective of video analysis is to detect the video shots and video objects automatically from compressed or uncompressed video sequences. Visual features are then extracted for characterizing these video shots and video objects.

- *Video Database Indexing Structure:* After high-dimensional visual features — such as colors, texture, shape and layout — have been extracted, they are properly indexed according to database indexing structures to support fast video access over large-scale video collections. When truly large-scale video data sets come into view, video database indexing can no longer be ignored for supporting effective content-based video retrieval and browsing (Fan et al., 2001a; Smeulders, Worring, Santini, Gupta, & Jain, 2000; Wu & Manjunath, 2001).

- *Video Database Retrieval and Browsing:* The objective of CBVR systems is to support retrieving relevant videos for a given query and browsing video contents according to users' interests (Fan, Ji, & Wu, 2001b; Fan Zhu, & Wu, 2002a; Fan, Zhu, Hacid, Wu, & Elmagarmid, 2002b; Fan, Zhu, Elmagarmid, & Aref, 2002c; Rui, Huang, & Mehrotra, 1997; Yeung, Yeo, Wolf, & Liu, 1995; Chen, Taskiran, Albiol, Delp, & Bouman, 1999; Smith, 1999; Zhong, Zhang, & Chang, 1996). How to evaluate the performance of the inherent retrieval and browsing techniques is also becoming an important research issue.

Most existing CBVR systems focus on video analysis, visual feature extraction, and supporting query by example. Few CBVR systems release their inherent video database indexing structures. Video database indexing, however, is becoming an important issue because traditional database indexing structures cannot be extended directly for video database indexing: the *curse of dimensionality* becomes a problem. In this chapter, we first review some existing CBVR systems and then propose a new framework towards more effective content-based video indexing and retrieval.

RELATED WORK

Much pioneer work on content-based video indexing and retrieval has been done in the past, but we cannot review all of the papers in this brief section because of the limitation on pages. We review pioneer work most relevant to the works proposed in *ClassView*. In this section, we give a brief review of the related work based on three components for supporting content-based video indexing and retrieval:

- *Visual Feature Extraction and Content Representation:* Content-based video analysis and visual feature extraction are the basic steps for building CBVR systems. Many pioneer works have been proposed to detect video shots and video objects automatically from compressed or uncompressed video sequences (Zhang, Kankanhalli, & Smolier, 1993; Meng, Juan, & Chang, 1995; Meng & Chang, 1995; Patel & Sethi, 1997; Swanberg, Chang, & Jain, 1992; Yeo & Liu, 1995; Fan, Yau, Aref, & Rezgui, 2000; Ahanger & Little, 1996; Alatan et al., 1998; Gunsel, Tekalp, & Beek, 1999; Meier & Ngan, 1998; Jaimes & Chang, 1999; Forsyth & Fleck, 1997; Fan et al., 2001e; Fan, Yau, Elmagarmid, & Aref, 2001c; Fan, Zhu, & Wu, 2001d; Gu & Lee, 1998; Guo, Kim, & Kuo, et al., 1999; Luo & Eleftheriadis, 2002).

In order to support shot-based video representation and indexing, Zhang et al. (1993) have proposed a novel bi-threshold technique. Yeo and Liu (1995) have also proposed a window-based video shot detection scheme. Swanberg et al. (1992) have suggested a knowledge-based scheme for shot detection. Patel et al. (1997) have also developed a novel shot detection algorithm via color histogram analysis. Chang et al. (1998) have also suggested a shot detection technique, which analyzes block-based coding types (Meng et al., 1995; Meng & Chang, 1995). Ahanger and Little (1996) review well the shot detection algorithms proposed in the early years. . In general, threshold setting plays a critical role in automatic video shot detection (Fan et al., 2000). The thresholds for shot detection should be adapted to the activities of video contents. It is impossible to use a universal threshold that can satisfy various conditions because the thresholds for different video sequences or even different video shots within the same sequence should be different. Fan et al. (2001a, 2000) have proposed an automatic shot-detection technique, which can adapt the thresholds for video shot detection according to the activities of various video sequences.

In order to support object-based video representation and indexing, several automatic and semi-automatic object extraction algorithms have been proposed: Alatan et al. (1998), Gunsel et al. (1999), Meier and Ngan (1998), Jaimes and Chang (1999), Forsyth and Fleck (1997), Fan et al. (2001e, 2001c, 2001d), Gu and Lee (1998), Guo et al., (1999), and Luo and Eleftheriadis (2002).

Meier and Ngan (1998) have developed a video object extraction technique via object plane detection. Fan et al. (2001e, 2001c, 2001d) have also proposed several techniques via spatiotemporal segmentation and model-based region aggregation. Jaimes and Chang (1999) have developed a novel model-based object detection technique. However, it is very hard — if not impossible — for current computer vision techniques to detect video objects automatically from a general video sequence without using domain knowledge (Jaimes & Chang, 1999; Forsyth & Fleck, 1997; Fan et al., 2001c, 2001d). Several semiautomatic video object extraction algorithms have also been developed by Fan et al. (2002a), Gu and Lee (1998), Guo et al. (1999), and Luo and Eleftheriadis (2002) to address this problem.

The main weakness of the shot-based approach is that shot-based global visual features are too general to characterize the semantic visual concepts associated with the video shots. The main weakness of the object-based approach is that automatic object extraction in general is an ill-defined problem because homogeneous regions in color or texture do not correspond to semantic objects directly (Jaimes & Chang, 1999; Forsyth & Fleck, 1997).

- *Video Database Retrieval and Browsing:* There are three widely-accepted approaches to access video in a database:

  (a) **Query-by-example** is widely used in the existing CBVR systems. Query-by-example is necessary in a situation where naive users cannot clearly describe what they want via keywords or they do not want to search a large-scale video database via hierarchical summary browsing. However, the query-by-example approach suffers from at least two problems. The first one is that not all database users have example video clips at hand. Even if the video database system interface can provide some templates of video clips, there is still a gap between the various requirements of different users and the limited templates that can be provided by the database interface. Naive users may prefer to query the video database via high-level semantic visual concepts or hierarchical summary browsing through the concept hierarchy of video contents. The major difficulty for the existing CBVR systems is that they are unable to allow users to query video via high-level semantic visual concepts and to enable concept-oriented hierarchical video database browsing (Fan et al., 2002b, 2002c).

  (b) **Query-by-keywords** is also used in some CBVR systems based on manual text annotation (Humrapur et al., 1997; Jiang & Elmagarmid, 1998). Keywords, which are used for describing and indexing videos in the database, are subjectively added without a well-defined structure by a database constructionist. Since the keywords used for video indexing are subjective, naive users cannot find exactly what they want because they may not use the same keywords as did the database constructionist. Moreover, manual text annotation is too expensive for large-scale video collections.

  (c) **Hierarchical browsing** is also widely accepted by naive Internet users for accessing text documents via *Yahoo* and *Google* search engines. Naive users (rather than using visual features or keywords to describe their requests) should browse the summaries, which are presented on different visual hierarchic concept levels. However, most existing CBVR systems do not support concept-oriented hierarchical video database browsing because of the lack of efficient visual summary presentation structure (Fan et al., 2002b, 2002c). In order to support video browsing, some pioneer works have been proposed in the past by Rui et al. (1997), Yeung et al. (1995), Chen et al. (1999), Smith (1999), and Zhong et al. (1996). However, these existing techniques focus only on browsing a video sequence and do not address how to support concept-oriented hierarchical video database browsing (Fan et al., 2002b, 2002c). These three video-access approaches have been treated independently, but it is very important to support them in the same CBVR system so that naive users can select convenient approaches to accessing video in databases.

- *Video Database Indexing Structure:* One common shortcoming of the existing CBVR systems is that only a few of them release their inherent video database indexing structures (Flickner et al., 1995; Fan et al., 2002b, 2002c). Video database indexing is becoming an important issue for supporting content-based video retrieval because the traditional database indexing structures suffer from the problem of dimensionality. Therefore, the cutting-edge research on integrating computer vision with database management deserves attention.

Figure 1a.   Content-Based Video Analysis Results — Shot Detection Results From a Movie

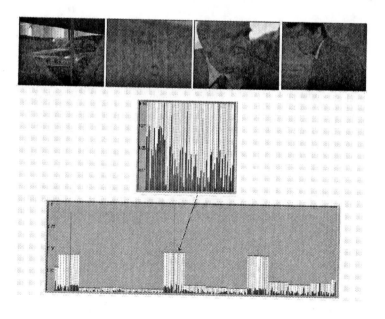

Figure 1b. Content-Based Video Analysis Results — Model-Based Object-Extraction Results from a MPEG Test Video

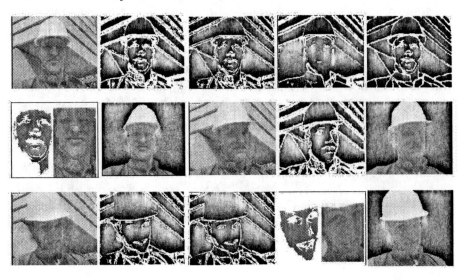

Figure 1c. Content-Based Video Analysis Results — Object-Extraction Results From a News Video via Human-Computer Interaction

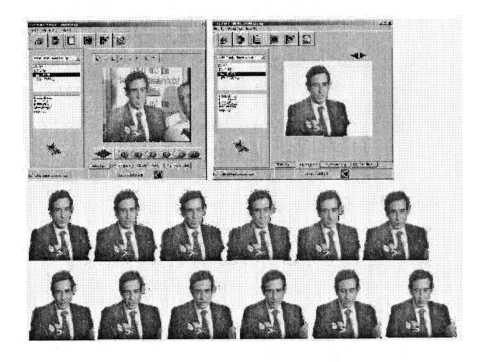

VIDEO CONTENT ANALYSIS
AND REPRESENTATION

Video analysis and feature extractions are necessary steps for supporting hierarchical, semantics-sensitive video classification, indexing, and access. In *ClassView*, a MPEG video sequence is first partitioned into a set of video shots by using our automatic video shot-detection technique. In order to adapt the thresholds to the *local activities* of different video shots within the same sequence, we use a small window (i.e., 20 frames in our current work), and the threshold for each window is adapted to its local visual activity (Fan et al., 2001a, 2002c). The video shot-detection results shown in Figure 1(a) are obtained from one of the video data sources used in our system. However, it is not necessary to use all these physical video shots for indexing and characterizing the semantic visual concepts associated with the corresponding MPEG video. For example, a one-hour MPEG movie may consist of hundreds of physical video shots, but some of them may not be relevant to the associated semantic visual concepts. Even with online relevance feedback, using the shot-based global visual features alone cannot be effective in characterizing the high-level visual concepts and in describing the intentions of naive users. It is necessary and desirable to understand the basic visual patterns (i.e., salient objects) that human beings actually use and how humans combine these basic salient objects when deciding whether two video shots are semantically similar (Fan et al., 2002b, 2002c; Mojsilovic, Kovacevic, Hu, Safranek, & Ganapathy, 2000; Luo & Etz, 2002). Detecting the basic salient objects that human beings use for judging semantically visual similarity is becoming very important to support content-based video retrieval. Based on this observation, some specific types of salient objects are extracted automatically from these physical video shots.

Automatic object extraction for supporting content-based video indexing and retrieval is very challenging. Fortunately, not all the objects in video need to be extracted and used for characterizing the semantic visual concepts because users may decide semantically visual similarity based on specific types of salient objects (Mojsilovic et al., 2000; Luo & Etz, 2002). Since objects for content-based video indexing applications are not necessarily the semantic objects from the human point of view (Smeulders, 2000), they can be specific types of salient objects which are meaningful for detecting and characterizing relevant semantic visual concepts. For example, human faces are good enough for detecting and characterizing the semantic visual concepts in a *news* video (Satoh & Kanade, 1997). Therefore, automatic salient object extraction is becoming possible for supporting content-based video indexing and retrieval by performing query concept classification.

Based on this observation, several *statistical object-specific functions* are defined in *ClassView*, and each function can provide one specific type of salient object. These statistical object-specific functions are obtained from the labeled training data sets (Fan et al., 2001c, 2001d; Mojsilovic et al., 2000; Luo & Etz, 2002). An obvious example of the statistical object-specific functions is the *statistical skin color map* for skin detection (Wei & Sethi, 1999). The number of the statistical object-specific functions depends upon how many types of salient objects will be used by naive users to specify their query concepts in our system. Our salient object extraction results are given in Figure 1(b). Since automatic object extraction in general is difficult among current computer vision techniques, we have also developed an interactive video object extraction technique. These experimental results are given in Figure 1(c) (Fan et al., 2002a; Gu & Lee, 1998; Luo & Eleftheriadis, 2002).

After the salient objects are extracted from the physical video shots, a set of shot-based and object-based visual features are extracted for enabling hierarchical shot representation and indexing. The physical video shots for each MPEG video are classified into two opposite classes, based upon their importance in characterizing associated semantic visual concepts: *principal video shots* versus *non-principal video shots*. If a physical video shot consists of any type of well-defined salient object, it is treated as the principal video shot for characterizing and accessing the corresponding MPEG video. In this way, a MPEG video is indexed and accessed hierarchically by its principal video shots as shown in Figure 2.

SEMANTIC VIDEO CLASSIFICATION

Several high-dimensional database indexing trees have been proposed in the past, and they are expected to be used for video database indexing (Bohn, Berchtold, & Keim, 2001); but they suffer from the problem of the *curse of dimensionality*. This is because the low-level visual features used for video representation and indexing are normally in high-dimensions. One reasonable solution is first to classify videos into a set of clusters and then to perform the dimension reduction on these clusters independently (Ng & Han; Thomasian et al., 1998). Traditional database-indexing trees may be used for indexing these video clusters independently with relatively low-dimensional features. However the pure feature-based clustering techniques are unsuitable for video

Figure 2.   The Proposed Video Representation and Access Scheme in ClassView

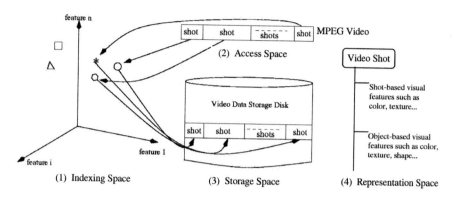

classification because of the semantic gap (Zhou, Vellaikal, & Kuo, 2000; Huang, Kumar, & Zabih, 1998; Sheikholeslami, Chang, & Zhang, 1998; Wang, Li, & Wiederhold, 2001; Minka & Picard, 1997; Vailaya, Jain, & Zhang, 1998; Yu & Wolf, 1995; Naphade & Huang, 2001). A decision tree classifier is very attractive for video classification via learning from the labeled training examples (Quinlan, 1986), but its internal nodes do not make sense for video database indexing. The semantics-sensitive video classifier is expected not only to be efficient for bridging the semantics gap, but also to provide an effective video database indexing scheme; thus the tree structure of the semantic video classifier should be related to the concept hierarchy of video contents (Fan et al., 2002b, 2002c; Miller, G., Beckwith, Fellbaum, Gross, & Miller K., 1990; Benitez, Smith, & Chang, 2001). Since it is very hard — if not impossible — for current computer vision and machine learning techniques to bridge the semantic gap in general, the concept hierarchy is domain-dependent.

After the principal video shots are obtained, we focus on generating semantic video scenes and upper-level visual concepts such as clusters. From the obtained principal video shots, more efficient database management structure can be supported. The semantic video classifier is built in a bottom-up fashion as shown in Figure 3. As introduced in Fan et al. (2002b, 2002c), the hierarchical tree structure of the classifier (i.e., *levels* and *nodes*) is first determined according to the domain-dependent concept hierarchy of video contents and is given by the domain experts or obtained via WordNet or MediaNet (Fan et al., 2002b, 2002c; Miller et al., 1990; Benitez et al., 2001). Once such hierarchical video classification structure is given, we use a set of labeled training examples to determine the discriminating features (i.e., feature subspace) and classification rules for each visual concept node via relevance analysis. For each visual concept node, a labeled training example exists in terms of a set of shot-based and object-based low-level visual features $\Xi = \{F_l \mid_{l=1}^{N}\}$ and the semantic label L provided by domain experts or naive users. There are two measurements for defining similarity among the labeled training principal video shots under the given visual concept node:

- Visual similarity via comparing shot-based and object-based low-level visual features;
- Semantic similarity via comparing high-level semantic labels (i.e., visual concepts).

The feature-based similarity distance $D_F(T_\delta, T_\gamma)$ between two principal video shots T_δ and T_γ is defined as:

$$D_F(T_\delta, T_\gamma) = \sum_{F_i \in \Xi} \frac{1}{\alpha_l} \cdot D_{F_l}(T_\delta, T_\gamma), \quad \sum_{l=1}^{N} \frac{1}{\alpha_l} = 1 \tag{1}$$

where $D_F(T_\delta, T_\gamma)$ denotes the similarity distance between T_δ and T_γ according to their l^{th} low-level visual feature F_l, α_l is the weight for the lth visual feature, Ξ is the set of original low-level visual features, and N is the total number of shot-based and object-based low-level visual features as described above and initially extracted for video shot representation.

The concept-based semantic similarity distance $D_S(T_\delta, T_\gamma)$ between two principal video shots T_δ and T_γ can be defined as:

$$D_S(T_\delta, T_\gamma) = \begin{cases} 0, & L_\delta = L_\gamma \\ 1, & otherwise \end{cases} \tag{2}$$

where L_δ and L_γ are the semantic labels for the principal video shots T_δ and T_γ. There are only two possibilities for the concept-based semantic similarity between two labeled principal video shots under the given semantic label for the corresponding visual concept node: *similar* versus *dissimilar*.

Relevance analysis is first used to remove the irrelevant features and to balance the importance among representative features (Rui et al., 1998) so that the feature-based visual similarity between two principal video shots may

Figure 3.   Bottom-Up Procedure for Building the Hierarchical Video Classifier, Where the Semantic Cluster May Include Multiple Levels According the Concept Hierarchy

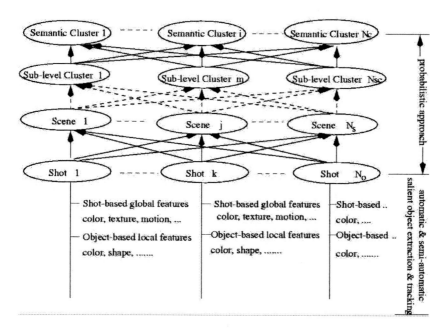

correspond to their concept-based semantic similarity. This step not only reduces the dimensions of the low-level visual features: it also rearranges the feature space to reflect major correlation patterns in data, ignoring smaller, less important variations. The visual concept nodes at the same visual concept levels (such as the semantic cluster level) are then characterized by different discriminating features with different levels of importance.

We model the *first classification* (from principal video shots to semantic scenes) by utilizing a set of object-based low-level visual features $X=(x_1, x_2, ..., x_m)$ and probabilities. We assume a mixture model to describe the shot distribution for each visual concept node in its weighted feature subspace — specifically, a multi-dimensional Gaussian distribution. The mixture probability function of the principal video shots residing in N_s semantic scene nodes is given by:

$$P(X) = \sum_{k=1}^{N_s} P(S_k)P(X \mid S_k, \omega_{s_k})$$

(3)

where $P(X|S_k, \omega_{s_k})$ is the conditional probability that a principal video shot with the object-based feature vector X belongs to a semantic scene S_k in its weighted subspace, ω_{s_k} is the set of dimensional weights for the semantic scene S_k, and $P(S_k)$ is the fraction of principal video shots assigned to the semantic scene S_k. The posterior probability $P(S_k|X, \omega_{s_k})$ for a principal video shot with the object-based feature value X to be assigned to the semantic scene S_k, can be obtained by:

$$P(S_k \mid X, \omega_{s_k}) = \frac{P(X \mid S_k, \omega_{s_k})P(S_k)}{P(X)} \tag{4}$$

In our current experiments, we assume that the discriminating features for characterizing high-level visual concept nodes in Figure 3 are independent. The multidimensional Guanssian distribution $P(X|S_k, \omega_{s_k})$ of the principal video shots residing in the semantic scene S_k can be defined by its centroid (mean) $\mu_{s_k} = \{\mu_{s_{k1}}, \ldots, \mu_{s_{ki}}, \ldots, \mu_{s_{kD_{sk}}}\}$ and variance $\sigma_s = \{\sigma_{s_{k1}}, \ldots, \sigma_{s_{ki}}, \ldots, \sigma_{s_{kD_{sk}}}\}$:

$$P(X \mid S_k, \omega_{s_k}) = \prod_{i=1}^{D_{sk}} \frac{1}{\omega_{s_{ki}}} \cdot \frac{1}{\sqrt{2\pi\sigma_{s_{ki}}^2}} e^{-\frac{1}{2\sigma_{s_{ki}}^2}(x_i - \mu_{s_{ki}})^2} \tag{5}$$

where D_{s_k} is the size of the discriminating visual features used for characterizing the semantic scene S_k. The multidimensional Gaussian distribution can then be simplified as:

$$P(X \mid S_k, \omega_{s_k}) = \prod_{i=1}^{D_{sk}} \frac{1}{\omega_{s_{ki}}} \cdot P(x_i \mid S_k, \omega_{s_{ki}}) \tag{6}$$

where $P(x_i \mid S_k, \omega_{s_{ki}}) = \frac{1}{\sqrt{2\pi\sigma_{s_{ki}}^2}} e^{-\frac{1}{2\sigma_{s_{ki}}^2}(x_i - \mu_{s_{ki}})^2}$ is the Gaussian distribution of

the principal video shots according to the dimensional feature x_i.

The Expectation-Maximization (EM) algorithm is used to determine the Gaussian parameters for each visual concept node (Fan et al., 2002b, 2002c). The EM derivation shows that the parameters μ_{s_k} and σ_{s_k} for the semantic scene S_k can be updated by maximizing the expression:

$$\sum_{p=1}^{N_p}\sum_{k=1}^{N_s} P(S_k \mid X_p, C_p)\log P(S_k \mid X_p, \omega_{s_k}) \tag{7}$$

where the training set of N_p examples with known semantic labels is indicated by: $\chi = \{(X_p, C_p)\} \mid_p^{N_p}$.

After the principal video shots are classified into the corresponding semantic scene nodes, they are then assigned to relevant high-level semantic visual concept nodes according to the domain-dependent concept hierarchy. The *second classification* (from semantic scenes to the corresponding semantic clusters) is modeled by a set of shot-based low-level visual features $Y=(y_1, y_2, ..., y_n)$ and probabilities:

$$P(C_j \mid Y, \alpha_{C_j}) = \frac{P(Y \mid C_j, \alpha_{C_j})P(C_j)}{\sum_{j=1}^{N_c} P(Y \mid C_j, \alpha_{C_j})P(C_j)} \tag{8}$$

where the prior probability $P(C_j)$ is obtained from the labeled training examples, and the conditional probability:

$$P(Y \mid C_j, \alpha_{C_j}) = \prod_{i=1}^{D_{C_j}} \frac{1}{\omega_{C_{ji}}} \cdot \frac{1}{\sqrt{2\pi\sigma_{C_{ji}}^2}} e^{-\frac{1}{2\sigma_{C_{ji}}^2}(y_i - \mu_{C_{ji}})^2}$$

is modeled as a Gaussian distribution in our current work. The parameters $\mu_{C_j} = \{\mu_{C_{j1}}, ..., \mu_{C_{ji}}, ..., \mu_{C_{jDC_j}}\}$ and $\sigma_C = \{\sigma_{C_{j1}}, ..., \sigma_{C_{ji}}, ..., \sigma_{C_{jDC_j}}\}$ for the semantic cluster C_j can also be determined via a similar approach as described by *Equation (7)*.

After the semantic classifier is obtained, the task of video classification is to assign an unlabeled principal video shot to the relevant visual concepts based on its low-level feature values. The process for semantic video classification (decision making) can be summarized as follows: Given an unlabeled principal video shot with m-dimensional object-based feature value $X=(x_1, x_2, ..., x_m)$ and n-dimensional shot-based feature value $Y=(y_1, y_2, ..., y_n)$, it is first assigned to the most relevant semantic scene S_k, and it is then assigned to the most relevant high-level visual concept nodes according to the domain-dependent concept hierarchy. Each step of this hierarchical classification procedure tries to find the best matching visual concept node that corresponds to the maximum posterior probability. The centroids and variances of the relevant visual concept nodes are also updated step-by-step by involving the new principal video shot. The video shot classification results for a medical domain are shown in Figure 4 and Figure 5.

VIDEO DATABASE INDEXING

After the semantic visual concepts have been obtained according to the domain-dependent concept hierarchy, we turn our attention to a way in which they may be used to provide more efficient video database indexing. Our multi-level video classifier can inherently support more efficient video indexing, where the parent-child relationships in the tree structure correspond to inter-level relationships in the domain-dependent concept hierarchy. As mentioned earlier, when the traditional database indexing trees are used for video

Figure 4. Semantic Scene Generation Results for Medical Videos where the Discriminable Regions such as Slide, Clipart, Blood-Red, Skin-Color, Human Faces, etc., are First Detected [These discriminable regions are then grouped into four semantic scenes according to pre-defined models (domain knowledge): (a) presentation, (b) dialog, (c) surgery, and (d) diagnosis.]

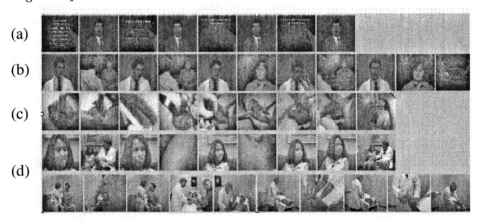

Figure 5. Semantic Scene of Surgery Generated from Medical Video, where the Salient Objects, Blood-Red Regions, are Identified

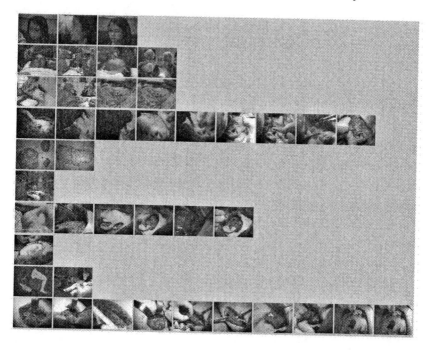

database indexing, they suffer from the *curse of dimensions* and the *semantic gap*. The semantic video classification procedure (as described earlier) has provided an approach to bridge the semantic gap, resulting in more meaningful partitions of video contents in the database. However, it is still difficult to use traditional indexing techniques to represent high-level visual concept nodes such as clusters (which are also used as database management units): semantically similar principal video shots may have large variations of distributions in the high-dimensional feature space, thus representing the boundaries of semantic visual concept nodes via rectangular or even spherical boxes, which will induce high overlap (Bohn et al., 2001).

In our hierarchical video database indexing structure (shown in Figure 6[a]), each high-level visual concept node (such as a cluster) is characterized by a subset of discriminating visual features, dimensional weights, and Gaussian distributions (e.g., defined by mean (centroid) and variance). Given the dimensional weighting coefficients $\{ \alpha_{C_{i_1}}, ..., \alpha_{C_{i_m}} \}$ for the semantic visual concept node C_i, the degree of importance of the visual features is also given. Bigger dimensional weighting coefficients mean that the corresponding visual features are more important in making the decision of similarity. We use Gaussian density to model the distribution of the principal video shots residing in each high-level visual concept node. For the semantic visual concept node C_i, centroid $\mu_{C_i} = \{\mu_{C_{i1}}, \ldots, \mu_{C_{ij}}, \ldots, \mu_{C_{im}}\}$ can be defined as:

$$\mu_{C_{ij}} = \frac{\sum_{h=1}^{N} z_{j,h}}{N} \tag{9}$$

where N is the total number of semantically similar principal video shots residing in the semantic visual concept node C_i, $z_{j,h}$ indicates the jth projected attribute of the shot-based or object-based visual features for the principal video shot h residing in the semantic visual concept node C_i, and $\mu_{C_{ij}}$ is its *projected centroid* on the jth dimension. The jth *dimensional variance* can then be defined as:

$$\sigma_{C_{ij}} = \frac{\sum_{h=1}^{N} \frac{1}{\alpha_{C_{ij}}} \cdot \left| z_{j,h} - \mu_{C_{ij}} \right|^2}{N} \tag{10}$$

where $\alpha_{C_{ij}}$ is the weight for the jth dimensional feature for the semantic visual concept node C_i.

The small value of $\sigma_{C_{ij}}$, indicates that (a) associated dimensional visual features are less important for representing the corresponding semantic visual concept; and (b) principal video shots are distributed more densely and cannot be separated efficiently by using the associated dimensional visual features. From a video database indexing point of view, the discriminating features selected for database indexing should have the following properties: (a) they recognize different principal video shots; (b) they are efficient enough to distinguish semantically similar principal video shots residing in the same semantic visual concept node. Based on the above discussion, visual features that have bigger dimensional weights should be selected for indexing the corresponding visual concept node (database management unit). Our dimension reduction (feature selection) technique via relevance analysis may consider users' subjectivity and is very attractive for video retrieval systems (Fan et al., 2001b).

After the discriminating features and their weights have been determined for each visual concept node, we then use the following novel techniques to support more efficient content-based video database indexing:

- A principal video shot corresponds to a data point (vector) in the high-dimensional feature space as shown in Figure 2. We warp the semantically similar principal video shots residing in the same visual concept node from their original high-dimensional feature space to a relatively low-dimensional compact subspace for the discriminating features: they can be close to each other in their warped-feature subspace, and the principal video shots from different visual concept nodes can be separated efficiently (Figure 7).
- We use a statistical model to represent and index the semantic visual concept nodes. The statistical model attempts to approximate data distributions (principal video shots in their warped feature subspace) with a certain degree of accuracy by a Gaussian function.
- We use geometric hashing to build the database indices for the high-level visual concepts. The following features are used to represent the semantic visual concept node Q:

semantic label L_Q, subset of discriminating features: Θ_Q
dimensions D_Q, weights $\alpha_Q = \{\alpha_Q | r \in \Theta_Q\}$
centroid $\mu_Q = \{\mu_{Q_1}, \dots, \mu_{Q_{D_Q}}\}$, variance $\sigma_Q = \{\sigma_{Q_1}, \dots, \sigma_{Q_{D_Q}}\}$

where L_Q is its semantic label (inherent within the concept hierarchy) for the corresponding visual concept node Q; Θ_Q is a subset of the discriminating features that are selected for characterizing the principal video shots residing in Q; D_Q is the number of its discriminating features; α_Q indicates the weights associated to these features; and μ_Q and σ_Q are used to define the Gaussian distributions $P(X| Q, \alpha_Q\}$ of the principal video shots in the corresponding visual concept node Q. The parameters Θ_Q, α_Q, and D_Q are used for defining the warped feature subspace that characterizes the corresponding visual concept node Q. The parameters L_Q, μ_Q, and σ_Q are used for defining the statistical properties of the principal video shots residing in the corresponding visual concept node Q.

The indexing structure consists of a set of separate indices for the visual concepts, and each visual concept node is connected to a single root node. The indexing structure includes a set of hash tables for different levels of the video database: a root hash table for keeping track of information about all semantic clusters in the database; a hash table in which each cluster may preserve information about all of its subclusters; and a leaf hash table for each subcluster, used for mapping its video scenes to the associated disk pages.

The semantic scene node (leaf node in the domain-dependent concept hierarchy tree) may consist of a large number of principal video shots. It is ineffective to use only one hash table to index large-scale principal video shots that reside in the same semantic scene node. The principal video shots residing in the same semantic scene node can be further partitioned into a set of groups according to their distributions, and each group is indexed by a hash table. This hierarchical partitioning procedure ends when the number of principal video shots in each group is fewer than a pre-defined threshold $\log N_i << D_i$ (Manolopoulos, Theodoridis, & Tsotras, 2000), where N_i represents the total number of principal video shots in the group and D_i represents the dimensions of discriminating features for the corresponding semantic scene.

Figure 6. (a) Hierarchical Database Indexing Structure; (b) Hierarchical Query Processing

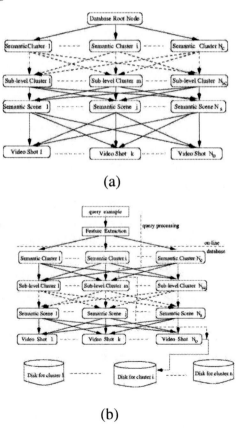

(a)

(b)

Figure 7. Feature Space Transformation for Supporting Better Cluster Representation: (a) Data Distributions for Two Clusters in the Original Representation Feature Space; and (b) Data Distributions for the Same Two Clusters in the Warped Low-Dimensional Feature Subspace

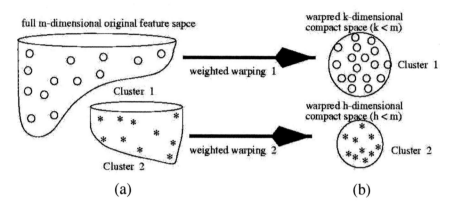

(a)   (b)

VIDEO DATABASE RETRIEVAL AND BROWSING

To answer a query-by-example, our query processor first extracts the object-based and shot-based low-level visual features $X=(x_1, x_2,..., x_m)$ and $Y=(y_1, y_2,..., y_n)$ from the query-example, and then compares them to those of the semantic clusters as shown in Figure 6(b). The similarity distance d_{q_i} between the query example and the center of the cluster C_i is defined as:

$$d_{q_i} = \sum_{r=1}^{n} \frac{1}{\lambda_{C_{i_r}}} \cdot d_r(y_r, \mu_{C_{i_r}})$$
(11)

$$\frac{1}{\lambda_{C_{i_r}}} = \begin{cases} \dfrac{1}{\alpha_{C_{i_r}}}, & if \; \alpha_{C_{i_r}} \in \Theta_{C_i} \\ 0, & otherwise \end{cases}$$
(12)

where $d_r(y_r, \mu_{C_{i_r}})$ is the similarity distance between the query example and the semantic cluster C_i according to their r^{th} dimensional representative feature; and Θ_{C_i} is the selected feature subset for the semantic cluster C_i. If:

$$d_{q_i} \le \sum_{r=1}^{D_{C_i}} \sigma_{C_{i_r}} \qquad (13)$$

then the query processor will subsequently obtain the posterior probabilities $P(C_i|Y,\alpha_{C_i})$ that the subject of the query example belongs to C_i.

$$P(C_i|Y,\alpha_{C_i}) = \frac{P(C_i)\prod_{j=1}^{D_{C_i}} \frac{1}{\alpha_{C_{ij}}} \cdot P(y_j|C_i,\alpha_{C_{ij}})}{\sum_{i=1}^{N_C} P(C_i)\prod_{j=1}^{D_{C_i}} \frac{1}{\alpha_{C_{ij}}} \cdot P(y_j|C_i,\alpha_{C_{ij}})} \qquad (14)$$

where $P(y_j|C_i,\alpha_{C_{ij}}) = \dfrac{1}{\sqrt{2\pi\sigma_{C_{ij}}^2}} e^{-\frac{1}{2\sigma_{C_{ij}}^2}(y_i-\mu_{C_{ij}})^2}$ can be obtained by using the

Gaussian distribution defined by the cluster centroid $\mu_{C_{ij}}$ and variance $\sigma_{C_{ij}}$. Similarly, we can also get the similarity distances and the posterior probabilities indicating that the query-example resides in the residue clusters. As shown in Figure 6(b), the cluster C_q, which has the smallest similarity distance and the maximum posterior probability with the query-example, is selected:

$$P(C_q|Y,\alpha_{C_q}) = \max\{P(C_i|Y,\alpha_{C_i})|i=1,...N_C\} \qquad (15)$$

where N_C is the total number of semantic clusters in the database. Similarly the query processor can sequentially find the relevant video scenes by using object-based low-level visual features $X = (x_1, x_2, ..., x_m)$.

In this query processing procedure, the system may find more than one cluster, subcluster, or scene that has the same or very close values of the posterior probability. This would indicate that the query-example resides in them. In this case, the system will query all relevant database management units in parallel. The final query results can be determined by human users via a browsing procedure or determined automatically by the system via a conjunction procedure. This parallel search procedure is meaningful because the same video scene may correspond to several different semantic concepts, classified into different semantic clusters by our video classifier (Section 4). A query-by-example from a medical video cluster is shown in Figure 8.

Our cluster-based indexing structure can also support *browsing-based video query*, where the user can first browse the visual summaries at the cluster level and then send his/her query to the relevant cluster. This browsing-based query can provide more relevant results because only the user knows what she/he wants.

As introduced above, each principal video shot inherits a hierarchy of semantic labels, which are labels of the corresponding nodes it belongs to in the proposed hierarchical video database model. A semantic label is also used as an attribute for video indexing so that a label-based semantic video query can also be supported in our system.

Most existing video retrieval systems do not support hierarchical browsing. Users, however, are not only interested in searching for specific videos (e.g., query-by-example). They would also like to browse and to navigate through video databases. A key issue to hierarchical video browsing is whether or not the clusters found make sense to the user and whether or not the browsing may be performed over IP networks. Such requirements have created great demands for effective and efficient approaches to organize summaries of the video contents at different database management levels. Browsing refers to a technique or a process by which users skip information rapidly and decide whether or not the content is relevant to their needs. Browsing video databases should be like scanning a table of contents or the index of a book — or flipping through the pages — to quickly get an overview of content and gradually focus on particular chapters or sections of interest (Yeung et al., 1995).

Our hierarchical video classification procedure has resulted in a hierarchical organization of video contents in a database. This hierarchical semantic video classification and organization technique can also support contextual understanding of the entire video contents in the database: it enables an efficient approach to hierarchical video browsing.

At the cluster level, we generate visual summaries by selecting representative video shots, which are closest to the centers of their subclusters. At the subcluster level, we use the *principal components* of the corresponding subcluster for visual summaries. The identification of principal components is very attractive for supporting high-level visual summarization. At the video shot level, we select key frames for visual summaries. Five types of browsing have been provided: browsing the whole video database via the summaries of all the semantic clusters, browsing the semantic clusters via the summaries of its subclusters, browsing the subcluster via the summaries of its video scenes, browsing the video scene via the summaries of its video shots, and browsing the video shot via its key frames. From the user's point of view, our multi-level video indexing and summarization system has the following advantages: (a) easy browsing and navigation through the hierarchical database indexing structure; (b) efficient retrieval; (c) ergonomic and friendly presentation of the database.

In our current implementation, browsing the whole video database is made possible by arranging available semantic titles into a cluster-based tree. Each cluster (root node) is represented by a semantic text title and a set of icon images (semantic visual template, seed of cluster, etc.) that are displayed at the higher level of the hierarchical browser. Users can get a rough sense of the video contents in a cluster without moving down to a lower level of the hierarchy. Browsing the selected semantic cluster is supported by partitioning the video contents in the same cluster into a set of subclusters (the icon video for each subcluster is also obtained). Browsing the selected semantic cluster, which is supported by arranging the available semantic icon videos into a tree, is similar to browsing the whole database. Browsing a single video sequence is, in some respects, a more complicated problem. The goal of the browser is to provide a mechanism by which a user can quickly (1) identify the content of a video to see if it is relevant or interesting and (2) find and view a relevant fragment of a video.

PERFORMANCE EVALUATION AND DISCUSSION

In this section, we present the results of an extensive performance analysis we have conducted to: (1) evaluate the effectiveness of this proposed semantic video classifier; (2) evaluate the performance of our hierarchical video indexing and retrieval system; and (3) evaluate the performance of our dimension reduction (feature selection) technique.

- *Semantic Video Classifier:* We have tested three video sources: *medical* videos, *news* videos, and *movies*. The average performance of our semantic video classifier is given in Table 1. Unfortunately, the performance of our current semantic video classifier depends upon the real distribution of the video data set. The *positive* and *negative* examples that are selected for determining the parameters for each internode of the semantic video classifier should differ sufficiently on their low-level visual features. The performance of our semantic video classifier can also benefit from the initial video segmentation results by detecting the salient objects. The average performance of video classification, which is based upon only the shot-based global visual features, is given in Table 2. One finds that by integrating video shots with salient objects, better results may be obtained.

$$\text{Missing Ratio} = \text{number of misclassified shots/total number of shots} \qquad (16)$$

The performance of our semantic video classifier also depends upon the number of clusters and the size of the training data set. A large-scale training data set can also improve the performance of our semantic video classifier as shown in Figure 9.

- *Cluster-Based Indexing:* The search time T_e for video retrieving from a large-scale database is the sum of two times: the time T_s for comparing the relevant videos in the database and (b) the time T_r for ranking the relevant results. If no database indexing structure is used for organizing this search procedure, the total retrieval time is:

$$T_e = T_s + T_r = N_T \cdot T_m + O(N_T \log N_T) \qquad (17)$$

where N_T is the number of videos in the databases, T_m is the basic time to calculate the low-level feature-based similarity distance between two principal video shots, and $O(N_T \log N_T)$ is the time to rank N_T elements.

Our multi-level video indexing structure can provide fast retrieval because only relevant database management units are compared with the query example. Moreover, only relevant features are selected for video representation and indexing. The basic time, therefore, for calculating the feature-based similarity distance is also reduced ($T_c, T_{sc}, T_s, T_o \le T_m$ because only the relevant features are used). The total retrieval time for our cluster-based indexing system is:

$$T_c = N_c \cdot T_c + N_{sc} \cdot T_{sc} + N_s \cdot T_s + N_o \cdot T_o + O(N_o \log N_o) \qquad (18)$$

where N_c, N_{sc}, N_s are the numbers of the nodes at the cluster level and at the most relevant subcluster and scene levels, N_o is the number of video shots that reside in the most relevant scene node, T_c, T_{sc}, T_s, T_o are the basic times for calculating the similarity distances in the corresponding feature subspace, and $O(M_o \log M_o)$ is the total time for ranking the relevant shots residing in the corresponding scene node. Since $(N_c + N_{sc} + N_s + N_o) << N_T$, $(T_c, T_{sc}, T_s, T_o) \le T_m$, thus $T_c << T_e$.

The average performance of the cluster-based indexing technique is shown in Figure 10.

- *Feature Selection (Dimension Reduction):* Our dimension reduction technique via relevance analysis also has the property of low computation cost as compared with other existing dimension reduction techniques (Thomasian, Castelli, & Li, 1998). The total cost of the existing SVD-based dimension reduction techniques is bound to $O(N_T \cdot m^2) + O(N_T \cdot m^2 \cdot N_C) + O(m \cdot N_C)$, where N_T is the total number of video shots in the database, N_C is the total number of possible clusters, and m is the total number of feature dimensions. The SVD techniques need $O(N_{C_i} \cdot m^2)$ for calculating the principal components of the ith cluster, where N_{C_i} is the total number of video shots in the ith cluster. The total cost of clustering is bound to $O(N_T \cdot m^2)$ because $\sum_{i=1}^{N_C} N_{C_i} = N_T$. The cost for SVD is bound to $O(\sum_{i=1}^{N_C} N_{C_i} \cdot D_{C_i}^2)$, and the cost for selecting the subspace dimensions is bound to $O(\sum_{i=1}^{N_C} D_{C_i})$. On the other hand, our dimension reduction technique reduces dimensions via relevance analysis according to dimensional weights, and its cost is bound to $O(m \cdot N_C)$. The performance of our dimension reduction technique is shown in Figure 11.

A classification accuracy for one-level and two-state images of greater than 90% may be achieved with our classification techniques (Wang et al., 2001; Minka & Picard, 1997; Vailaya et al., 1998). As compared with traditional one-level and two-state semantic image classification techniques, one can find that the accuracy ratio for our hierarchical semantics-sensitive video classifier is not perfect — as we expected. The reasons are:

- The relevance analysis has been integrated with the EM algorithm to bridge the semantic gap by exploiting the statistical properties of the semantically similar principal video shots, but there is a semantic gap between the low-level visual features and the high-level visual concepts. Thus using the statistical properties of these low-level visual features to characterize the relevant semantic visual concepts may not be the best solution to bridge the semantic gap.
- It is not the best solution to use the feature weighting technique to bridge the semantic gap, especially when low-level visual features are unsuitable for characterizing relevant visual concepts. The concept-based semantic similarity among these training examples is too label-intensive: the manual

Figure 8. The Feature-Based Retrieval Results from the Surgical Cluster

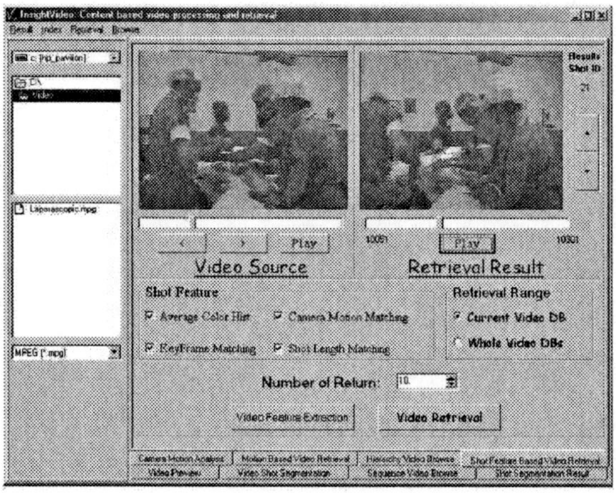

labels may be defined by domain experts or naive users according to semantic categorizations instead of to visual perceptions.

- The accuracy of our semantic video classifier also depends upon the distribution of the training example set. Some selected training examples may be irrelevant to the corresponding visual concept, thus resulting in poor performance.

- As shown in Figure 9, the performance of our video classifier depends upon the size of the training data set. A large training data set often increases the accuracy of the classification. It is very expensive, however, to obtain large-scale training example sets. The limited size of the training data set for each specific visual concept node depends upon the dimensions of its discriminating features and the number of its relevant sub-level visual concept nodes.

Table 1. The Average Performance of Our Semantic Video Classifier, Integrating Shot-Based Global Visual Features with Object-Based Local Visual Features

Test Data Type	Test Data Number	Concept Levels	Missing Ratio
Medical Videos	1200	3	26.8%
News Videos	1100	3	37.6%
Movies	3500	4	46.32%

Table 2. The Average Performance of the Video Classifier When Using Only Shot-Based Global Visual Features

Test Data Type	Test Data Number (shots)	Concept Levels	Missing Ratio
Medical Videos	1200	3	39.8%
News Videos	1100	3	41.7%
Movies	3500	4	42.4%

- Our hierarchical semantics-sensitive video classifier focuses on addressing the video classification problem with multiple levels (i.e., concept hierarchy) and multiple states (i.e., each visual concept cluster consists of multiple sub-level clusters). Variances of the low-level visual features for the semantically similar principal video shots may be very large, resulting in poor performance. One simple but reasonable solution treats the hierarchical video classifier as a set of independent one-level and two-state classifiers. Each semantic visual concept in our hierarchical semantics-sensitive video classifier is generated by a specific one-level and two-state classifier, but the relationships among these visual concepts on the

Figure 9. The Classification Accuracy Based on Different Training Data Size, Where Accuracy = 1 - Missing Ratio

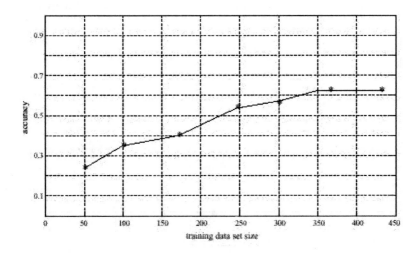

Figure 10. The Average Performance of Recall versus Precision for Cluster-Based Indexing Technique with Different Structures of the Classifier: (a) Classifier Includes Three Concept Levels; (b) Classifier Includes Four Concept Levels

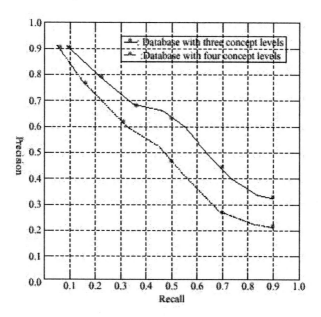

Figure 11. The Performance Comparison Between our Relevance-Based Dimension Reduction Technique and the Traditional SVD-Based Technique (we use solely the principle features in our experiments)

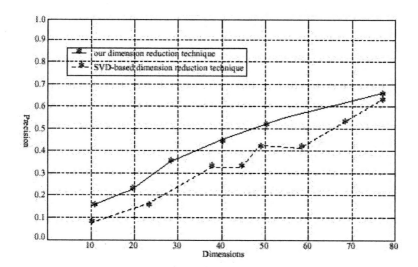

same level are lost. Generated visual concepts may have heavy overlaps in their low-level feature spaces.

- The single principal video shot may consist of multiple semantic visual concepts and induce very different subjective interpretations. The concept-based semantic similarity between the labeled principal video shots suffers from the subjectivity problem.

CONCLUSION AND FUTURE WORKS

We have proposed a novel framework, called *ClassView*, to make some advances in overcoming the problems suffered by existing content-based video retrieval systems. A hierarchical semantics-sensitive video classifier is proposed to shorten the semantic gap between low-level visual features and high-level semantic concepts. The hierarchical structure of the semantics-sensitive video classifier is derived from the domain-dependent concept hierarchy of video contents in a database. Relevance analysis is used to shorten the semantic gap by selecting discriminating visual features of suitable importance. The Expectation-Maximization (EM) algorithm is used to determine the classification rule for each visual concept node. A hierarchical video database index and summary presentation technique is also proposed to support more effective video access over a large-scale database. Integrating video querying with video browsing has provided great opportunity for supporting more powerful video search engines.

While we are not claiming to be able to solve all the problems related to content-based video retrieval, we have made some advances toward the final goal — the most nearly human-level video retrieval using the domain-dependent concept hierarchy. The following research issues should be addressed in the future to avoid the limitations of our hierarchical semantics-sensitive video classification and indexing techniques:

- Research in semantics-sensitive video classification is currently limited by the relative lack of large-scale labeled training data sets. It would be beneficial to generate classification rules by integrating unlabeled video clips with limited labeled video clips. Since unlabeled training examples may consist of different visual concepts, they will not follow joint probability and they may also degrade classification performance. A good solution for this problem should be found before using unlabeled training examples.
- Video characterization and classification via integration of multiple media

— video, audio, and textual information such as closed captioning — will provide more meaningful results. At the same time, it is urgent to address problems concerning the normalization of multiple cues and the automatic determination of their importance for semantic visual similarity judgment.

- High-dimensional visualization techniques should be developed for evaluating the real performance of our semantic video classifier. The basic assumption for semantic video classification is that semantically similar principal video shots residing in the same semantic visual concept node should be close to each other in their warped feature subspace, even though they may be far away each other in their original feature space. Moreover, the proposed high-dimensional visualization technique should have the capacity to visualize data distribution within warped feature subspace.

- Video database access control is also becoming a very important issue now because video data are used for different objectives. Different user-classes should have different access capabilities to particular levels of videos within databases or even within differing quality levels of the same video titles. The common weakness of existing CBVR systems is that they do not address the problem of content-based video database access control.

- It is very important to enable real-time updating of pre-determined feature subspaces, dimensional weights, classification rules, or even the inherent concept hierarchy according to the user's subjectivity for large-scale video databases. Our hierarchical video database indexing structure can support more effective video retrieval and concept-oriented hierarchical video database browsing, which makes it viable for supporting online relevance feedback. It may achieve more effective query optimization for large-scale video databases. The final users will ultimately evaluate the performances of the inherent video database representation and the indexing model, semantics-sensitive video classification under the given database model, query optimization, and concept-oriented hierarchical video database browsing for content-based video retrieval. It is very important to study human factors in supporting content-based video retrieval through this proposed prototype system.

REFERENCES

Ahanger, G., & Little, T.S. (1996). A survey of technologies for partitioning and indexing digital video. *Journal of Visual Communication and Image Representation, 7*, 28-43.

Alatan, A., Onural, M., Wollborn, R., Mech, E., Tuncel, & Sikora, T. (1998). Image sequence analysis for emerging interactive multimedia services - the European COST 211 framework. *Circuits and Systems for Video Technology, 8*, 802-813.

Benitez, A.B., Smith J.R., & Chang, S.-F. (2001). MediaNet: A multimedia information network for knowledge representation.

Bohn, C., Berchtold, S., & Keim, D. (2001). Searching in high-dimensional spaces: Index structures for improving the performance of multimedia databases. *ACM Computing Surveys, 33*, 322-373.

Carson, C., Belongie, S., Greenspan, H., & Malik, J. (1997). Region-based image querying. *IEEE Workshop on Content-Based Access of Image and Video Libraries.*

Cascia, E., & Ardizzone. (1996). JACOB: Just a content-based query system for video database.

Chang, S.F., Chen, W., Meng, H.J., Sundaram, H., & Zhong, D. (1998). A fully automatic content-based video search engine supporting spatiotemporal queries. *Circuits and Systems for Video Technology, 8*, 602-615.

Chen, J.-Y., Taskiran, C., Albiol, A., Delp, E. J., & Bouman, C. A. (1999). ViBE: A compressed video database structured for active browsing and search. *Multimedia Storage and Archiving Systems* IV, *3846*, 148-164.

Deng, Y., & Manjunath, B.S. (1998). NeTra-V: Toward an object-based video representation. *Circuits and Systems for Video Technology, 8*, 616-627.

Fan, J., Aref, W.G., Elmagamid, A.K., Hacid, M.S., Marzouk, X. & Zhu (2001). MultiView: Multi-level video content representation and retrieval. *Journal of Electronic Imaging, 10*, 895-908.

Fan, J., Ji, Y., & Wu, L. (2001). A content-based video database system: Content analysis, clustering, representation and indexing. *Journal of Visual Communication and Image Representation, 12*, 306-347.

Fan, J., Yau, D.K.Y., Aref, W.G., & Rezgui, A. (2000). Adaptive motion-compensated video coding scheme towards content-based bitrate allocation. *Journal of Electronic Imaging, 9*, 521-531.

Fan, J., Yau, D.K.Y., Elmagarmid, A.K., & Aref, W.G. (2001). Image segmentation by integrating color edge detection and seeded region growing. *Image Processing, 10,* 1454-1466.

Fan, J., Yu, J., Fujita, G., Onoye, T., Wu, L., & Shirakawa, I. (2001). Spatiotemporal segmentation for compact video representation. *Signal Processing: Image Communication, 16,* 553-566.

Fan, J., Zhu, X., & Wu, L. (2001). An automatic model-based semantic object extraction algorithm. *Circuits and Systems for Video Technology, 11,* 1073-1084.

Fan, J., Zhu, X., & Wu, L. (2002). Accessing video contents through key object over IP. *Multimedia Tools and Applications, 18.*

Fan, J., Zhu, X., Elmagarmid, A.K., & Aref, W.G. (2002). Class view: Hierarchical video shot classification, indexing and accessing. *Multimedia, 4.*

Fan, J., Zhu, X., Hacid, M.-S., Wu, L., & Elmagarmid, A.K. (2002). Cluster-based indexing of video databases towards more efficient retrieval and browsing. *Image Processing, 11.*

Flickner, M., Sawhney, H., Niblack, W., Ashley, J., Huang, Q., Dom, B., Gorkani, M., Hafner, J., Lee, D., Petkovic, D., Steele, D., & Yanker, P. (1995). Query by image and video content: The QBIC system. *IEEE Computer, 38,* 23-31.

Forsyth, D., & Fleck, M. (1997). Body plan. *Proceedings of CVPR,* (678-683).

Gu, C., & Lee, M.C. (1998). Semantic segmentation and tracking of semantic video objects. *Circuits and Systems for Video Technology, 8,* 572-584.

Gunsel, B., Tekalp, A.M., & Beek, P.T. (1999). Content-based access to video objects: temporal segmentation, visual summarization, and feature extraction. *Journal of Electronic Imaging, 7,* 592-604.

Guo, J., Kim, J., & Kuo, C.-C.J. (1999). SIVOG: Smart interactive video object generation system. *ACM Multimedia,* 13-16.

Huang, J., Kumar, S.R., & Zabih, R. (1998). An automatic hierarchical image classification scheme. *ACM Multimedia.*

Humrapur, A., Gupta, B., Horowitz, C.F., Shu, C., Fuller, J., Bach, M., Gorkani, & R. Jain. (1997). Virage video engine. *Storage and Retrieval for Image and Video Databases,* 188-197.

Jaimes, A., & Chang, S.-F. (1999). Model based image classification for content-based retrieval. *Proceedings of SPIE.*

Jain, A.K., Vailaya, A., & Wei, X. (1999). Query by video clip. *ACM Multimedia Systems, 7,* 369-384.

Jiang, H., & Elmagarmid, A.K. (1998). WVTDB — A semantic content-based video database system on the world wide web. *Knowledge and Data Engineering, 10*(6).

Luo, H., & Eleftheriadis, A. (2002). An interactive authoring system for video object segmentation and annotation. *Signal Processing: Image Communication, 17,* 559-572.

Luo, J., & Etz, S.P. (2002). A physical model-based approach to detecting sky in photographic images. *Image Processing, 11,* 201-212.

Manolopoulos, Y., Theodoridis, V.J., & Tsotras. (2000). *Advanced Database Indexing.* Kluwer Academic Publishers.

Meier, T., & Ngan, K.N. (1998). Automatic segmentation of moving objects for video object plane generation. *Circuits and Systems for Video Technology, 8,* 525-538.

Meng, J., & Chang, S-F. (1995). CVEPS — A compressed video editing and parsing system. *ACM Multimedia.*

Meng, J., Juan, Y., & Chang, S-F. (1995). Scene change detection in a MPEG compressed video sequence. SPIE Symposium on Electronic Imaging: Science and Technology-Digital Video Compression: Algorithms and Technologies.

Miller, G., Beckwith, R., Fellbaum, C., Gross, D., & Miller, K. (1990). Introduction to WordNet: An on-line lexical database. *International Journal of Lexicography, 3,* 235-244.

Minka, T.P., & Picard, R.W. (n.d.). Interactive learning using a society of models. *Pattern Recognition, 30.*

Mojsilovic, A., Kovacevic, J., Hu, J., Safranek, R.J., & Ganapathy, S.K. (2000). Matching and retrieval based on the vocabulary and grammar of color patterns. *Image Processing, 9,* 38-54.

Naphade, M.R., & Huang, T.S. (2001). A probabilistic framework for semantic video indexing, filtering, and retrieval. *Multimedia, 3,* 141-151.

Ng. R., & Han, J. (n.d.). Efficient and effective clustering methods for spatial data mining. *Proceedings of VLDB.*

Patel, N.V., & Sethi, I. K. (1997). Video shot detection and characterization for video databases. *Pattern Recognition, 30,* 583-592.

Pentland, A., Picard, R., & Sclaroff, S. (n.d.). Photobook: Content-based manipulation of image databases. *International Journal of Computer Vision, 18,* 233-254.

Quinlan, J. (1986). Induction of decision trees. *Machine Learning, 1*, 81-106.

Rui, Y., Huang, T.S., & Mehrotra, S. (1997). Constructing table-of-content for videos. *ACM Multimedia System, 7*, 359-368.

Rui, Y., Huang, T., Ortega, M., & Mehrotra, S. (1998). Relevance feedback: A power tool for interactive content-based image retrieval. *Circuits and Systems for Video Technology, 8*, 644-655.

Satoh, S., & Kanade, T. (n.d.). Name-It: Association of face and name in video. *Proceedings of Computer Vision and Pattern Recognition.*

Sheikholeslami, G., Chang, W., & Zhang, A. (1998). Semantic clustering and querying on heterogeneous features for visual data. *ACM Multimedia.*

Smeulders, A., Worring, M., Santini S., Gupta A., & Jain R. (2000). Content-based image retrieval at the end of the early years. *Pattern Analysis and Machine Intelligence, 22*, 1349-1380.

Smith, J.R. (1999). VideoZoom spatial-temporal video browsing. *Multimedia, 1*(2).

Swanberg, S., Chang, C.F., & Jain, R. (1992). Knowledge guided parsing in video databases. *SPIE Proceedings of Electronic Imaging.* Sciences and Technology.

Thomasian, A., Castelli V., & Li. C.-S. (n.d.). Clustering and singular value decomposition for approximate indexing in high dimensional space. *Proceedings of CIKM*, (201-207).

Vailaya A., Jain, A., & Zhang, H.J. (1998). On image classification: City versus landscape. *Proceedings of the IEEE Workshop.* Content-based Access of Image and Video Libraries, 3-8.

Wang, J.Z., Li J., & Wiederhold, G. (2001). SIMPLIcity: Semantics-sensitive integrated matching for picture libraries. *Pattern Analysis and Machine Intelligence, 23*, 947-963.

Wei, G., & Sethi, I.K. (1999). Face detection for image annotation. *Pattern Recognition Letters, 20*, 1313-1321.

Wu, P., & Manjunath, B.S. (n.d.). Adaptive nearest neighbor search for relevance feedback in large image database. *ACM Multimedia.*

Yeo, B.-L., & Liu, B. (1995). Rapid scene change detection on compressed video. *Circuits and Systems for Video Technology, 5*, 533-544.

Yeung M., Yeo, B.-L., Wolf, W., & Liu, B. (1995). Video browsing using clustering and scene transitions on compressed sequences. *Multimedia Computing and Networking, 2417*, 399-413.

Yu, H., & Wolf, W. (n.d.). Scenic classification methods for image and video databases. *Proceedings of SPIE, 2606*, 363-371.

Zhang, H.J., Kankanhalli, A., & Smoliar, S.W. (1993). Automatic partitioning of full-motion video. *ACM Multimedia Systems, 1*, 10-28.

Zhang, H.J., Wu, J., Zhong, D., & Smoliar, S. (1997). An integrated system for content-based video retrieval and browsing. *Pattern Recognition, 30*, 643-658.

Zhong, D., Zhang, H.J., & Chang, S.-F. (n.d.). Clustering methods for video browsing and annotation. *Proceedings of SPIE*, (pp. 239-246).

Zhou, W., Vellaikal, A., & Kuo, C. (n.d.). Rule-based video classification system for basketball video indexing. *ACM Multimedia.*

Chapter VIII

Evaluating Graph Drawing Aesthetics:
Defining and Exploring a New Empirical Research Area

Helen C. Purchase
University of Glasgow, Scotland

ABSTRACT

This chapter describes a long-term project that investigates the validity of the design principles — not from the perspective of computational efficiency, but from the perspective of human comprehension — upon which many automatic graph layout algorithms are based. It describes a framework for experimentation in this area, the overall methodology used throughout, as well as the details of the experiments themselves. It shows the development of the empirical ideas and methods as the project matured and provides reflections on each experiment, demonstrating the difficulty of initiating a new experimental research area. The chapter suggests how the current results should best be interpreted, as well as ideas for future work in this area.

INTRODUCTION

This chapter describes a long-term project that investigates the validity of the design principles — not from the perspective of computational efficiency, but from the perspective of human comprehension — upon which many automatic graph layout algorithms are based.

There are two main objectives of the chapter:

- to summarise empirical work the author has done on the effectiveness of 2D graph drawing aesthetics; and
- to describe the process of initiating a new experimental research area, developing a framework for empirical studies within the area with specific reference to the experimental methodology and statistical analysis issues involved.

BACKGROUND

A *graph* is a set of nodes (representing objects) and edges (representing relationships between the objects). Graphs may be represented in diagonal matrices, with each node being associated with both a row and a column and each edge being represented by a positive value in the cell that links two nodes. However, graphs are more typically represented as node-edge diagrams (called *graph drawings*). Figure 1 represents three different renderings of the same graph structure.

The process of creating a graph drawing from an underlying graph structure is known as *automatic graph layout*. Many graph layout algorithms exist (Battista et al., 1994) and for many years, researchers have been devising increasingly efficient and elegant algorithms for the production of graph drawings. At the annual Graph Drawing symposium, researchers present their

Figure 1. Three Representations of the Same Graph

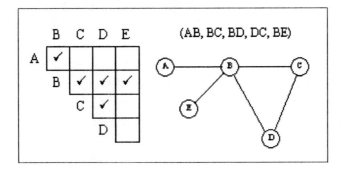

newest layout algorithms, or their variations on existing algorithms. (This forum typically comprises approximately 30 papers, of which only a few do not present a new algorithm.)

These algorithms are typically valued for their computational efficiency and the extent to which they conform to one or more standard layout design principles (called *aesthetic criteria*). Examples of such criteria include minimising the number of edge crosses, maximising the display of symmetric structures, and maximising orthogonality (the property of fixing edges and nodes to an invisible underlying unit grid). Designers of graph layout algorithms claim that by optimising these measurable aesthetics and producing 'nice' graph drawings, the graph information is easier to read. Prior to 1995, these claims had not been empirically tested with respect to human studies.

The author initiated a new empirical research area in 1995: that of attempting to validate these graph drawing aesthetics, not with respect to computational efficiency, but solely with respect to human understanding. The project has so far investigated the following areas with human empirical studies:

- effectiveness of several aesthetic criteria in the performance of graph theoretic tasks;
- effectiveness of several layout algorithms in the performance of graph theoretic tasks;
- human preference for different aesthetic criteria in the layout of software engineering diagrams;
- effectiveness of several aesthetic criteria in the performance of software engineering tasks;
- effectiveness of several layout algorithms in the performance of social network analysis tasks.

In addition, to support the empirical studies, the project produced definitions of computational metrics for measuring aesthetic presence, independent of the structure of the underlying graph structure.

The aim of this chapter is two-fold:

- To summarise and integrate the results of some of these empirical studies in an attempt to give a 'big-picture' overview of this new research area. Six experiments are described.
- To demonstrate the process of building a new empirical research area (including the production of an empirical framework, discussion of the mistakes made, and a description of the experimental methodological and statistical analysis decisions required).

While the specific details of some of the experiments presented in this chapter have been published elsewhere, this chapter also includes descriptions of the unpublished pilot studies that informed the experimental design and reflections on the ideas and methods used as the project matured.

EXPERIMENTAL ISSUES

Aesthetics

Designers of graph drawing algorithms tend to optimise certain aesthetics and claim that by doing do, the resultant graph drawing helps the human reader to understand the information embodied in the graph. The aesthetic criteria considered in this project were all extracted from the research literature on automatic graph layout algorithms. The set of aesthetics addressed in each experiment differs: at the start of the project, only a few common aesthetics were considered; the later experiments include a wider range.

The graph-drawing aesthetics considered in the experiments described in this chapter are:

- *(c) edge crosses:* the number of edge crosses should be minimized (Reingold & Tilford, 1981).
- *(m) minimum angles:* the minimum angle between edges extending from a node should be maximised (Coleman & Stott Parker, 1996; Gutwenger & Mutzel, 1998).
- *(b) bends:* the total number of bends in polyline edges should be minimised (Tamassia, 1987).
- *(ndis) node distribution:* nodes should be distributed evenly within a bounding box (Coleman & Stott Parker, 1996).
- *(el) edge lengths:* edge lengths not be too short, nor too long (Coleman & Stott Parker, 1996).
- *(ev) edge variation:* edges should be of similar length (Coleman & Stott Parker, 1996).
- *(f) flow:* directed edges should, as much as possible, point in the same direction (Waddle, 2000).
- *(orth) orthogonality:* nodes and edges should be fixed to an orthogonal grid (Tamassia, 1987; Papakostas & Tollis, 2000).
- *(sym) symmetry:* where possible, a symmetrical view of the graph should be displayed (Eades, 1984; Gansner & North, 1998).

Metrics

The measurement of these aesthetic criteria within a graph drawing is often done informally and may differ among algorithms. There is no standard, objective way for analysing a graph drawing with respect to the presence of different aesthetics. Trivial counting methods may be used for simpler aesthetics (for example, counting the number of intersecting edges or the number of edges which point in the same direction), but continuous measures are necessary so that analysing a drawing with respect to an aesthetic is not merely a binary decision. Thus, it is desirable that a drawing is not considered 'orthogonal' or 'not orthogonal', but is rather described according to the extent to which the drawing conforms to the orthogonality aesthetic (that is, the drawing may be considered to have 65% presence of orthogonality).

In defining new continuous metrics for aesthetic criteria, two particular issues arose:

- The metrics need to be scaled, so that they all lie within the same range. This enables aesthetic presence comparisons between drawings of graphs of different size and structure. For example, a drawing of a graph with 150 edges of which five intersect would need a lower aesthetic presence value of the crossing aesthetic than a drawing of a graph with 10 edges of which seven intersect.

- Many of these aesthetics are difficult to measure by trivial computational methods. For example, satisfying the orthogonality aesthetic needs to be more than merely putting the nodes and edges onto an underlying grid: the resolution of the grid needs to be optimal according to the number of nodes, and the angular deviation of any edges that do not lie on the grid needs to be taken into account.

Early in the project, unscaled metrics for crosses, bends, and symmetry were defined for use in experiments 1 and 2 (Purchase, Bhanji, Cohen, & James, 1995). These definitions were altered so that scaled values were produced, and the second version of the symmetry metric was extended to take more account of symmetric sub-graphs (Purchase & Leonard, 1996). Together with a further three metrics (orthogonal, min angle, and flow), these adapted formulae were used in experiments 3, 4, and 5a (Purchase, 2002).

EXPERIMENTAL FRAMEWORK

It became clear during the early experiments that there were several different approaches that could be taken to experimentation in this area. As this was a new research area, there was no existing literature to which the various experiments could be related, so a new evaluation framework was defined as part of this project. This framework was based on three dimensions relevant to determining the experimental form for an investigation of graph drawing algorithms:

- *Usability measurement:* The usability of a graph drawing can be measured in many different ways: two common methods are *performance* (subjects perform better on a given task using one drawing than when using another) and *preference* (subjects express personal preference for one drawing over another).
- *The nature of the graph:* There are two types of graphs that can be used in the experiments: abstract (the information in the graph has no reference to the real world, referred to as a *syntactic* graph) and domain-specific (the graph represents a domain, for example, data-flow or transport networks, referred to as a *semantic* graph).
- *The effect being investigated:* There are two ways in which graph drawing layout can be investigated: by considering the usability effect of the individual *aesthetics* or by looking at the usability of complete *algorithms* (which produce drawings conforming to different aesthetics to varying degrees).

This framework allows many different avenues of empirical study to be followed. While an experiment on algorithms has been conducted (Purchase, 1998) and preference data has been collected (Purchase, Carrington, & Allder, 2002), this chapter concentrates on performance and aesthetics experiments, both syntactic and semantic.

The forms of the experiments reported in this chapter are shown in Table 1.

Experimental Method

While the methodology for each of the experiments described below was specifically designed for the type of evaluation required, the underlying method is the same. A set of diagrams of the same graph was produced according to different aesthetic presences (for example, one graph drawing would have no crossing edges while another would have many). Experimental participants would be asked to perform a task using the drawings. The data collected was analysed to determine whether or not there was a significant difference in the performance of participants between different diagrams of contrasting aesthetic presence.

Table 1.   The Form of the Different Experiments, According to the Experimental Dimensions

Experiment	Usability measurement	The nature of the graph	The effect being investigated
1	performance	syntactic	3 aesthetics
2	performance	syntactic	3 aesthetics
3	performance	syntactic	5 aesthetics
4	performance	semantic (class diagrams)	4 aesthetics
5a	performance	semantic (UML class diagrams)	5 aesthetics
5b	performance	semantic (UML class diagrams)	7 aesthetics (perceptual)
6	performance	semantic (UML collaboration diagrams)	6 aesthetics (perceptual)

Most of the experiments were conducted using a within-subject methodology, with each subject performing a task using all of the experimental diagrams. One of the experiments uses a between-subject methodology (experiment 4), in which participants were divided into eight groups, with each participant group being given the same one drawing as the other people in that same group.

STRUCTURE OF THIS CHAPTER

This first part of this chapter will summarise all the experiments performed in this project so far: first describing the syntactic experiments, followed by the semantic ones. The order of the presentation of the experiments is roughly chronological (with the exception of experiment 4, which was performed between experiments 2 and 3). Presenting the experiments chronologically demonstrates the development of this new research area, shows how each experiment built on the results (or problems) of the prior one, and reveals the lessons learned along the way.

The second part of this chapter presents a general overview of the experimental results, reflections on the experimental processes and designs, and suggestions as to future avenues for research in this area.

THE SYNTACTIC EXPERIMENTS

Pilot Experiment 1 (Purchase, 1995)

This was the first experiment that was performed, and it was intended to be a pilot study. The aim of the experiment was to explore the relevant issues relating to aesthetic variations, experimental methodology, and graph-based tasks. We hoped to gain a better understanding of what would be required in our later, more formal experiments.

The experimental drawings were defined by the following features:

- The aesthetics considered: *bends, crosses, symmetry.*
- The variations for each of these aesthetics: *few, many.*
- The graphs used: *dense* (20 nodes, 32 edges), *sparse* (20 nodes, 21 edges).

There were therefore 12 drawings in total (for example, *sparse-bends-few, dense-crosses-many, etc.*). These drawings were drawn by hand, so that they conformed to the required aesthetic variations. The variations were measured by hand: the number of edge crosses were counted, with a three-way intersection counting as three crosses. The range of edge crosses in the drawings was 0-42. The number of edge bends were counted, with only bends with angles less than 150° included. The range of edge bends in the drawings was 0-30. We defined a symmetry metric that identified symmetric sub-graphs around multiple axes in the drawing and counted the edges mirrored around each axis. The range of the symmetry metric in the drawings was 0-51. Figure 2 shows the *dense-crosses-many* drawing.

Three different questions were asked of each of the 12 graph drawings. For example:

1. How long is the shortest path between node J and node G?
2. What is the minimum number of nodes you would need to remove in order to disconnect nodes F and B, such that there is no path between them?
3. What is the minimum number of edges you would need to remove in order to disconnect nodes E and A, such that there is no path between them?

The graphs were designed so that for each of the three question types pairs of nodes could be identified that would give a range of answers. As each question type was asked for each drawing, we needed to be sure that the answer to each question type was not always the same. The answer differed according to which node pair was used in the statement of the question. For the first question, four node-pairs could give the answers 2,3,4,5; for the second question, node pairs were identified that gave answers of 0,1,2; and for the third question, the possible answers were 0,1,2,3. The graphs included an independent smaller sub-graph of four nodes, so that the answer to questions 2 and 3 could be 0. Care was taken to ensure that in defining the node pairs corresponding to the three answers to question 3 (the minimum number of edges to be removed to disconnect two nodes), the answers to the questions were not easily determined by the degree of either of the nodes.

This experiment was paper-based: the subjects were given a booklet of the following structure:

- instructions;
- six pages of two graphs drawn three times each, with all three questions asked of all six drawings: these drawings were for practice only;
- a small word puzzle that served as a filler task;
- 12 pages showing the 12 experimental drawings, with all three questions asked of all 12 drawings (these drawings were in a different random order for each subject).

The data collected were the correctness of the subjects' answers and the length of time it took for them to complete the questions for each experimental diagram.

As this was only a pilot test, only five subjects took part in the experiment and the data was not analysed statistically. Five different experimental booklets were produced, each with a different random order for each subject. In addition, the questions themselves were randomised: although the same three question types were asked of each drawing, the pair of nodes chosen for each question was randomly selected from a list of node-pairs. This ensured that any variability in the data could not be explained by varying difficulty of the questions.

A within-subjects analysis method was used to reduce any variability that may have been attributable to differences between subjects (e.g., age, experience). Any learning effect was minimised by the inclusion of practice graphs and the random order of the graph drawings.

Most of the answers that the subjects gave to the three questions were correct. Although the accuracy and time data was not analysed, some qualitative data was collected from the subjects in the form of general comments: these revealed that the *crosses-many* drawings were considered more difficult than the *bends-many* drawings. There were no comments about symmetry.

The lessons we learned from this pilot study were how important it is for the experimental instructions to be very clear and unambiguous and for examples of the required tasks (with their correct answers) to be provided at the start of the experiment. We also discovered that timing by observation is very difficult and inaccurate. Most importantly, we learned the significance of controlling confounding factors. For example, we realised that if we wished to compare subjects' performance on the *sparse-bends-few* drawing with their performance on the *sparse-bends-many* drawing, then it was important that both these diagrams had the same number of crosses and the same symmetry metric measurement.

The graphs used in this experiment were of two kinds — we included an independent smaller sub-graph of four nodes (B,H,I, and J in Figure 2), so that the answer to questions 2 and 3 could be 0. The main problem was that if one of the nodes referred to in node in question 2 was in this smaller independent graph, and it was also referred to in question 3, the answer was obvious. Many subjects also commented that they found this sub-graph very confusing, and none of the graphs used in further experiments included an independent sub-graph.

Experiment 2 (Purchase, Cohen, & James, 1997)

This experiment built on the experience of the pilot study: it considered the same three aesthetics and used adapted versions of the drawings produced for the pilot study. However, an additional aesthetic variation was introduced, an interim *some* measurement. Thus, for each of the three aesthetics — for the sparse graph — three drawings were produced (for example: *sparse-bends-few, sparse-bends-some, sparse-bends-many*). There were therefore 18

Figure 2. The Dense-Crosses-Many Drawing Used in Pilot Experiment 1

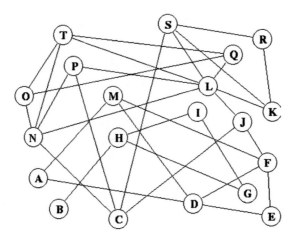

experimental graph drawings. The same methods for measuring the aesthetic variations were applied, the drawings were controlled for confounding factors (all other aesthetics being kept at zero), and the ratio between *few/some/many* was the same for all three aesthetics. Figure 3 shows the *sparse-symmetry-some* drawing, and indicates the axes around which local symmetry was measured. The same three graph-theoretic questions as were used in the pilot experiment were used as the experimental task.

As we were running the experiment formally for the first time, we needed to clearly define our hypotheses:

- Increasing the number of edge bends in a graph drawing decreases the understandability of the graph.
- Increasing the number of edge crosses in a graph drawing decreases the understandability of the graph.
- Increasing the local symmetry displayed in a graph drawing increases the understandability of the graph.

The methodology was similar to that used in the pilot experiments, although this time we wished to fix the time that the subjects spent answering the questions for each diagram and to collect accuracy data only. We used trials of this method to determine an appropriate time limit. This time limit was different depending upon whether the sparse graph (30 seconds) or the dense graph (45 seconds) was used. We separated the experimental diagrams and ran two experiments: one for the sparse graph and one for the dense graph (for which there were nine experimental drawings each).

For each of the two experiments, the subjects were given a booklet of the following structure:

- instructions, including definitions and worked examples;
- six practice drawings, with all three questions asked of each;
- a small word puzzle that served as a filler task;
- nine pages showing the nine experimental drawings, with all three questions asked of each.

There were 49 subjects for the dense graph and 35 for the sparse graph. As before, the order of the experimental drawings was randomised for each subject. There were the same constraints on the nodes selected for each question as in the pilot study, except that as the independent sub-graph had been removed, no question had 0 for its correct answer.

As in the pilot test, a within-subjects analysis method was used. The control variables were the graphs themselves and the time allowed for each drawing. The independent variables were the number of bends, the number of crosses, and the value of the symmetry metric. The dependent variable was the accuracy data.

We collected accuracy data from both experiments. As the *few/some/ many* variations measurements were ordinal and not continuous (i.e., the numerical difference in aesthetic variation between *few* and *some* is not necessary — the same as the difference between *some* and *many*), we could not use parametric statistical methods. Instead, we ranked each student's accuracy on each experimental drawing on a 1 to 3 scale, giving the drawing that they performed best a score of 1, and the drawing that they performed least well a score of 3 (with tied values recorded where necessary).

For our statistical analysis, we used the Friedman two-way analysis of variance-by-ranks method, which is used when a number of matched ordinal samples are taken from the same population. The aesthetic variations were ordinal, and the samples for each metric were matched as all values of each metric were tested on every subject. The Friedman test was used to determine the χ^2 value for each aesthetic for each of the two graphs, which implied that the probability that the ranked data was produced by chance. For those aesthetics for which the probability of the ranked accuracy data having been produced by chance was less than 0.05, observation of the average accuracy

Figure 3. The Sparse-Symmetry-Some Drawing Used for Experiment 2, Showing the 6 Axes of Symmetry Used for Calculating the Symmetry Metric

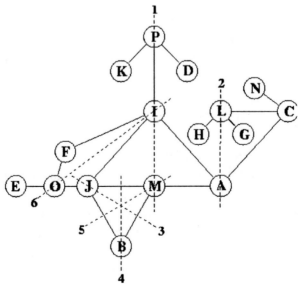

Figure 4. Accuracy Results for the Dense Graph in Experiment 2

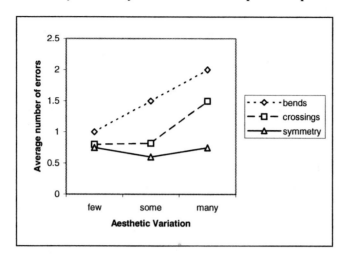

for the relevant drawings could tell us whether or not the direction of the accuracy difference followed that predicted by our hypotheses. Figure 4 and Figure 5 show the charts representing the average accuracy and response times.

For both the sparse and dense graphs, our bends and crosses hypotheses were confirmed. There was no significant result for symmetry. There was very little variation in the average accuracy between the *few/some/many* symmetric variations, as most students made very few errors on the symmetric diagrams. This meant that the time limit given for these symmetry diagrams was too long:

Figure 5. The Accuracy Results for the Sparse Graph in Experiment 2

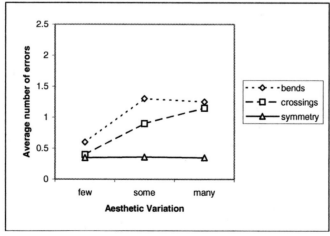

the students had sufficient time to answer the questions correctly (this is known as a "ceiling effect").

One of the main lessons learned from this experiment regarded controlling opposing potential confounds. In controlling the diagrams for the experiment, we avoided potential interaction between the aesthetics by having no variation of two aesthetics while varying the third. For example, all the graph drawings that varied the number of bends had no crosses and a zero value for symmetry. There is a potential conflict here between the nature of our three hypotheses: with bends and crosses, the hypothesis was that *increasing* their number would result in increased errors. However, the symmetry hypothesis was that *decreasing* the amount of symmetry would increase the errors. By keeping the number of crosses and bends at zero for the symmetrical graph drawings, the drawings made simpler. However, keeping the symmetry metric at zero made the bends and crosses drawings more complex. It is therefore no surprise that a ceiling effect was observed with the reading of the symmetry drawings when the same time period was being used for reading all the graphs of the three aesthetics.

Another important problem was revealed in this experiment. One of the subjects commented that much of the time was spent locating the two nodes whose labels corresponded with those stated in the question. This was an experimental design error, inappropriate when time was an important factor in the experiment. In subsequent experiments, no nodes were labeled, and the nodes relevant to the question were highlighted in black.

Another issue that arose out of this experiment was the difficulty of manual timing when a paper-based experiment is used, and we also questioned the effectiveness of the current metric used to determine the extent of symmetry in the drawing.

Experiment 3 (Purchase, 1997)

This third experiment considered the three aesthetics used earlier (crosses (c), bends (b), and symmetry (s)); and introduced two more: maximizing minimum angles (m) and increasing orthogonality (o). Two variations for each aesthetic were considered: a + version (assumed to be easy to read), and a – version (assumed to be difficult to read). Only one graph was used, with 16 nodes and 28 edges. There were therefore 10 experimental graph drawings (for example, c+, o-, m-). Like the previous experiments, answering the three graph theoretic questions was the experimental task, and suitable node pairs were identified that could give a range of answers to the three questions.

One of the ways in which this experiment was different from the previous ones was in the use of a full set of aesthetic metric definitions. Aesthetic metric formulae that measured the aesthetic presence of all five of the aesthetics to be considered were defined: these could be applied to any graph drawing of any graph and were scaled to lie between 0 and 1 to allow for numerical comparison. This set of aesthetics included an updated definition of symmetry, which takes into account the perceptual affect of symmetry of bends and crosses (Purchase & Leonard, 1996).

In creating the experimental diagrams, the aesthetic variations were carefully controlled: while it was impossible to always have the metric values of the other four aesthetics identical in any aesthetic variant pair, we ensured that they lay within a reasonable 'neutral' range according to that aesthetics' distribution. We were also more careful about the definition of our extremes: the drawings named with a + (e.g., $c+$, $o+$) were assumed to be easy to read. In some case this means having a high aesthetic presence (e.g., orthogonality); in other cases it means having a low aesthetic presence (e.g., crosses). We therefore introduced the terms "bend-less" and "cross-less" to refer to these two aesthetics so that all five aesthetic hypotheses could state that the increase of the aesthetic would improve understanding. Figure 6 shows the experimental graph drawings and their associated aesthetic values.

The other main difference between this experiment and the former ones was the use of an experimental online system. The methodology was similar. The experimental system presented

- instructions, including definitions and worked examples;
- six practice drawings, with all three questions asked of each;
- a small logic puzzle that served as a filler task;
- ten experimental diagrams, which were each displayed three times, one for each question.

All 30 instances of the diagram/question combinations were presented in random order; thus, the three questions for the m- diagram were not necessarily asked consecutively. The diagrams were also given a random orientation, apart from the highly orthogonal one, which was randomly rotated by a multiple of 90°. The nodes on the drawings were unlabeled, and the two nodes relevant to each question were highlighted on the screen (thus removing the search time that was included in the prior experiments). The subjects typed their answers to the questions.

There were 55 subjects in this experiment. The online system collected the subject answers to each diagram/question pair and the time taken for the subject to answer each question.

This was again a within-subject methodology: the controls were the graphs and the other four aesthetics for each aesthetic variant pair, the independent variable was the aesthetic variation within each pair, the dependent variables represented the accuracy of subjects' answers to the questions as well as the time taken to answer each question.

As we had measured both accuracy and response time, we had two measures of understanding. These were treated independently in the statistical analysis, although it may have also been useful to consider the correlations between time and accuracy to see to what extent we could consider these measures independently. This was not done for this experiment. As there were only two variations for each aesthetic, we could use a parametric test as the measurable difference between the two variations is not important.

For both time and accuracy, we performed t-tests for each of the five aesthetics, to see which of our five hypotheses were confirmed. We found that the bends and crosses hypotheses were supported for accuracy and that the crosses and symmetry hypotheses were supported for response time. There was no support for orthogonality or for maximising the minimum angle.

We also performed a Tukey pair-wise comparison for both time and accuracy on both the set of "– drawings" and the set of "+ drawings". This statistical test indicates which of an ordered set of results are significantly different from each other and takes into account the Bonferroni correction that is usually applied when data is being used more than once in repeated statistical tests. The results of this test revealed that the c- (lots of crosses) drawing took significantly more time and had a lower accuracy than all other (–) versions of the graph. In addition, the highly symmetric $s+$ drawing took significantly less time than the minimum angle $m+$ and orthogonality $o+$ drawings.

The main lesson extracted from this experiment concerned the limitations of the formal experimental method: in order to run a well-controlled and valid experiment, the context in which the experiment needs to be run constrains the extent to which the conclusions can be generalised. This experiment used only one set of subjects (computer science students); there were only two variations for each aesthetic; the aesthetic variations were measured by metrics that may not have corresponded with perception; only one graph of a particular size and structure was used; and only three questions of limited scope were asked. The constraints of this experiment imply that, while the results are useful, they cannot necessarily be generalised to encompass larger graphs, graphs of very different

Figure 6. Graph Drawings Used in Experiment 3 with their Aesthetic Metric Values (Note that although the nodes are labeled in this figure, the nodes were blank when the drawings were displayed on the screen, with the two nodes relevant to the current question highlighted.)

graph		bend-less	cross-less	minangle	orthog	sym
b+	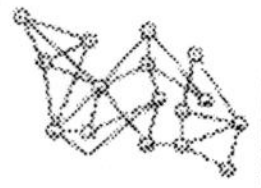	0.96	0.97	0.38	0.27	0.75
b-	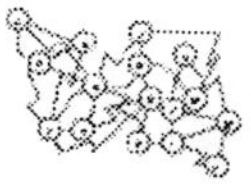	0.47	0.99	0.44	0.28	0.71
c+	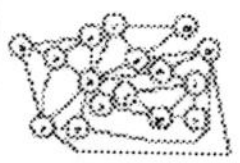	0.82	1	0.46	0.33	0.63
c-	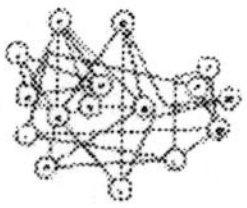	0.87	0.88	0.35	0.29	0.84
m+	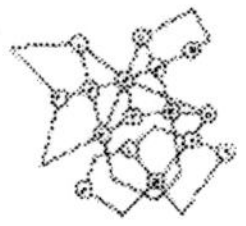	0.71	0.98	0.62	0.22	0.74
m-	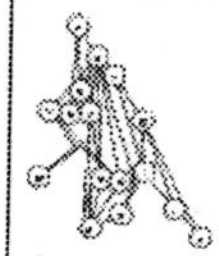	0.82	0.98	0.16	0.26	0.79
o+	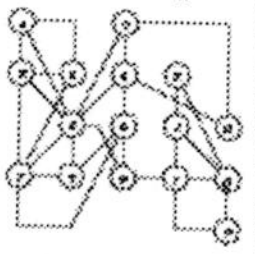	0.82	0.98	0.42	0.46	0.73
o-	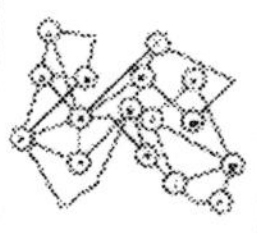	0.82	0.98	0.41	0.21	0.68
s+	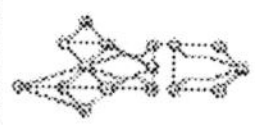	0.77	0.99	0.57	0.29	0.96
s-	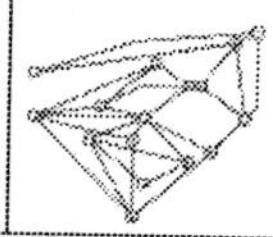	0.87	0.99	0.44	0.25	0.00

structures, or graphs used for different purposes. The danger was that, in presenting this work to researchers in graph layout who had never had their aesthetic assumptions experimentally challenged before, the researchers would generalise these results further than is appropriate simply because they are the sole experimental results in this area.

THE SEMANTIC EXPERIMENTS
Pilot Experiment 4 (Purchase, Grundon, & Naumann, 1996)

Having worked on abstract graphs, we then extended our efforts to semantic graphs — graphs which relate to some real-world domain. This pilot semantic experiment first explored three experimental methods for testing graph drawing aesthetics in the area of software-engineering diagrams and then ran one experiment to test the effects of four aesthetics (bends, crosses, orthogonality, and upward-flow).

The semantic notation chosen was object-oriented class diagrams based on the Booch notation (Booch, 1994), which was adapted for our purposes to suit Smalltalk code. The notation was made more graph-like (using ellipses instead of clouds, adapting the font variations used to illustrate the class type, etc.). The notation was therefore sufficient to describe the code while being uncluttered by unnecessary syntax that was irrelevant to our research questions regarding aesthetic variations. A brief tutorial handout was prepared for all subjects, explaining the notation to be used in the experiment and how it related to object-oriented design.

Three initial methodologies were attempted in a preliminary study which collected no data, did not use aesthetic-variant drawings, and whose aim was to identify an appropriate method for semantic aesthetics experiments.

For the first method, the task the subjects needed to perform was code adaptation. They were given the class and scenario diagrams for a system and the matching code (system A). They were also given the class and scenario diagrams for a similar system (system B). Both systems were key-access systems with identical functionality but with different underlying structures, the information being either centralised or distributed. The subjects' task was to adapt the system A code so that it represented the diagrams given for system B and to demonstrate the identical functionality when the new code is executed. The dependent variable was the time taken to complete the task. We tried this method with five subjects, four of whom took well over an hour to complete the task, while the fifth (an expert) took 35 minutes. We concluded that this adaptation task was inappropriate for experimental purposes, as it was too heavily influenced by subjects' prior coding experience and did not rely enough on actual use of the diagrams where the aesthetic variation to be tested would be represented.

The second method required subjects to identify mistakes in given code. They were given a brief textual description of the system, a class diagram representing the structure of the system, and a code listing. Within 15 minutes, they needed to identify as many errors in the code as they were able in relation to the diagram. We hoped that this task would require more from the subjects in terms of understanding the class diagram than the prior pilot experiment had done. The dependent variable was the number of mistakes identified in the given time. We tried this method with only one subject, but this was sufficient to highlight its problems. Subjects need to look at *all* the code — even that containing no errors. They may also (rightly or wrongly) identify errors that were not part of our intended list and that are unrelated to any need to understand the diagram. We felt that we still needed to find a methodology that relied more on understanding the diagrams.

The third method was the one ultimately chosen for the pilot experiment. It required subjects to match diagrams with code.

We used the two systems — A and B — which were designed for the first method investigated above. The two systems had identical functionality with different underlying structures. Each of these systems was represented by a class diagram and a code listing. Figure 7 shows the class diagram for system A. The subjects were given the two diagrams and the two code listings and were told to match the diagrams to the code. So as not to bias their decisions, the diagrams and listing were not referred to by any ordinal scale (for example, by letters or numbers), but were colour coded. We also did not give any indication that there would be a perfect two-way match between the two diagrams and two code listings. Subjects were therefore asked to say whether the pink code corresponded with the green diagram, the blue diagram, or neither diagram; and whether the yellow code corresponded with the green diagram, the blue diagram, or neither diagram.

We considered four aesthetics (bends, crosses, orthogonality, and up-ward-flow), each with two aesthetic variations (*few/-, many/+*). Thus, there were eight diagrams of system A (*Ab+ Ab- Ac+ Ao- etc.*), and eight diagrams for system B (*Bb+ Bb- Bc- Bo- etc.*). The diagrams were produced according to existing aesthetic metric formulae, with appropriate controls.

The dependent variable was the time taken for the subject to get the correct answer (as measured by experimenter observation): subjects submitted their solutions to the experimenter repeatedly until told that the answer was correct. The data from subjects who appeared to be using a quick trial-and-error method were eliminated.

As the task was more complex than the three graph-theoretic questions used in the syntactic experiments (taking approximately 30 minutes), a be-tween-subjects methodology was used. Thus, each subject was randomly paired with a particular aesthetic variation (e.g., *b*+), and used only the two diagrams associated with that variation (*Ab*+ *and Bb*+). There were six subjects for each of the eight aesthetic variations, yielding a total of 48 subjects.

The between subjects t-test statistical analysis on the data, used to determine whether the different presence of the aesthetics had any effect on the time taken to complete the task, revealed no significance at all. There was very little variation in the data. Variation that did exist was attributed to chance.

With regard to the methodologies investigated in this experiment, we learned that repeatedly submitting results until getting a correct answer clouds the data and that the more well-defined the task, the better the experiment. Adapting code is a loosely defined task; matching two diagrams with code listings is much more well-defined.

Figure 7. The Smalltalk Application Domain Used in Pilot Experimentat 4

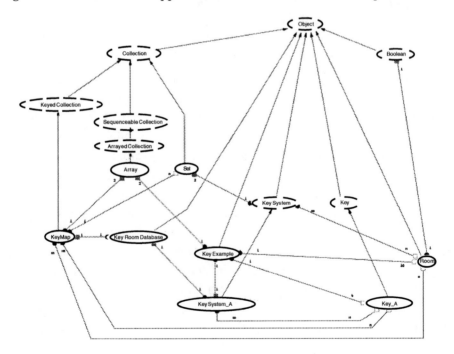

The most important lesson we learned from investigating all three methodologies and from running the one experiment was the difficulty of running valid between-subjects experiments. For a complex domain such as understanding object-oriented programming, the expertise variability between subjects is likely to be so great that comparing their performance on the same task is clearly inappropriate. Even if a pre-experiment tutorial is provided to ensure that all subjects have the same base level of domain-specific knowledge for a programming task, there is still likely to be substantial subject variability that will make the data meaningless.

Experiment 5a (Purchase, McGill, Colpoys, & Carrington, 2001)

For our first formal semantic aesthetics experiment, we used an adaptation of the matching experiment described in experiment 4. Our domain consisted of UML class diagrams (Rumbaugh et al., 1999), and five aesthetics were considered: bends, node distribution, edge variation, flow, and orthogonality. As the prior experiments had given strong support for removing edge crosses, this aesthetic was not included in the list and no experimental diagrams included crosses.

The hypotheses for our experiment follow:

- Increasing the number of bends in the representation of associations in an UML class diagram decreases the understandability of the classes and the relationships in the application.
- Placing the visual objects representing classes in a UML class diagram such that they are evenly distributed over the drawing area increases the understandability of the classes and of the relationships in an application.
- Representing associations in an UML class diagram with lines of similar length increases the understandability of the classes and of the relationships in an application.
- Representing the direction of associations and inheritances in an UML class diagram with arrows that point in the same direction increases the understandability of the classes and of the relationships in an application.
- Placing the visual objects representing associations, inheritances, and classes in an UML class diagram on an underlying unit grid increases the understandability of the classes and of relationships in an application.

The application domain was a simple UML class diagram of 13 objects and 17 edges that modeled a small information technology company. A textual specification in simple English was produced which matched this class diagram. The experimental task was to match this specification against a set of experimental diagrams, indicating whether or not each diagram matches the specification.

For each of the five aesthetics, a "low-effect" (-) and a "high-effect" (+) version of the diagram was produced. To ensure that there were no confounding factors among aesthetics, ranges were controlled as much as possible. For example, to remove any confounding factors in a diagram pair for a particular aesthetic, the measurement of all other aesthetics were kept within a "middle-effect" range. A control diagram that conformed to a "middle-effect" range for all the aesthetics as much as possible was also created. There were therefore a total of 11 correct experimental diagrams. Aesthetic presence was measured using computational metrics, and Figure 8 shows the aesthetic values for each of the experimental diagrams.

Ten incorrect diagrams were created by randomly changing the origin or destination of one relationship per diagram. The layouts of the incorrect diagrams were visually comparable to those of the correct diagrams: as we did not intend to analyse the responses to the incorrect diagrams, their layout was not important. However, it was important to include incorrect diagrams in the experimental set so that the correct answer to each diagram presented was not the same. These incorrect diagrams to had to be visually comparable to the

Table 2. The Computational Aesthetic Values for Experiment 5a Diagrams

Diagram	Aesthetic				
	bends (b)	orthogonality(o)	edge variation (ev)	node distribution(n)	direction of flow (f)
b+	1	0.43	0.66	0.59	0.6
b-	0.71	0.46	0.64	0.56	0.6
o+	0.85	0.70	0.66	0.56	0.4
o-	0.85	0.32	0.64	0.56	0.6
ev+	0.85	0.44	0.74	0.59	0.6
ev-	0.85	0.41	0.55	0.59	0.6
n+	0.85	0.41	0.66	0.73	0.4
n-	0.85	0.48	0.64	0.45	0.6
f+	0.85	0.44	0.65	0.59	1
f-	0.85	0.46	0.66	0.59	0
control	0.85	0.45	0.66	0.57	0.6
example	0.85	0.44	0.66	0.56	0.6

correct diagrams so that they could not be identified by mere visual pattern matching.

The first phase of the experiment was preparation: subjects were given a brief UML tutorial which explained the meaning of UML class diagrams and, using a simple example, described its semantics. Subjects were not expected to have any prior knowledge of UML and this tutorial provided all the UML background information that they required for the experimental task. A worked example demonstrated the task that the subjects were to perform, presenting a small specification with four different diagrams. It indicated whether or not each diagram matched the given specification. Care was taken to ensure that neither the tutorial nor the worked example would bias the subjects towards one layout over another.

As part of this preparation, subjects were also given an UML class diagram (which conformed to a 'middle effect' for all the aesthetics) of the application domain and the accompanying textual specification (this was the specification against which they would need to match the experimental diagrams). The subjects were asked to study this specification closely and to memorise it if possible.

The second phase of the experiment was conducted online: UML diagrams were presented in turn on the screen, and subjects needed to press 'Y' or 'N' depending on whether or not they thought the diagram matched the specification. A copy of the specification was propped up against the computer for quick reference. Pilot tests had revealed that 50 seconds was a suitable cut off time for each diagram; therefore if a subject had not responded within 50 seconds, the next diagram was presented and an incorrect answer recorded. The practice diagrams helped the subjects get used to this cut-off time. The diagrams were presented in blocks of eight, with a rest break between each block (the length of which was controlled by the subject).

The experimental diagrams were presented in random order for each subject: the set of diagrams included two instances of each of the 11 correct diagrams and one instance of each of the incorrect diagrams — 32 in total. Sixteen practice diagrams were presented at the start of the experimental session (the data for these was not collected).

A within-subject methodology was used to reduce any variability that may have been attributable to differences between subjects: thus, each subject's performance on one layout was compared with his or her own performance on an alternative layout. The practice diagrams and random order of presentation helped counter any learning effect.

Thirty subjects took part in this experiment. Both response time and accuracy data for the 11 correct diagrams were collected. We used a t-test to analyse both the response time and accuracy data for each of the five aesthetics independently, using the 'middle effect' diagram as the middle variation point for all of the aesthetics. We realised after analysing the data that a non-parametric test would have been more appropriate: the three variation measures were ordinal and not continuous, similar to experiment 2.

There was no significance in the accuracy data. In the response time data, the only significant results were that the middle effect diagram had the best performance for bends and edge variation and for flow (the upward direction produced the quickest response). The results were confusing and contradictory.

In reassessing the diagrams that we used for this experiment, we felt that the problem was in the measurement of the presence of the aesthetics. The computational metrics, while useful for measuring the aesthetics from a computational point of view, may be less useful for measuring perceptual aesthetic presence from a human point of view. For example, the orthogonality metric measures the extent to which the nodes and edges are placed along an underlying unit grid, but the human perception of orthogonality in a diagram may not match the numerical value produced by the metric. This phenomenon may particularly be the case for aesthetics that are global — those that require an overall assessment of the entire diagram (for example, orthogonality, symmetry, or node distribution).

We therefore decided to run the experiment again. This time we used a different set of diagrams created according to humans' perception of the presence of each aesthetic in the diagrams, rather than according to the defined metrics.

Experiment 5b (Purchase, McGill, Colpoys &Carrington, 2001)

The methodology for this experiment was identical to that used in experiment 5a, and the same UML application domain was used. The difference was in the way in which aesthetic presence within the experimental diagrams was determined.

Seven aesthetics were considered in this experiment: bends, node distribution, edge variation, direction of flow, orthogonality, edge lengths, and symmetry — each with three variations. For each aesthetic, three diagrams were created by hand: low-effect (-), middle-effect (0), and high-effect (+). To confirm that these diagrams had an appropriate amount of low-, middle- and high-effect of the aesthetics and that the aesthetics were appropriately controlled, simple perception experiments were performed with 10 subjects. The subjects were asked to rank sets of three diagrams according to the presence of the aesthetic. For example, a subject was shown the $n+$, $n0$, and $n-$ diagrams and asked to rank them according to the extent of even node distribution in the diagrams. The possible confounds of symmetry and orthogonality were also addressed in these interviews. For example, the subjects were asked to rank the $n+$, $n0$, and $n-$ diagrams according to symmetry, the desired result being that they would find it difficult to do so. We needed to ensure that a difference in performance on the node distribution diagrams could not be attributed to differences in symmetry and orthogonality. The bends and flow aesthetics were not perceptually tested in the production of the diagrams, as their presence is better assessed computationally (for example, by counting the number of bends or by counting the number of edges pointing upwards). However, the bends and flow diagrams were tested for possible symmetry and orthogonality confounds. Figure 9 shows the *flow+* (consistent direction of flow) diagram.

Note that the decision to measure aesthetic presence by perception rather than by computational measures introduces a new feature into the three-dimension experimental framework described at the beginning of this chapter (usability measurement, the nature of the graph, and the effect being investigated). If the effect being investigated is that of individual aesthetics, then the method by which that aesthetic presence is measured is another dimension of the experiment.

The same methodology, preparatory materials, online system that we used in experiment 5a was used once again. Thirty-five subjects took part. The same 10 incorrect diagrams from experiment 5a were used. The 21 correct and 10 incorrect diagrams were each presented once in the online task: a total of 31 experimental diagrams. Pilot tests indicated that a reduced cut-off time of 40 seconds would be more appropriate than the 50 seconds used previously.

As before, both response time and accuracy data for the 21 correct diagrams was collected. We used t-tests for each aesthetic (although a non-parametric test and pair-wise analysis would have been more appropriate).

The only significant results obtained supported the hypothesis that reducing the number of bends improves both time and accuracy. There were some confusing results regarding edge variation that showed the middle effect variation to be worse (with respect to response time only).

While it is tempting to say that no aesthetics matter (apart from reducing the number of bends, which matters only a little), our view is that there are other

Figure 8. The Flow+ Class Diagram Used in Experiment 5b

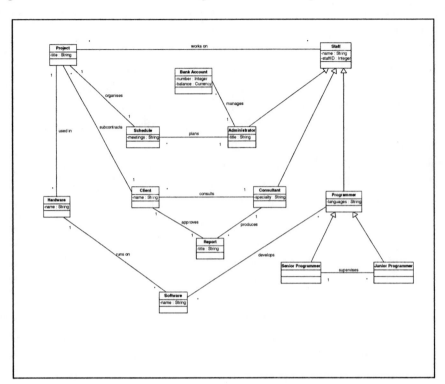

issues that need to be considered. In particular, the notion of semantic grouping, where related (but unconnected) objects are placed in close proximity, must be addressed.

One of the main lessons we learned from these two experiments was the limitation in the production of the experimental materials: we considered (and tried to control for) seven aesthetics, but there are many other visual features regarding diagram layout for which we did not control. For example, some subjects said that they found the task easier if the classes in the diagram were presented in the same vertical order as shown on the textual specification. We think that visual proximity of semantically related objects might also affect performance (Petre, 1995); this and other visual features (for example, the amount of white space, ratio of diagram width to diagram height, left-to-right placement of nodes, etc.) were not considered at all in our controls. It became clear that it would be impossible to identify (and control for) all the possible layout aesthetics that may affect comprehension of the diagram, and this was revealed as a limitation of using a formal experimental method that requires strict controls.

Statistical lessons that we learned included the necessity to identify whether a parametric or non-parametric test is required. We questioned the usefulness of a pair-wise test if more than two variations have been used: multiple t-tests need to be adjusted according to the Bonferroni correction; pair-wise tests (for example, Tukey), automatically take that correction into account.

We also considered more closely than before the potential interaction between accuracy and response time (as indicated by linear correlations). If a significant correlation exists between these two measures of understanding for any of the experimental diagrams, then the importance of any significant results for that aesthetic in either of the measures is reduced.

Experiment 6 (Purchase, Colpoys, McGill & Carrington, 2002)

Our most recent experiment uses the same overall methodology as experiment 5b, but in the domain of UML collaboration diagrams. Six aesthetics were considered: node distribution, edge variation, direction of flow, orthogonality, edge lengths, and symmetry. Each of these had three variations (+, 0, -, and nd+ which represents a diagram with a high node distribution). Flow had four variations, depending upon the position of the actor in the diagram (a total of 19 experimental diagrams). Figure 10 shows the UML collaboration diagram with even node distribution.

The UML collaboration diagram used in the experiment represented a simple preferential voting system and comprised an actor, 10 objects, 17 edges and 22 messages. Perception pre-tests were used with eight subjects to validate the hand-drawn diagrams and to ensure their conformance with the required aesthetic variations (in the same manner as in experiment 5b). Ten incorrect diagrams were produced by randomly changing the origin or destination of one link per diagram. The layouts of the incorrect diagrams were visually comparable to the correct diagrams.

The same preparatory and online experimental process was followed: this time the subjects needed to match a pseudo-code listing with the collaboration diagram. Thirty-five subjects took part. There were 16 practice diagrams and 29 experimental diagrams (19 correct and 10 incorrect). The cut-off time was 60 seconds.

The statistical method used in this experiment was more appropriate for ordinal variations and for pair-wise analysis of data. We used the Friedman test for each aesthetic (for both response time and accuracy) to determine whether there was any variation in the data. If we found variation, we used a non-

Figure 9.   UML Collaboration Diagram Used in Experiment 6, with a Balanced Node Distribution (nd+)

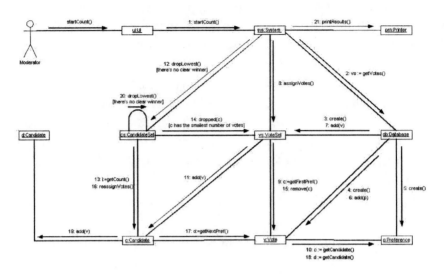

parametric version of the Tukey pair-wise comparison test — the Nemeyi test (Zar, 1999) — to determine where the differences lay.

Figure 11 and Figure 12 represent the data from the experiment. The only significant results we obtained were with edge variation, and these were contradictory (*ev0* is slower than *ev+*, and *ev-* is less accurate than both *ev+* and *ev0*). However, there was a significant linear correlation between time and accuracy for the *ev0* diagram, which makes the data for edge variations difficult to interpret.

Figure 10.   Response Time Results for Experiment 6

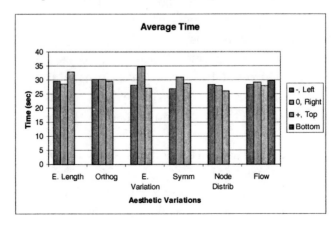

Figure 11. Accuracy Results for Experiment 6

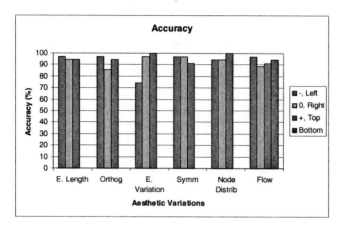

One problem made obvious in this experiment was that of trying to cover more than one hypothesis in a single experiment. In all of our experiments, we have addressed more than one aesthetic; and in this particular one, we were looking at six in total. While this is an efficient way to consider several aesthetics, it can cause problems with methodology (for example, choice of time cutoff and choice of errors introduced into the incorrect diagrams) and with the interpretation of results.

RESULTS AND REFLECTIONS

These experiments have covered the investigation of graph drawing aesthetics in several ways and have produced both useful and confusing results (see Table 3). It became clear very early in the project that reducing the number of edge crosses was by far the most important aesthetic criterion and that reducing the number of bends was also important. The results for other aesthetics are less convincing: edge variation and flow gain some support within the UML domain, but the evidence is far from overwhelming.

We believe that there are other influences that need to be considered:
- The notion of a possible 'critical mass' for any of the aesthetics should not be ignored. A small number of edge crosses may be acceptable if, by including them, a high degree of symmetry can be portrayed; but once the number of edge crosses exceeds a critical mass the crosses aesthetic takes a higher priority over symmetry.

Table 3. A Summary of the Results of the Experiments

Experiment	Nature of the graph	Aesthetic	Result
1	syntactic	Pilot experiment only: insufficient data points for analysis	
2	syntactic	bends	hypothesis confirmed
		crosses	hypothesis confirmed
		symmetry	no significant result
3	syntactic	bends	hypothesis confirmed
		crosses	hypothesis confirmed
		minimum angle	no significant result
		orthogonality	no significant result
		symmetry	hypothesis confirmed
4	semantic (class diagrams)	Between subjects analysis: subject variation produced invalid data	
5a	semantic (UML class diagrams)	bends	contradictory result
		edge length variation	contradictory result
		direction of flow	hypothesis confirmed for upward direction
		node distribution	no significant result
		orthogonality	no significant result
5b	semantic (UML class diagrams)	bends	hypothesis confirmed
		edge length	no significant result
		edge length variation	contradictory result
		direction of flow	no significant result
		node distribution	no significant result
		orthogonality	no significant result
		symmetry	no significant result
6	semantic (UML collaboration diagrams)	edge length	no significant result
		edge length variation	contradictory result
		direction of flow	no significant result
		node distribution	no significant result
		orthogonality	no significant result
		symmetry	no significant result

- There are many other visual properties that it would be impossible to control to ensure that the data collected can be considered valid within the confines of the formal experimental method. We controlled for features like node size, edge width, etc.; but we did not consider other syntactic features such as white space or semantic features such as node proximity. It would be impossible to identify *all* the potential visual influences and be able to control them effectively.

The results presented here do not include results from preference data collected in experiments that also form part of this project (Purchase, Carrington, & Allder, 2002). The results from the preference experiments indicated that subjects' preference does not always match performance: the aesthetics that subjects prefer are not always the aesthetics that result in improved performance.

Although what has been learned about graph drawing aesthetics may be considered limited in its scope and in its ability to be generalized, much has been learned about experimenting in this area and about the process of defining a new empirical research area. We made many mistakes along the way, and our results need to be interpreted in the context of the particular method used in the experiments. The most important experimental issues that emerged include:

- the importance of providing preparatory materials that are easy to understand, that include very clear definitions of all the concepts required for the task, and that present a clear worked example of the task that the subjects are to perform (with the correct answer and explanation);
- the importance of having a very clearly defined experimental task that does not require skills unrelated to the research question (for example, a task that requires subjects to write a program is much less clearly defined than a task that requires subjects to answer yes or no to a question);
- the importance of defining the experiment clearly with respect to hypotheses, variables (independent, dependent and control), within-subject or between-subject design, quantitative or qualitative data when writing for publication;
- the importance of choosing the correct statistical tests: the distinction between parametric and non-parametric data and the use of pair-wise comparison tests when more than two variations are used.

Most importantly, we realised the necessity of presenting the results of these experiments in such a way that they are not generalized beyond what is appropriate. It was important to state clearly the limitations of each experiment and to present the analysed data separately from our own interpretation of it. By making a clear distinction between the actual data that was obtained from the experiment, and what this data meant to us, we allowed the readers of our publications to consider the factual data independently of our opinion, and therefore gave them the opportunity to form their own conclusions.

FUTURE TRENDS

The graph-drawing community, who seek empirical validation of their assumptions, has welcomed the results of this project. However, it is plain that the results of each of these experiments are limited by the necessary constraints of formal experimentation and that this work could continue in the same vein for a long time to come. However, there are two important alternate routes that this research may take:

- Perceptual and Cognitive issues: The main problem with the experiments is that they are purely concerned with behaviour. Thus, while the experiments show that crosses are indeed detrimental to the understanding of a graph drawing, we cannot say why this is the case from the point of view of what is currently known about both perceptual visual processes and cognition. There is a substantive literature on perceptual and cognitive models. Integrating this existing theory with our experimental results would not only enable us to explain the results, but it may provide a predictive model by which a user's performance in a graph that has a high presence of a particular aesthetic may be predicted with reference to the model. Some initial work has recently been performed in this area: Ware, Purchase, Colpoys and McGill (2002) recently ran an experiment that hypothesized the effect of the angular continuity of a path in a shortest path task, based on knowledge of perception of continuity. They found that the angular continuity was indeed an important factor.
- Real-world tasks: The experiments have all been run in limited environments with artificial tasks. For this kind of research to be truly useful for the development of practical software systems that include automatic graph layout algorithms, investigations of real world use 'in the field' are important. Real-world experiments are more difficult to run: they are more time-consuming on the part of both experimenter and participants and the data collected is less quantitative, less easy to characterize, and less easy to analyse. There is a decreased chance of recruiting a sufficient number of participants for statistical analysis, and it may therefore be more difficult to convince others of the validity and of the ability to generalize the results.

This project has revealed a great deal, both about the worth of existing graph drawing aesthetics and about the process of empirical studies. The former is of interest to the designers of graph drawing algorithms; the latter is of interest to experimental psychologists. Two other communities that could also be served if the research were to be focused differently are cognitive scientists and the designers of domain-specific diagram support software.

ACKNOWLEDGMENTS

With thanks to: Peter Eades, who initially suggested this research area, and who has been supportive throughout; those who assisted with the overall approach and aims of the experiments (Robert Cohen, David Carrington);

those who prepared experimental materials and ran experiments (Shelina Bhanji, Murray James, Steven Grundon, Daniel Naumann, Jo-Anne Allder, Linda Colpoys, Matthew McGill); those who assisted in defining aesthetic metrics (Shelina Bhanji, David Leonard); those who took part in the experiments (many students in the School of Information Technology and Electrical Engineering at the University of Queensland over several years); institutions who provided resources for this project (The Australian Research Council, The University of Queensland).

REFERENCES

Booch, G. (1994). *Object Oriented Programming With Applications.* Wesley, MA: Addison-Wesley.

Coleman, M., & Stott Parker, D. (1996). Aesthetics-based graph layout for human consumption. *Software – Practice and Experience, 26*(12), 1415-1438.

Di Battista, G., Eades, P., Tamassia, R., & Tollis, I. (1994). Algorithms for drawing graphs: An annotated bibliography. *Computational Geometry: Theory and Applications, 4,* 235-282.

Eades, P. (1984). A heuristic for graph drawing. *Congressus Numeratum, 42,* 149-160.

Gansner, E., & North, D. (1998). Improved force-directed layouts. *Proceedings of the Graph Drawing Symposium 1998* (364-373) Springer-Verlag.

Gutwenger C., & Mutzel, P. (1998). Planar polyline drawings with good angular resolution. In S.H. Whitesides (Ed.), *Proceedings of Graph Drawing Symposium 1998,* (167-182). Montreal, Canada: Springer Verlag.

Papakostas, A. & Tollis, I. (2000). Efficient orthogonal drawings of high degree graphs. *Algorithmica,* (1), 100-125.

Petre, M. (1995). Why looking isn't always seeing: Readership skills and graphical programming. *Communications of the ACM, 38*(6), 33-44.

Purchase, H.C. (1997). Which aesthetic has the greatest effect on human understanding? In G. Di Battista (Ed.), *Proceedings of Graph Drawing Symposium.* Montreal, Canada: Springer-Verlag.

Purchase, H.C. (1998). Performance of layout algorithms: Comprehension, not computation. *Journal of Visual Languages and Computing, 9,* 647-657.

Purchase, H.C. (2002). Metrics for graph drawing aesthetics. *Journal of Visual Languages and Computing, 13*(5), 501-516.

Purchase H.C., & Leonard D. (1996). *Graph Drawing Aesthetic Metrics.* Technical report 361. The University of Queensland.

Purchase H.C., Bhanji, S., Cohen R.F., & James, M.I. (1995). *Validating Graph Drawing Aesthetics: A Pilot Study.* Technical report 336. The University of Queensland.

Purchase, H.C., Carrington, D.A., & Allder, J-A. (2002). Graph l aesthetics in UML diagrams. *Journal of Graph Algorithms and Applications, 6*(3), 255-279.

Purchase, H.C., Cohen, R.F., & James, M. (1997). An experimental study of the basis for graph drawing algorithms. *ACM Journal of Experimental Algorithmics, 2*(4), 1-17.

Purchase, H.C., Colpoys, L., McGill, M., & Carrington, D. (2003). Graph drawing aesthetics and the comprehension of UML collaboration diagrams: An empirical study. Work in progress.

Purchase H.C., Grundon, S. & Naumann, D., (1996). *Exploring Graph Drawing Aesthetics in Object-Oriented Diagrams.* Unpublished research report and data. The University of Queensland.

Purchase, H.C., McGill, M., Colpoys, L., & Carrington, D. (2001). Graph drawing aesthetics and the comprehension of UML class diagrams: An empirical study. In P. Eades & T. Pattison (Eds.), *Proceedings of the Australian Symposium on Information Visualisation,* (129-137). Australian Computer Society.

Reingold E., & Tilford, J. (1981). Tidier drawings of trees. *IEEE Transactions on Software Engineering, SE-7* (2), 223-228.

Rumbaugh, J., Jacobson, I., & Booch, G. (1999). *The Unified Modeling Language Reference Manual.* Reading, MA: Addison Wesley-Longman.

Tamassia, R. (1987). On embedding a graph in the grid with the minimum number of bends. *SIAM J. Computing,* (3), 421-444.

Waddle, V. (2000). Graph layout for displaying data structures. *Proceedings of the Graph Drawing Symposium 2000.* Williamsburg, VA: Springer-Verlag.

Ware, C., Purchase, H.C., Colpoys, L., & McGill, M. (2002). Cognitive measurements of graph aesthetics. *Information Visualization, 1*(2), 103-110.

Zar, J. H. (1999). *Biostatistical Analysis.* 4th ed. New York: Prentice-Hall.

SECTION III

MULTIMEDIA AND NEW MEDIA

Chapter IX

Client and Server Side Programming Concepts Incorporating Macromedia Flash

Robert Barone
Buffalo State College, USA

ABSTRACT

This chapter demonstrates the usefulness of Macromedia Flash MX as a medium for providing interactive content. The motivation for using Flash is presented first. This is followed by an overview of Flash, a brief illustration of Flash's animation ability, and a straightforward example of data communication from a Flash movie to an external server-side script. Furthermore, basic concepts of object-oriented programming are introduced within the context of the application. The similarity of Flash's ActionScript to other object-oriented scripting languages is mentioned, and the important non-linear aspect of program development using Flash is pointed out. It is intended that an understanding of Flash's underlying principles make it more accessible to a larger audience of web designers and developers.

INTRODUCTION

Macromedia Flash MX is much more than a graphic arts program. This multimedia application allows the designer and the developer the ability to create a true and unique graphical user interface (GUI). This GUI can be precisely programmed to support end-user interactivity. Flash is not limited to the World Wide Web although it has found tremendous applications in this arena.

The general perspective of this chapter is to discuss Macromedia Flash as a tool for the delivery of multimedia content via the World Wide Web. In addition, object oriented programming and server-side scripting will also be addressed within and related to the context of this application.

BACKGROUND

Flash employs vector graphics as the primary medium in content delivery. Vector graphics are described by mathematical formulas. These formulas provide a blueprint to the video processor of the client computer. The video processor constructs a raster image based on the formulas. Raster graphics are bitmapped images. They are composed of pixels that require a large number of bits to convey the information. File sizes are inherently larger, even when compression techniques (jpeg, etc.) are utilized. Although they suffer from aliasing, vector graphics are scalable and retain information when enlarged. Raster graphics are not scaleable, and they become unable to interpret when enlarged. Flash also makes use of streaming. The information contained in the streaming wave file is displayed in the browser as it is received. The browser does not wait for the entire contents of the file to be downloaded first. These two features — vector graphics and streaming — combine to make Flash a successful medium for providing multimedia content. Furthermore, the programming aspect of Flash further enhances and extends the usability of websites by bringing interaction to the forefront.

The physical medium or channels comprising the Internet are composed of everything that is available in our society and that is currently being used for communication. From twisted pair telephone wires, coaxial cable television, optical fiber, wireless and satellite transmission — all mediums are used. As file sizes and the number of users increase, the physical medium reaches capacity and becomes strained. File size reduction is an alternative to infrastructure replacement. In other words: since the pipe cannot always be made larger, the content must be made smaller.

Other issues influencing the desire for smaller file sizes are related to the client. Not everyone using the Internet has cutting-edge technology. Many users are leery of upgrading their browsers, other software, or hardware. There are individuals using exactly what came out of the box, and they feel neither need nor want to invest money for an upgrade. Until something breaks or a catastrophe occurs, they remain entrenched.

Engaging technophobes and technocrats simultaneously requires finesse on the part of the web design and development team. A commercial site does not want to lose customers because its site takes too long to load or lacks engaging content.

Flash has found a unique place in this venue by bridging the gap between users of outmoded technology and those of the cutting edge.

TWO FLASH VIGNETTES

Since there is a plethora of authoritative text books available on the subject and space considerations dictate constraint, a thorough treatment of any one topic is prohibitive. In addition, Flash provides comprehensive documentation and tutorials in the form of PDF files available on the installation disk. These are also duplicated in the browser environment through the help menu. The reader should take the time to become familiar with the on-line lessons as well as the built-in tutorials.

Flash, with each new version, has evolved at a considerable pace. Originally the user interface was predominantly a menu driven program; now the user interface is palette-oriented, which seems the trend in contemporary graphical authoring and editing. A short history of Flash is available at http://www.flashmagazine.com/html/413.htm.

The primary drawback of using palettes to interface with the program is the amount of real estate consumed on the computer monitor. A 19-inch or larger monitor is recommended, and two monitors are preferred. Flash displays the work area, called the stage; the timeline, which dictates the animation sequence; and the palettes used for editing. Palettes can be switched on and off or floated to increase work area but, in general, this needlessly increases the learning curve.

Concepts in Flash are essentially hierarchical in organization. Simply drawing on the stage with any of the tools creates a drawing object. These are the basic building blocks of a Flash movie. Objects can be selected, copied, grouped, transformed, skewed, stacked, deleted, or otherwise mutated. Essentially any designer's demands can be met with the drawing object.

The next level of hierarchy is the symbol. If the desire is to motion animate (motion tween) the drawing object, the object must first be converted to a symbol. Interestingly, shape morphing (shape tweening) is performed on a drawing object. There is a subtle importance here that cannot be underestimated. Once a symbol is created it is automatically placed inside a container known as the library. If the designer wishes to re-use the symbol, it is dragged and dropped from the library onto the stage. Multiple occurrences of the symbol on the stage are referred to as instances of the symbol. An instance on the stage may be thought of as pointing to the symbol in the library. Since the symbol is only stored once and reused many times in the form of an instance, file size remains at a minimum. Another advantage is file-to-file reusability of symbols. A library from one Flash file can be opened in a completely separate file and the symbols reused.

There are three symbol types: Movie clip, button, and graphic. Movie clips are self-contained Flash movies that can be treated as instances. Once on the stage, they cycle through their animation sequences independently of the main movie. Movie clips are also programmable. Buttons maintain an up state, an over state, a down state, and a hit state. The first three states can be animated. Buttons are also programmable. Graphic symbols are simply used to create motion tweens and are not programmable in the sense that an Action cannot be directly attributed to one.

The stage also maintains a hierarchy in the form of layers. Think of the stage as a deck of playing cards (a typical analogy). Each card in the deck is a layer. The card at the top is the highest in the hierarchy, and those underneath it are lower in the hierarchy. Typically one animation per layer is the rule. It is not enough to recognize that a symbol must be on the stage to work with: identifying the corresponding layer it resides in is just as important.

The timeline is the backbone of a Flash movie. A celluloid film strip is composed of still images that are rapidly moved across a movie projector to give the illusion of continuous movement. The same is true of a Flash movie. Each layer has a timeline that is subdivided into frames. A symbol is placed into a layer. Movements of symbols on the stage are broken across a series of frames in the layer's timeline. As the software play head moves from one frame to the next, the symbol is given the illusion of movement. When the play head reaches the last frame it loops back to the beginning and replays — unless a programmable command is given to interrupt the process. Consequently certain symbols can be programmed via the timeline, directly via their instance on stage, or both. The developer must distinguish between these programming concepts as well as those of the Actions and objects that can be attributed in a given situation. This ability simultaneously causes Flash to exhibit a steep learning curve; and yet, when mastered, be very versatile in the end result.

Creating a Simple Motion Tween

Normally, several housekeeping tasks would normally be performed before actually creating an animation in Flash. These would include naming the file, setting the movie properties, naming the layer, and so forth. To simply illustrate the concept, however: open Flash MX, select the oval tool, and draw an oval on the stage.

Notice that Layer 1 is highlighted and that the first frame of the timeline is occupied with a solid circle. The solid circle indicates that this frame is a keyframe. Keyframes are the principle frames created by the designer. Before the oval object can be animated, it must be converted into a symbol. Using the Arrow Tool, highlight the oval with the mouse. From the Insert Menu choose Convert to Symbol... or press function key F8. Choose Graphic as the behavior, and accept the default name or change it if you prefer.

A symbol has now been created from the drawing object. The symbol is stored in the library. What is being manipulated on the stage is the instance. To observe the symbol in the library, simply press CTRL+L. Once viewed, dismiss the Library window.

To continue with the animation process, click in frame 15. From the Insert Menu choose Keyframe. Notice that Flash inserts a solid circle in frame 15 to indicate the keyframe.

Click in frame 15 of the timeline to isolate it. It is important that frame 15 be selected and isolated form the others so that it does not influence them. Use the Arrow Tool and move the symbol instance to another location on the stage.

Using the mouse, drag the play head across all the frames of the timeline. Notice that frames 2 through 14 are imitations of keyframe 1. A keyframe directly influences all subsequent frames until a new keyframe is inserted or ordinary frames are deleted. The last frame in a sequence of frames influenced by a keyframe has a white rectangle in it.

Select any ordinary frame between the two keyframes and from the Insert Menu choose Create Motion Tween. A successful Motion Tween will have frames 1 through 14 colored blue, with an arrow extending through them. An unsuccessful Motion Tween will have frames 1 through 14 colored blue, with a dotted line extending through them.

Using the mouse, drag the play head across all the frames of the timeline. Notice that the symbol instance moves with each successive frame. The nomenclature is well known from Disney Studios. The master animator or designer creates the keyframes. Flash fills in all the in-between frames or tweens. Hence, motion tween.

From the Control Menu choose Play to observe the timeline directly or Test Movie to preview the finished product.

Text effects elicit much attention. Only a glimpse of the capabilities can be addressed here, however, due to space limitations. The important consideration when creating motion tweens with text is that text must be set to Static in the Properties palette, and it must be broken apart into drawing objects before conversion into symbol(s) (from the Modify Menu, choose Break Apart CTRL+B). After the text has been broken apart, individual letters or groups of letters must be converted into symbols for animation. Each symbol representing a letter or group of letters should be placed subsequently into its own layer.

Communication from a Flash Movie

A Flash movie is created in a file with the extension .*fla*. This file can create many other file types that can be seen in the Formats tab of the Publish Settings dialog box. The Publish Settings dialog box can be accessed by way of the File Menu. For Web delivery, common types are .*html* and streaming wave file .*swf*. The client's browser requests the html from the server. Once the browser has loaded the html file, the html file calls the streaming wave file from the server.

Communication back to the server now requires programming the Flash movie. There are several possibilities. Nevertheless, communication from inside a Flash movie to a server side script via a Flash UI Component will be considered. On the server side, ASP (Active Server Pages) will be treated. This is an arbitrary choice (other server side scripting languages may also be used).

The idea here parallels the concept of creating an ordinary FORM tag in a traditional HTML page, using POST method to send the data collected in the FORM to a server side script that processes it.

The serve side script will process the data and respond in many different fashions. It may create an HTML page and send it back to the browser, or it may store the data in a database manager first and then send a page back to the client. There are many variations of theme depending upon the web application.

Flash incorporates a programming language known as ActionScript. ActionScript, like many other scripting languages, is considered loosely-typed. This means that variables do not have to be declared before they are used and that the data type stored in a variable may change depending upon how the logic flows. Scripting languages are also interpreted — not compiled. This means that they are executed one line at time by a program known as an interpreter. The interpreter for ActionScript is part of the Flash player. When a new version of Flash is introduced there inevitably exists new ActionScript, which must be supported under a new player; hence, a player upgrade is expected. In contrast, a strongly-typed language demands that all variables and their associated data types are identified before they are used. An example of a strongly-typed language is C++. In C++ the programmer creates a file known as source code. Source code is examined by a compiler and if it is syntactically error-free, an executable file in the native machine language of the processor is created for execution. Compiled code is faster in execution than is interpreted code.

In ActionScript, as in ASP, the developer is handed an object toolbox to use. The Flash architects have designed an immense collection of functions and objects that can be utilized to manipulate instances of symbols. Once the concept of using an object in a program is understood, what remains is becoming familiar with all of the different objects and conditions that affect the object and its usage.

ActionScript also provides traditional programming elements: a simple sequence of statements, branching or decision making statements, and looping statements. Variables are used to store numbers or text and, when a large number of variables are needed, data structures such as arrays are introduced. Functions allow the program to be broken into smaller, more manageable, sections of code. In ActionScript, functions are absolutely essential because they isolate a section of code that is called by name to perform a specific task related to the event that called it. An example of an event is the clicking of a button or menu item.

An object is a programming element that has an appearance at any particular point in time and the ability to react to external input. Consider the instance of the symbol created in the motion tween example above. Its appearance or state at any particular moment can be described by its size, color, and location on the screen. If it is programmed to change color or to load a URL when clicked, it would be reacting to external input. Not all objects are as easily grasped, especially when they exist only by definition in the lines of program code; yet their essence is still the same.

To help understand the following tutorial, become familiar with the following: Introduction to Components Tutorial provided with Flash; and Chapter 17 of the Using Flash help file (Using Flash, 2002), found in the C:\Program Files\Macromedia\Flash MX\PDF folder. Chapter 17 refers specifically to a file named FormExample.fla that can be found in the C:\Program Files\Macromedia\Flash MX\Tutorials\Components folder. This file is not treated in the tutorials, but it contains a wealth of information.

In order to complete this tutorial, an account on an NT server is needed. ASP is also supported on the Linux server platform, but it needs additional software (http://wwws.sun.com/software/chilisoft/) installed by the server administrator.

Collecting data from a group of radio buttons is investigated here. A radio button group was chosen because it did not receive full attention in the tutorial or in the sample file. (In academic settings, it is the cornerstone of multiple choice examinations.)

The approach here is simple, yet illustrative. The Flash movie is a group of four radio buttons and one push button component. By their nature only one radio button in the group can be selected. After selection the data is transmitted from the Flash movie to an ASP page residing on the server. In this example, the ASP page simply echoes the data back to the client's browser.

Creation of the Flash Component Interface

Open Flash MX and choose Save As ... from the File menu. Name the file radioTest1.fla and store it in a favorite folder. Three layers will be needed for this interaction. The first layer will house the radio buttons and the push button components. The second layer will be used to store the main body of code that forms the heart of the interaction. The third layer will be used to store code that calls or references functions contained in the main body of code. By double clicking directly on a Layer name, it becomes editable. Rename the top Layer buttons following Macromedia conventions: the second Layer allActions; and the bottom Layer formActions. Each of the layers should contain one keyframe.

If the component palette is not visible choose Components under the Window menu. Make sure the buttons layer is selected by clicking once on it and then dragging an instance of a radio button to the stage.

This action immediately places the component information of a radio button group in the Library (CTRL+L) into a folder entitled Flash UI Components. In order to see the component in the Library, the folder in which it resides must be expanded by double clicking it. Double click to expand this folder inside the Library, and then drag and drop three more instances of the radio button component to the stage. Do not drag from the Components Palette — this will defeat the purpose.

By using the Arrow Tool and the Align palette found in the Window menu, the four radio buttons can be arranged in a vertical group on the stage.

Drag and drop a Push Button from the Flash UI Components palette to the stage, again in the buttons layer. When the application is active, clicking this button will execute code that will POST the data from the Flash movie to the ASP page.

Before code can be added, the radio buttons themselves must first be configured to provide data. It is interesting to note that they will not provide the data directly to the server side script file. Within the Flash movie, "behind the scene" so to speak, the data must first be transferred to a user-defined program object, which in turn must transfer the data to an ordinary variable. Data in this variable is finally transferred from the Flash movie to the ASP script via the POST method.

Assuming the radio buttons are stacked vertically, select the top radio button and examine the Properties palette. In the Properties palette change the Label from Radio Button to uppercase A: the Group Name from RadioGroup to radioOne; and the Data from blank to lower case a. Leave the other items — Initial State, Label Placement, and Change Handler — as is.

For the other three radio buttons, the Group Name will always be radioOne; the Labels will be uppercase B, C, and D; and the Data will be lowercase b, c, and d, respectively. The uppercase letters are visible to the user. The lowercase letters are the data. Additional text for questions and answers can be appended via static text.

Next configure the Push Button component by clicking on it. In the Properties palette, change the Label from Push Button to choose and the Click Handler from blank to onPress. The Click Handler is a function that needs to be coded. The name onPress was chosen arbitrarily. This is the name of a programmer defined function and could have been named whatever the programmer desires.

The code must now be entered. The formActions layer will contain one function call. This is where program execution starts because this is where the function is called or referenced. There will be three functions. The functions themselves will be defined in the allActions layer. The first function, named Initialize, will ready an object. This object accepts one of the lowercase (a, b, c, or d) depending on which radio button was selected in the group. The second function, named getSelect, will transfer the data from the radio button group to the programmer-defined object. And the third function, onPress, will transfer the data first from the object to a variable, and then from the Flash movie to the server side script.

Select the first frame of the formActions layer. Open the actions palette, select expert mode (CTRL+Shift+E), and type initialize();. It is extremely important to observe syntax.

Select frame one of the allActions layer and enter the code shown in Figure 1 (enter one statement per line).

The initialize() function performs two actions. The first, following Macromedia's technique as outlined in the FormExample.fla file, is to insure that the function is referenced once only. This is achieved by setting the Boolean variable init to *true* when the function is initially referenced. Subsequent calls will automatically return to the function call without executing the next segment of code. Notice the Boolean variable init was not declared or identified before it was used. In addition, init was not initialized to *false*. This is an example of loosely-typed script.

Figure 1. ActionScript for Frame One of the AllActions Layer

```
function initialize()
{
    if (init)
    {
        return;
    }//endif
init = true;
myData = new Object();
}// end initialize

function getSelect()
{
    myData.select = radioOne.getValue();
}// end getSelect

function onPress()
{
    getSelect();
    aVar = myData.select;
    getURL("http://facstaff.buffalostate.edu/baronera/asp-bin/flashTest.asp",
    "_blank", "POST");
}// end onPress
```

The next segment of code, myData = new Object(); initializes an object used for storing the transferred data from the radio button. The object name is myData. This identifier is arbitrary and could have been named myDataObject instead. Keep in mind that reserved words in ActionScript appear blue in the editor window.

The next programmer defined function is named getSelect(). This function assigns the data from the radioOne object using the ActionScript provided method named getValue() to the select property of the object myData. The actual data transferred from the radioOne object are the lower case letters a, b, c, or d.

Notice that the myData object has a programmer-defined property named *select*. Again, this is an identifier chosen by the programmer. Also note that the property does not have to be defined or identified to the program before it is used. It is simply called into existence when needed by the program. This is another example of loosely-typed script.

The last function, onPress(), calls the getSelect() function to first transfer data from the radioOne object to the myData object. Then, the data stored in the select property of the myData object is assigned to a variable named aVar.

Finally, the getURL function takes every variable defined in the time line and, using the POST method, transmits the data to an ASP script file named flashtest.asp. In this case the only variable is aVar. The file should be saved and an .html and .swf file published.

The ASP Script

The code for the ASP file flashTest.asp can be created in a text editor (Luce, 2001). The code is found in Figure 2.

An ASP page is essentially an HTML page with embedded script. The script may be JavaScript or, as in this case, VBScript. The important thing is that the script makes use of ASP objects.

By examining the code in figure two it can be seen that there are basically two major sections to the file. The first is a small amount of VBScript at the beginning, and the second is simple HTML. The concept is elegant. The server uses the VBScript and the ASP request object to retrieve the data POSTed from the Flash movie. The server then constructs an HTML page in server memory using the HTML present in the file as a template. When the VBScript embedded in the HTML portion is encountered, the data POSTed from the Flash movie is substituted. The server constructs the entire HTML page first, substituting the data, and then sends it back to the client.

Figure 2.   Code for the ASP File FlashTest.asp

```
<%@ LANGUAGE="VBScript" %>
<%
Option Explicit
Response.Buffer = TRUE
Dim vntRadio
vntRadio = Request.Form("aVar")
%>
<HTML>
<HEAD>
<TITLE>getURL Test</TITLE>
</HEAD>
<BODY>
<CENTER>
You selected <B><%= vntRadio %>
</B><BR><BR></B>
</CENTER>
</BODY>
</HTML>
```

The two most basic ASP objects are the request and response objects. Also note that the VBScript is enclosed between <% and %> tags. The Option Explicit statement demands that all variables be declared or identified before use. The Response.Buffer = TRUE statement causes the server to create the entire page in server memory before it is sent back to the browser. The statement Dim vntRadio identifies or declares a variable named vntRadio. The assignment statement, vntRadio = Request.Form("aVar") makes use of the ASP request object. The method Form() takes the data POSTed in the Form collection and stores it in the variable vntRadio. Notice that the variable name in the argument of the Form() method is aVar. This is exactly the same name used in the ActionScript of the Flash movie. It is not a coincidence. When transferring data via the POST method the variable name and corresponding data combine into what is referred to as a name-value pair. On the server side, the ASP Request object makes use of the Form() method to read the name-value pair and to assign it to a local variable. On the server side the variable names must identically match those POSTed from the client.

In this simple yet illustrative example the data is echoed back to the browser using the ASP response object. Here, a shorthand version of the response object is used <%= vntRadio %>. This is equivalent to Response.Write(vntRadio).

The entire process can be summarized as follows. The designer and developer create a Flash movie using Components. In this example the file is named radioTest1.fla. From this file, radioTest1.htm and radioTest1.swf are published. Using a text editor, an ASP file named flashTest.asp is created. The three files — radioTest1.htm, radioTest1.swf, and flashTest.asp — must be placed on the server.

The client will request radioTest1.htm, which in turn is used to stream radioTest1.swf into the browser. The user will select one radio button in the group and click the push button. This will send the selected radio button data to the file flashTest.asp at the server. The file flashTest.asp will retrieve the data and generate an HTML page in the server's primary memory. When the page is completely constructed, based on the HTML supplied in the flashTest.asp file, the server automatically sends the HTML back to the client's browser.

SOLUTIONS AND RECOMMENDATIONS

On the client side, the application needs to be expanded by creating more frames with radio button groups, i.e., questions. As the user enters a question, a Push Button code would take the user to the next question and simultaneously store the selected data. An additional Push Button on each page would take the user backwards through the questions. The Push Button on the last page would POST all the data to the ASP file.

On the server side, instead of passing the information directly back to the user, the ASP file would write the data to a database manager. The database manager can be programmed to grade the exam.

A further extension of the application would allow the user to see the graded exam results. After the data has been sent from the Flash movie, the user would be given one more page with which to interact. This page would have a push button that allows the user to retrieve the results from the database manager. The Push Button would request a separate ASP page that would read the data from the database manager and write the data back to the client.

FUTURE TRENDS

From an educational point of view, Flash provides an excellent vehicle for the illustration of object-oriented concepts and techniques. There are so many aspects of ActionScript that there are entire textbooks devoted exclusively to this topic. (In the past, only a chapter or two would have been devoted to ActionScript.) It is obvious that the developer side of Flash is just as important as the design side. Using Flash on the server side will become more and more accepted. This will allow even more dynamics and interaction on the part of the user. Flash can also be used as a stand-alone vehicle for the delivery of multimedia content. One of Flash's strengths is its ability to provide a self-contained multimedia experience. A weakness is its awkwardness in communicating data outside its own environment. As noted here the process, even using a simple function, is a bit cumbersome. The Components that have been introduced with Flash MX have taken a good step toward streamlining this process—there is always room for improvement. As part of the learning curve the developer must accept that certain objects and variables must be defined in the Properties palette and not necessarily in the code. This non-linear approach to programming is alien at first, yet necessary. Flash's user interface has made great strides in accommodating the designer and one hopes that in future versions, the developer will find it easier as well. Increasingly, the application is definitely becoming a standard against which others will be measured.

CONCLUSION

Although brief, some very basic concepts regarding this application have been investigated. Design-oriented concepts such as symbols, layers, tweening, and the library have been investigated. Developer-oriented concepts such as object methods and functions have also been looked at in both ActionScript and ASP. Close comparison between the two should give the reader an indication of current paradigms in web scripting.

The vastness of this application cannot be understated. A person or team must be devoted almost exclusively to this application if the full potential is to be realized. Great strides can be made, however, by an individual with the desire to learn more.

REFERENCES

Luce, T. (2001). *Developing Web Applications with ASP*. El Granada: Scott/Jones, Inc.

Macromedia Flash MX Help File (2002). *Using Flash, Macromedia Flash MX*. San Francisco, CA: Macromedia.

Chapter X

Everything That Can Communicate Will:
Aspects of Digital Asset
Alignment and Management

Ben Howell Davis
Davis International Associates, USA

ABSTRACT

The concept of aligning and managing digital assets is a reaction to the evolution of digital production and digital networks. The understanding of this evolution is rooted in experiences in library and museum communities, the digital solutions and design disciplines, the communications and entertainment industries, and law. Aligning and managing digital assets is predicated upon the notion that everything that can communicate will and, in a sense, begins to approach what neuroscience has been telling us for quite some time — that everything actually does communicate in some way or other. There are a number of levels of digital assets. Digital assets are created and maintained in support systems architecture, in digital production tools, in digital content development, in taxonomy development, in user destination designs, in audience interactions, and in legal monitoring. Being digital means everything can be accounted for, everything can communicate, everything has value, and everything can last. Acquiring, merging, or divesting a digital enterprise requires comprehensive digital asset management at every level.

NO THERE THERE

Digital communication has become ephemeral content. There is no object, such as a bound book or celluloid film; rather, content exists as a digital asset to be accessed. The issues are how to make the digital assets accessible, how content can be widely distributed, and how the components that created the content can be reused. There are a number of misconceptions about digital asset production and distribution that should be acknowledged:

- Digital asset creation costs less than physical analog production. Digital asset creation can be more expensive than physical production depending upon what kind of strategic treatment the material is given.
- Digital asset creation is easier than that of older physical forms. Digital asset production is often not easier than traditional mediums because there are so many new options available in the digital realm.
- Digital asset production is as coherent as traditional forms. Digital is evolving as it is being understood, which makes it very difficult to know exactly what the best choices are at any given moment.

Traditional publishing practices have radically changed. Pricing-based units of information (books), libraries as distributors, intellectual property, royalties, marketing as the primary means of stimulating sales, and the shifts away from container-based infrastructures like the packaging of paper books have all altered the practices of publishing.

What have been required are strategies for going between object-based and content-based pricing. Transitional strategies include providing individual and institutional access to electronic materials, developing digitized content, digital access tools, and the consumer purchase of print as well as electronic forms. The development of digital accounting standards and digital intellectual property rights are paramount in digital asset management processes. In digital asset creation novelty becomes the required. The rapid demand for hyperlinks, interactive graphics, full motion video, and sound on the Web are all evidence of novel ideas becoming standards.

Digital technology facilitates the creation and exchange of data, information, and knowledge across ever expanding networks. This condition raises issues in digital asset liquidity, digital asset continuity, and digital viability for utilizing assets for prediction, risk analysis, and decision making,

What are the current technical requirements for digital alignment? What are the strategic forces shaping architecture asset management? What do digital assets actually represent? What may the economics of digital asset management become? How can an organization position itself to make maximum use of digital assets in the future?

WHAT IS DIGITAL ASSET ALIGNMENT?

Digital alignment is the seamless coordination of digital liquidity, digital continuity, and digital viability. Digital liquidity refers to the ways in which digital assets are created and used. Factors that influence the degree of liquidity are strategic plans for maximizing a return on the initial investment in digital production; anticipated types of screen destinations such as mobile, PC, broadband and/or print; plans for re-purposing various types of production; and interface design.

Digital continuity refers to how digital assets are stored and accessed. The longevity of digital materials is a topic of high interest. Digital technology produces fragments of projects in great quantity. Strategic planning for format conversion, migration, and usage frequency involves understanding and implementing evolving standards, metadata, storage formats, and search/access tools that involve sophisticated common vocabularies. Attention to digital continuity ensures the long-term use of assets.

Digital viability is concerned with how the use of assets is measured. Increasingly, the digital enterprise must justify budgetary expenditures for liquidity and continuity methods and practices. Tools for measuring return on investment, tools for modeling opportunities, and tools for risk analysis and decision making are beginning to be developed to track the viability of assets into the future.

Enterprises that manage digital liquidity, continuity, and viability create architectures of assets that must be aligned and integrated so that assets communicate on all three levels. Committing to digital solutions that seamlessly address these concerns is serious, core business practice. Solutions need to be considered for proactive management of digital assets that focus on reducing production costs and creating new revenue opportunities, as well as protecting content. Digital inventories are ever expanding. The growing usage of the Web, e-commerce, broadband, the proliferation of peripheral media devices, the consumer demand for streamlined access to exciting new forms of content, the increasing deployment of streaming media, the necessity for legal protection of assets, and the quest for new revenue streams and improved workflow efficiency all require deep solution strategies.

The focus on efficiencies is especially relevant. Efficiencies maximize production budgets, prevent asset loss or redundant asset production, ensure asset availability for cross-platform distribution, provide security for valuable assets, support partner relationships, and provide platform specific access modes for internal or business to business (BtoB) operations. Successful digital alignment and management allows the realization of new revenue opportunities, protects asset rights, tracks asset usage, and allows for incremental asset utilization.

Currently, industry terminology for systems that manage digital liquidity, continuity, and viability are Digital Asset Management (DAM), Content Management Systems (CMS), and Digital Rights Management Systems (DRM).

Digital Asset Management systems digitize physical media assets into storage systems. These systems leverage metadata structures to support asset cataloging and rights licensing policies. Content Management Systems (CMS) support Digital Asset Management by providing intelligent access tools to asset storage and archival facilities. Content Management Systems also enable edit capabilities to support the pre- and post-production phases of content development. Digital Asset Management and Content Management Systems identify most valued assets based on liquidity, reusability, scalability, interoperability, and accessibility. They design asset cataloging and metatagging foundations, digitize and archive priority assets, create core licensing rules, and identify critical legacy system integration initiatives. *DAM/CMS* validate current core technologies, search features, processes, rules, manage risks of asset loss or redundancies, ensure asset availability for cross platform distribution, and ultimately optimize user experience.

Digital Rights Management (DRM) solutions help to solve legal and logistical business problems through asset security and rights protection. Digital Rights Management solutions control asset usage and enable the collection of usage fees. Digital Rights Management implements asset tracking, builds order management, enforces access, enables cross-markets with partners and enterprise divisions, and bills for asset usage. DRM encourages the exploration and implementation of various tools for securing assets, creates new business models around monetization and digital distribution of content, and enables licensing/syndicating content and/or interactive programs. It can facilitate wireless/e-games (subscription, pay-per-use) and the creation of custom applications for classroom learning, airlines, and entertainment venues. DRM can facilitate ad-wrapped content, product placement, merchandising, allow for consumer data collection and targeted marketing, implement usage tracking systems, capture user profile information, and monitor and bill for usage.

REQUIRED INFORMATION SYSTEMS

Digital content is content that is understood at a human level and, simultaneously, understood and interpreted on the computer level. This is the distinguishing factor of digital asset production. Unlike a printed work, digital information simultaneously interacts with humans and with computer systems. With the advent of the World Wide Web, an electronic publication speaks to the world of humans as well as to the world of computer systems. The depth of asset creation is staggering. The communication alignment is absolutely essential.

The technologies that support "containerless content" are network systems. Networked digital technology used for production and distribution is a multi-layered system. There is a standard *seven-layer* (level) technical model[1] for networked digital technology that describes ways in which lower levels affect higher levels and ways in which higher levels do not (and cannot) know the details of lower levels.

The lower levels provide common functionality that can be used by different implementations of the higher levels. The standard levels are traditionally numbered from the bottom (1) to the top (7), the top being what the system user sees and interacts with. Levels 8 to 10 are here added to represent additional concerns, now apparent in digital asset creation and distribution. Everything starts with the physical (machines, wires, etc.), so that is why it is level 1.

Top
10. **Distribution:** Web, warehouse, navigation schemes, strategic design, graphic look and feel, audience mediation, content administration, and maintenance.
9. **Content and medium:** appropriate media, writing, editing, design, development, production, and marketing.
8. **Production application:** specific programming for publishing, metadata, and conversion from print to electronic.
7. **Application:** Layer where instructions or requests are received and executed at the operating system level.

6.   **Presentation:** File Transfer Protocol program and Netscape browser window.

5.   **Session:** Individual connection to network.

4.   **Transport:** TCP (Transmission Control Protocol), which works over IP (Internet Protocol).

3.   **Network:** Includes routing, IP network addresses, and everything else needed to make the Internet work no matter what specific network technologies are at the lower levels.

2.   **Datalink:** Includes Ethernet protocol or PPP (Point to Point Protocol) over a T-1 line.

1.   **Physical:** Machines, cables, wires, etc.
     Bottom

Hardware engineers deal with level 1. Systems engineers commonly speak of working on a layer 2 or 3 problem. Communications engineers deal with levels 4 and 5. A user or an applications developer interacts with the top levels 7 through 10, which represent access (a login window, for instance) to the application (Netscape) and content (electronic book).

The digital production may use application-layer software to display or to interact (link) with other material. The electronic author can use application software to "write" material that is interactive.

The final material, however, has been shaped based on its content, not by arbitrary uses of the lower technology. The electronic author need not technically know how any of the underlying levels work, but he/she must be aware of the potentials and limitations of levels 7 through 10 in order to make judgments on how to treat content. Authored material is administrated into various schemes for navigation purposes and for visual impact at the distribution level.

The top three (8 to 10) levels must work in parallel. Content must be developed and seamlessly created for the specific medium in which it will be distributed. Content creators must work directly with applications developers and distribution designers. Users interact with content, pass communication back to content creators who interact with applications to apply feedback to improve infrastructure, and so on down the chain. Ultimately something may affect hardware as a final solution to a content reaction — a new scanner is needed because users do not like the quality of a digital image, for instance.

At every level a different form of digital asset is created and will require maintenance over time.

An electronic article comparing an impressionist painter to a post-impressionist painter might instruct a person to access related images by expressionist painters. An interpreted applet (small, one-function application) would instruct a computer to pass data to a network server (which can be anywhere in the world) to access the file of images as can the reader of the article.

Digital assets are " architected" as well as authored. That is, the content is designed so that it communicates with the computer on whatever level necessary to make the content perform for the user. Adding a "link" to a text is now a common "information architecture" on the Internet that makes the computer layers perform in such a way as to connect the user to some other system, document, or program. At the same time, it transports the reader to other content separate from the document with which he/she is involved.

DIGITAL ASSET COMPLEXITY

It should become obvious that digital assets are created at every level of systems architecture. Until very recently, digital assets were mostly thought of as content or as electronic publication. In the most general sense, an electronic resource that requires "editorial review" is a digital "publication". Publications are assets, products that an organization puts forth as a representation of its commitment to a field or area of business endeavor. As long as editorial review is involved in the production of an information resource, that resource can be viewed as a publication asset of an organization.

Other electronic information assets may not require editorial review in that they are software developments that require code review. The search engine developed for the Getty's *Bibliography of the History of Art* (BHA), the *Getty Provenance Index,* and *Avery Index to Architectural Periodicals* CDs is an example of this type of software asset. Because all of these projects are capital publication projects (the CDs are sold), the search engine can be considered a capital asset because it is the necessary software that allows the databases to function as a searchable publication.

The search engine software is in a category of medium or long-term capital asset. This is essentially a subclass of fixed assets that are neither working capital nor fixed capital. These assets are not furniture, equipment, or publications. This class of asset is a form of intellectual property similar to a patent. Third-party costs for developing these kinds of assets can be amortized over fixed periods and may be tied to the economic life of a product such as a book, which may remain in print for five or 10 years. Other costs that may fall into this category of capital assets might include online versions of capital publications, whose longevity is tied to the longevity of the print version. A system could be developed to track this process whereby electronic asset closeouts would parallel print publication closeouts.

ECONOMICS OF DIGITAL ASSETS

The price determinants of digital assets are the presentational demands of the material, production demands, the scope of services that the material may support, how long those services need to be maintained, the anticipated uses of the material, and the breadth of the targeted audience.

A long-range planning time frame of twelve to eighteen months is very important for digital asset production. It is the amount of time needed to synchronize pricing determinants with possible shifts in the market.

There are a variety of cost-recovery models for digital publications:

- CD-ROM/DVD products with proprietary interfaces and licenses for single computer/user rights
- CD-ROM/DVD products with proprietary interfaces and network licenses
- CD-ROM/DVD delivery of projects on local servers under domain or subnet restrictions
- Internet publications on FTP (File Transfer Protocol) sites
- Internet publications with Gopher interfaces
- Online projects with proprietary interfaces and time-base charges
- Online (non-Internet) projects with proprietary interfaces and multiple tier-based charges (shopping cart model: each abstract at x rate, each article at y rate, etc.)
- Internet projects with Web interfaces and multiple tier-based charges (shopping cart model: each abstract at x rate, each article at y rate, etc.)
- Internet projects with Web interfaces under password-restricted access and simultaneous-user restrictions
- Internet projects with Web interfaces under domain-access models price-based on full-time enrollment
- Internet projects with Web interfaces under domain-access models with site-license restrictions on usage of materials
- Internet projects with Web interfaces under domain-access models with usage unrestricted

Change may be very near in the form of "micropayments"[2]. Charges for digital information could start as low as two hundredths (0.02) of a cent. They would be a very swift debit/credit transactions at very low transaction costs — a 10th of a cent and up, depending upon security, volume, and speed. And they would be done by automated systems. Micro-payments would be necessary in a "disintermediated" system — a system that is direct to the consumer via electronic delivery.

Prices are dependent upon transaction costs; the costs of shipping, storage, markup, promotion, advertising, and storage; as well as production costs such as editing, markup/typesetting, and server. In the micro-payment scenario, transaction costs will drop to virtually nothing and micro-payments will allow instantaneous payment, thus taking the billing costs out of the charge.[3] In the new micro-payment option, transaction and intermediation costs plummet; and prices become dictated by the nature of publisher, author, and content, almost exclusively. In the micro-payment world there could be:

- Five- or 10-year cost recovery timetable, without any significant cost for storage
- Continuous-update subscriptions
- Fragment fees of 0.02 worth per paragraph, section, article, or segment
- Variable quality with expense based on the desired quality of resolution
- Image with explanatory background for extra cost
- Pricing by audience demand
- Pricing by audience type
- Pricing by time in broad or narrow increments of minutes, days, month
- Shareware knowledge
- Pricing by knowledge level/filtration/server processing
- Pricing by update frequency
- Institutional discounts
- Association membership discounts

Standard variables such as content, the audience, the author's demands, and the ongoing costs are now compounded by a potential for a wide variety of consumer desires unique to electronic publishing, such as print on demand or usage of portions or fragments of publications. The new demands on the producer may be:

- Development of support infrastructure
- Explanatory material
- Ethical choices regarding prices
- Acquisition strategy changes
- Rethinking of the "unit" (the book, periodical, etc.)
- Flexibility of production

- Direct relationship with customer
- Multiple intermediaries
- Subsidiary rights/contractual diversity
- Micro-royalty mechanisms

ART COLLECTIONS vs.
INDUSTRY COLLECTIONS

It is instructive to understand the differences between traditional cultural museums/archives and industrial collections. In museums individual objects are of value and increase in value over time, requiring stable long-term systems of asset management. Industry Archives are composed of individual objects, groups of objects, production artifacts, and marketing materials that can be of value depending on historic and market demands. Industry Archives require variable, flexible, scalable, strategic systems for asset evaluation and management.

An arts organization is unique in that it functions as a school, a museum, a library, a laboratory, and a fiduciary. It is public and private, academic and corporate in its management. It serves both the general public and a variety of highly specialized audiences, from art historians to the general public. It may give grants, sell products, and distribute products freely as a public service. The introduction of networked digital technology into the organization will affect internal and external communications, publishing, record keeping, accounting, financial services, and investing activities. The following partial list offers an example of the complexity and number of computing systems in an arts organization:

- General computers, servers, network and telecommunication systems
- Collections management systems
- Public kiosks
- Visitor reservations system
- Contact management and mailing list system
- Facilities work order management systems
- Human Resources Management Systems
- Financial Information Systems
- Library and collection management systems
- Specialized database systems
- Web browsers
- Image Collection Systems

- Subscription system
- Publication inventory and fulfillment systems
- Bookstore inventory systems
- Web e-commerce

At some point, most of these systems will need to communicate with each other in order to have an efficient means for cataloging, researching, producing, advertising, distributing, archiving, accounting, rights verification, revenue projection, licensing, and communication, both internally and externally. These systems will be the infrastructure of intranet, extranet, and Internet[4] use of digital publications.

SHAPING FORCES

Digital production appears to be shaped by eight forces, all of which are necessary to production and distribution. All of these forces seem to be constantly changing and shifting.

- **Concept:** Information design — the future of words and images in the digital domain. These are the creative factors that drive the initiation, development, and implementation of digital resources.
- **Product:** Editorial, time constraints, physical media limitations such as the capacity of a CD-ROM/DVD; non-physical media such as the Web, etc. These are the realities that constrain the form of the final product.
- **Accounting:** Capital and operating expenses, revenue, online subscription, license fees, budgeting for maintenance of digital material over time, etc. These are the constraints that determine the asset status and future re-purposing of digital assets.
- **Legal:** Intellectual property such as copyright, trademark, licensing agreements. These are the risk factors inherent in doing business as a digital producer.
- **Technical:** Software and hardware required, bandwidth limitations, future opportunities, etc. These are both the opportunities and the constraints inherent in free-market technology.
- **Archival:** Asset management, preservation, re-use, record keeping, etc. These are the long-term realities of committing assets to a digital form.
- **Transactional:** E-commerce, advertising, promotion, audience data gathering, etc. An ever-evolving electronic marketplace requires participation in order to gain competence.

- **User:** Audience, communication, relationship building, marketing, etc. These are the forces of individual choice, mass appeal, and asset value.

All of these forces make some kind of demand upon technical infrastructure, as well as shape the quality of the product. All of these forces have to be considered when creating and implementing information architecture as well as content. The forces must be integrated, both technically and conceptually, for successful production.

INTEGRATION OF FORCES

A brief look at the history and evolution of the *Bibliography of the History of Art* (BHA) and the *Thesaurus of Art and Architecture* (AAT) from print publications to electronic publications gives an interesting perspective on how electronic publishing has occurred at the Getty Center.

Cumulative reference works such as bibliographies and thesauri are naturals for the digital domain because they are works that are essentially never complete. Their contents accumulate from a variety of sources, and they are published at regular intervals. The BHA, for instance, was created in 1991 by merging two older bibliographies: the *Repertoire d'Art and Archeologie* (RAA) and the *International Repertory of the Literature of Art* (RILA)[5]. Both of these bibliographies continued to be in print until 1989. The BHA was begun as a print publication in 1991 and was still in print as of November 2000, when the final print edition (Volume 9) ended the print publication. The merged RILA and RAA as part of BHA began a parallel CD-ROM publication in 1991. This electronic version also became online resources with the Research Library Group (RLG) and Questel in France in 1996. The Getty and the French organization Institut National de l'Information Scientifique et Technique (INIST) of the Centre National de la Recherche Scientifique (CNRS) also became joint copyright owners of the BHA in 1991.

All of this is to point out that the BHA began as two print publications merged into a third print publication, which then took on a parallel electronic production that has now resulted in a quarterly CD-ROM edition of the BHA, two archival CD-ROMs of RILA and RAA, and online versions hosted by third party vendors with joint copyright held by French and American entities. The print component of the mix will be discontinued in favor of the CD-ROMs and online access to the material.

The production of the BHA CD-ROM had its editorial offices in Williamstown, Massachusetts. (This has since moved to the Getty Center in late

2000.) It does the data compilation at the Getty Research Institute in Los Angeles; data processing for the CD-ROM at Inforonics in Littleton, Massachusetts; the CD-ROM packaging at Getty Trust Publication Services in Los Angeles; the CD-ROM production coordination at Co-Operations in Portland, Oregon; the disc manufacturing at Sony in Oregon; and the distribution through the Getty Trust Publications warehouse in Calabasas, California. Although the entire process appears quite cumbersome, in the electronic publication world it is not unusual at all. In fact, over the years of its electronic incarnation, the process has been quite efficient and cost-effective. The BHA returns revenue from the CD-ROMs and online royalties are significant enough to cover CD-ROM production costs.

The process successfully accommodates all the forces that shape an electronic publication from concept to user. The BHA conforms to the force matrix:

- **Concept**: Large-scale bibliographic database for the study of the history of art
- **Product**: CD-ROM and online subscription
- **Accounting**: Capital publication, capital cumulative asset, sold and licensed
- **Legal:** Joint international copyright
- **Technical:** Based on software engine held jointly by publisher and vendor
- **Archival**: Cumulative update that can migrate to any digital media – currently CD-ROM and online access
- **Transactional:** CD-ROM subscription, third-party nonexclusive online license with royalties
- **User:** Well-established user base with good new user market opportunities — need for the publication and information never becomes dated

The *Art and Architecture Thesaurus* (AAT) celebrated its 10th anniversary in 1990 with the print publication by Oxford University Press. Development of the idea began in 1979-1980 and took 10 years to bring to press.[6] The thesaurus, like the bibliography, embraces the cumulative reference concept and collaborative authorship style that make it a natural for digital publication. It collects synonyms for describing works of art and architecture from a variety of international sources, vets the terminology, and establishes standard vocabularies. The decade after its inception witnessed the development of the microcomputer, the proliferation of online databases, and the beginnings of collection management software. This had an effect on the automation of art and architecture collections. From its beginning, the AAT was thought of as a standard vocabulary tool for the new electronic databases. The notion of a print version was somewhat secondary to the necessity for an electronic version. Researchers and scholars, in describing their work, had clearly articulated the problems:

- The agony of tracking down information when indexes are inadequate
- The difficulty of organizing visual and written information
- The threat of loosing information due to lack of certainty of what the information is called in different indexing systems
- The impossibility of finding what you need in unindexed archives[7]

The AAT first appeared as a three-volume print publication in 1990. In 1992 the *Authority Reference Tool* (ART) software was created to allow computer access to the data in the first edition. By the time the second edition was published in 1994, ART was improved to allow immediate access to the data, to make it easy to navigate through the thesaurus, and to make it possible to copy terms from the thesaurus to a database record. This last feature made the AAT a production tool as well as a reference tool.

ART was designed to run on PC-DOS or MS-DOS and was never updated for Windows 95 or Windows NT. Since 1996 it has not been very useful. Since 1997 the AAT has been available as a licensed download from the Getty website without any accompanying software. Licensees incorporate it into their own software applications or have an interface built for it. The AAT was also prototyped as a filtering agent for search engines in 1997-1998 and proved very successful as a way to narrow searches on the Internet. This last application has carried the AAT from a print publication to a computer application to an Internet browser to an Internet search enhancement. The *Art and Architecture Thesaurus* is a prime example of the way developments in technology parallel the utility of a cumulative reference literary form. If we apply the forces matrix to the AAT:

- **Concept:** Large-scale thesaurus for art and architecture terminology
- **Product:** Licensed download
- **Accounting:** Capital cumulative asset, licensed
- **Legal:** Getty copyright
- **Technical:** hierarchical text, no software
- **Archival:** Cumulative update that can migrate to any digital media — currently as ftp access
- **Transactional:** Nonexclusive license for sliding scale of fees

- **User:** Well-established user base with good new user market opportunities — including search engine market, need and information never becomes dated

The examples of the BHA and the AAT are important on many levels. They make the case that publishing does not mean books per se. Publishing means the shaping of content. Content created to perform in the constraints of the paper page may be freed by digital publishing to become not only new content, but a variety of new opportunities as well.

Both of these examples point to larger issues having to do with production. Digital transmittal, the integration of publication databases, online licensing, conversion of pre-press materials to a variety of formats, issues of digital workflow, archiving, re-purposing, dynamic publication catalogs, third-party agreements, and how to establish criteria for deciding what form a publication might take are all concerns that make managing aligning digital assets critical.

Production of digital assets may take place internally within an organization's IT group and may be done in cooperation with a number of design and research groups. A Digital Asset Services Group might review and comment on contracts, agreements, permissions, and licenses for distribution of electronic products as a responsibility of managing most fiscal aspects of a publications budget. Publication Services may, when appropriate, research and recommend third-party distribution opportunities such as licensing existing products to Internet content service providers.

Digital Asset Services could research and propose projects that will facilitate efficient infrastructure such as the electronic vendor transmittal system for moving manuscript materials to printers via the Internet, online licensing, or database integration projects.

Digital Asset Services could work closely with the intellectual property manager of a legal department to ensure that all digital products are properly registered and annotated.

THE FUTURE

One area that will be increasingly important to the future of digital asset production is an inventory of intellectual property rights for materials in electronic form. In its broadest implication, an intellectual property assessment generally means determining:

(1)   whether or not you have all the necessary rights to exploit an item in whatever venue or media you intend to use it (print, electronic, advertising, performance, etc.); and

(2)   whether or not you have taken or can take the necessary steps to adequately protect the item from unlawful use by others in current and future media.

The answers to these questions will depend, to a large extent, on the way an organization decides to use its intellectual properties. At this point, it is difficult even to estimate the scope or cost of this kind of review without knowing how complex the histories of the various properties are. A complete review might focus on the developers and/or creators of the items, their relationships to the organization at the time the items were acquired or developed (e.g., employees, contractors, or contributors, etc.), and the sort of agreements they have or had with the organization.

Some initial issue spotting could be done before a definitive plan was implemented. For instance, a sample of properties from the various parts of the organization could be looked into as a way to model the process. The range of intellectual property issues is broad and could include:

*   Publications
*   Public Affairs materials
*   Contemporary works
*   Web materials
*   Contracts
*   Licenses
*   Scholarly works
*   Agreements
*   Software
*   Library materials

Typically the process for developing successful communications architecture alignment involves intensive strategic planning including an asset inventory, a needs assessment, a thorough understanding of existing systems and practices, and an examination of data collection criteria. Planning and preparing reviews of standard vocabularies for describing assets, reviewing standards for continuity and longevity, understanding cross-media definitions, and applying insights into methods and practices are critical. Solutions require defining requirements and alignments and, in most cases, customization of systems and configurations.

POLICY FOR
INFORMATION ARCHITECTURE

Organizational information systems need to be interoperable, have consistent technical compatibility for future relationships, and develop a core of criteria for judging functionality. Resources for production, development, communication archiving, and accounting — both financial and intellectual property accounting — become increasingly dependent upon consistent overall technology architecture. Internal and external uses of digital material have effects upon intellectual property rights, storage and preservation of digital assets, leveraging advantages vis-à-vis Internet use, and the strategic long-term goals and mission of the organization. The organization's digital library and asset management systems, electronic publishing initiatives, image delivery systems, digital archives, and cumulative digital assets will need to be seen as threads that require careful management. New threads are constantly being added, such as Customer Relations Management systems (CRM).

When customer call centers began using software to collect data on each caller, computer telephony integration (CTI) became a business function. The logical extension of this became CRM (Customer Relationship Management) with the move of the CTI database information back into the organization. Managing relationships with customers is not a new idea, but the notion of a level of sales automation with CRM is irresistible. This means that information from the sales force could be retained and potentially used to guide product development. Costs are attached to integrating CRM systems with existing IT systems; aligning information architectures, and creating links to other digital assets, content, and rights management systems. Systems alignment and integration costs can be three to five times the costs of initial CRM licensing. CRM has to be thought of strategically rather than a repository for customer data. CRM is most effective when it wins new customers and retains existing ones. CRM can prompt sales people with information significant to customers needs and lifestyles, including dates and events that personalize the customer experience. Continuing Education departments at some universities are beginning to use CRM systems to track what courses students have taken and inform them of new offerings that may be of interest to their career directions. The notion that continuing education is "life-long learning" makes CRM an attractive tool for retaining students far into the future and keeping enrollment at peek levels. The education consumer is not a new idea for universities, but CRM makes it possible to communicate with students in a substantive way that provides the university with data on educational trends while encouraging brand loyalty from customers. The data that these CRM systems generate is invaluable in marketing campaigns and kept over long periods, can reveal potential sources of future revenue as well as guide institutional investment.

THE NEW PAST

With the advent of digital technology, the great variety of options open to creating content in different forms is constantly expanding. Asset production now includes knowledge of complex digital systems, electronic distribution, industry directions, and vision of future opportunities. This is especially true where highly sophisticated development requires that everyone involved must understand something about every aspect of a digital project — from the mission of the organization to the nature of source material as well as the quality of design, production, distribution, audience, and technology. The client and the service are merged by alignment in digital communication. The continuity of the resulting assets is rapidly becoming a new kind of digital currency.

ENDNOTES

[1]   In the 1980s the European-dominated International Standards Organization (ISO) began to develop its Open Systems Interconnection (OSI) networking suite resulting in the Basic Reference Model, or *seven-layer model*. (From *Connected: An Internet Encyclopedia*, www.freesoft.org/CIE).

[2]   From Michael Jensen, Director of Publishing Technologies for National Academy Press, 1997. Since Jensen's lecture at the Getty in 1997, ebrary, Inc., an electronic publisher associated with Adobe Systems, Inc., has begun (June 2000) to institute the micro-payment concept for accessing online materials by allowing users to copy parts of free documents for a minimum payments of 15 cents per page. Payment is made with the on-line equivalent of a phone card.

[3]   When databases provide human-free billing, the phone bill will drop even further.

[4]   Intranet for internal uses, Extranet for uses with external partners, collaborators, etc., and Internet for the global public.

[5]   RAA began in 1910 and gained the support of the CNRS in 1963 to become fully automated in 1973. The print edition was issued from 1910-

1990. RILA began in 1975 and merged with RAA in 1989. The print edition was issued from 1975-1989.

[6]   The 1994 second edition of the AAT is still available from Oxford University Press in five volumes for $395.00.

[7]   The J. Paul Getty Trust Bulletin (Fall 1987): 4-5, *Introduction to the Art and Architecture Thesaurus,* 2nd ed., "The History of the AAT," by Toni Petersen, 1994.

REFERENCES

Connected: An Internet Encyclopedia. At: www.freesoft.org/CIE.

Davis, B. H., & MacLean, M. (2000). *Time and Bits: Managing Digital Continuity.* Los Angeles: J. Paul Getty Trust Publications.

Getty Research Institute. (2002). *Art and Architecture Thesaurus.* Los Angeles: J. Paul Getty Trust Publications.

Getty Research Institute. (2002). *Bibliography of the History of Art.* Los Angeles: J. Paul Getty Trust Publications.

Petersen, T. (1994). The history of the AAT. *Introduction to the Art and Architecture Thesaurus.* 2d ed. Los Angeles: The J. Paul Getty Trust Bulletin.

Chapter XI

Analysis of Musical Content in Digital Audio

Simon Dixon
Austrian Research Institute for Artificial Intelligence, Austria

ABSTRACT

*Automatic analysis of digital audio with musical content is a difficult —
but important — task for various applications in computer music, audio
compression, and music information retrieval. This chapter contains a
brief review of audio analysis as it relates to music, followed by three
case studies of recently developed systems which analyse specific aspects
of music. The first system is BeatRoot, a beat tracking system that finds
the temporal location of musical beats in an audio recording, analogous
to the way that people tap their feet in time to music. The second system
is JTranscriber, an interactive automatic transcription system, which
recognises musical notes and converts them into MIDI format allowing
interactive monitoring and correction of the extracted MIDI data via a
multimedia interface. The third system is the Performance Worm, a real
time system for visualisation of musical expression, which presents in real
time a two-dimensional animation of variations in tempo and loudness.*

INTRODUCTION

The history of audio analysis reveals an intensely difficult, laborious, and error-prone task, where analysis tools have proved helpful but final measurements have been based mostly upon human judgement. Only since the 1980s has it become feasible to process audio data automatically with computers; and as it developed, audio content analysis took an important place in the emerging fields of computer music, audio compression, and music information retrieval. That the field is reaching maturity is evident from the recent international standard for multimedia content description (MPEG7), one main part of which relates to audio (ISO, 2001).

Audio content analysis finds applications in automatic indexing, classification, and content-based retrieval of audio data, such as in multimedia databases and libraries. It is also necessary for tasks such as the automatic transcription of music and for the study of expressive interpretation of music. A further application is the automatic synchronisation of devices such as lights, electronic musical instruments, recording equipment, computer animation, and video with musical data. Such synchronisation might be necessary for multimedia or interactive performances or for studio post-production work.

In this chapter, we restrict ourselves to a brief review of audio analysis as it relates to music, followed by three case studies of recently developed systems which analyse specific aspects of music. The first system is BeatRoot (Dixon, 2001a, c), a beat tracking system that finds the temporal location of musical beats in an audio recording, analogous to the way that people tap their feet in time to music. The second system is JTranscriber, an interactive automatic transcription system (Dixon, 2000a, b), which recognises musical notes and converts them into MIDI format, displaying the audio data as a spectrogram with the MIDI data overlaid in piano-roll notation. It allows interactive monitoring and correction of the extracted MIDI data. The third system is the Performance Worm (Dixon, Goebl & Widmer, 2002), a real time system for visualisation of musical expression. It presents in real time a two dimensional animation of variations in tempo and in loudness (Langner & Goebl, 2002).

BACKGROUND

Sound analysis research has a long history, which is reviewed quite thoroughly by Roads (1996). The problems that have received the most attention are pitch detection, spectral analysis, and rhythm recognition — areas which correspond respectively to the three most important features of music: melody, harmony, and rhythm.

Pitch detection is the estimation of the fundamental frequency of a signal, usually assuming it monophonic. Methods include time domain algorithms such as counting of zero-crossings and autocorrelation; frequency domain methods such as Fourier analysis and the phase vocoder; and auditory models, which combine time and frequency domain information based on an understanding of human auditory processing. Although these methods are of great importance to the speech-recognition community, there are few situations in which a musical signal is monophonic. This pitch detection, therefore, is less relevant in computer music research.

Spectral analysis has been researched in great depth by the Signal-processing community, and many algorithms are available which are suitable for various classes of signals. The short-time Fourier transform is the best known of these; but other techniques, such as wavelets and signal-specific time-frequency distributions, are also used. Building upon these methods, the specific application of automatic music transcription has a long research history (Moorer, 1975; Piszczalski & Galler, 1977; Chafe, Jaffe, Kashima, Mont-Reynaud, & Smith, 1985; Mont-Reynaud, 1985; Schloss, 1985; Watson, 1985; Kashino, Nakadai, Kinoshita, & Tanaka, 1995; Martin, 1996; Marolt, 1997, 1998; Klapuri, 1998; Sterian, 1999; Klapuri, Virtanen, & Holm, 2000; Dixon, 2000a, b).

Certain features are common to many of these systems: producing a time-frequency representation of the signal; finding peaks in the frequency dimension; tracking these peaks over the time dimension to produce a set of partials; and combining the partials to produce a set of notes. The differences between systems are usually related to the assumptions made about the input signal (for example the number of simultaneous notes, types of instruments, fastest notes, or musical style) and the means of decision making (for example heuristics, neural nets, or probabilistic reasoning).

The problem of extracting rhythmic content from a musical performance, and in particular finding the rate and temporal location of musical beats, has also attracted considerable interest in recent times (Schloss, 1985; Longuet-Higgins, 1987; Desain & Honing, 1989; Desain, 1993; Allen & Dannenberg, 1990; Rosenthal, 1992; Large & Kolen, 1994; Goto & Muraoka, 1995, 1999; Scheirer, 1998; Cemgil, Kappen, Desain, & Honing, 2000; Eck, 2000; Dixon, 2001a). Previous work had concentrated on rhythmic parsing of musical scores lacking the tempo and timing variations that are characteristic of performed music. In the last few years, however, these restrictions have been lifted; tempo and beat tracking systems have been developed, working successfully on a wide range of performed music.

Despite these advances, the field of performance research is yet to experience the benefit of computer analysis of audio; in most cases, general purpose signal visualisation tools combined with human judgement have been used to extract performance parameters from audio data. Only recently are systems being developed which automatically extract performance data from audio signals (Scheirer, 1995; Dixon, 2000a). The main problem in music signal analysis is the development of algorithms to extract sufficiently high level content from audio signals. The low level signal processing algorithms are well understood; but they produce inaccurate or ambiguous results, which can be corrected given sufficient musical knowledge (such as that possessed by a musically literate human listener). This type of musical intelligence is difficult to encapsulate in rules or in algorithms that can be incorporated into computer programs. In the following sections, three systems are presented, each taking the approach of encoding as much as possible of the intelligence within the software and presenting the results in a format that is easy to read and to edit via a graphical user interface (the systems can be used in practical settings). This approach has proved to be very successful in performance research (Goebl & Dixon, 2001; Dixon, Goebl, & Widmer, 2002; Widmer, 2002).

BEATROOT

Compared with complex cognitive tasks such as playing chess, beat tracking (identifying the basic rhythmic pulse of a piece of music) does not appear to be particularly difficult, as it is performed by people with little or no musical training who tap their feet, clap their hands, or dance in time with music. However, while chess programs compete with world champions, no computer program has been developed which approaches the beat tracking ability of an average musician. Recent systems, however, are approaching this target. In this section, we describe BeatRoot: a system which estimates the rates and times of musical beats in expressively performed music (for a full description see Dixon, 2001a, c).

BeatRoot models the perception of beat by two interacting processes: the first finds the rate of the beats (tempo induction), and the second synchronises a pulse sequence with the music (beat tracking). At any time, there may exist multiple hypotheses regarding each of these processes, which are modeled by a multiple agent architecture in which agents representing each hypothesis compete and cooperate to find the best solution. The user interface presents a graphical representation of the music and the extracted beats and allows the user to edit and recalculate results based upon the editing.

BeatRoot takes as input either digital audio or symbolic music data (such as MIDI). This data is processed off-line to detect salient rhythmic events, and the timing of these events is analysed to generate hypotheses of the tempo at various metrical levels. The stages of processing for audio data are shown in Figure 1, and will be described in the following subsections.

Onset Detection

Rhythmic information in music is carried primarily by the timing of the beginnings (onsets) of notes. For many instruments, the note onset can be identified by a sharp increase in energy in the frequency bands associated with the note and with its harmonics. For percussion instruments — piano, guitar and drums — the attack is sharp enough that it can often be detected in the time domain signal, making possible an extremely fast onset detection algorithm. This algorithm is based on the "surfboard" method of Schloss

Figure 1. System Architecture of BeatRoot

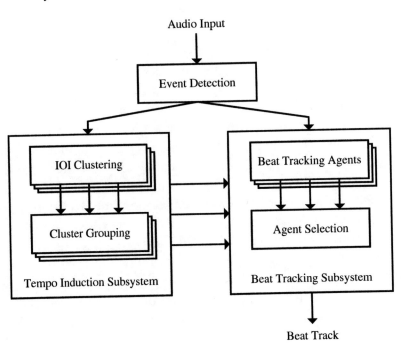

(1985), which involves smoothing the signal to produce an amplitude envelope and finding peaks in its slope using linear regression. Figure 2 shows the original signal with the smoothed amplitude envelope drawn in bold over it, with the peaks in the slope shown by dotted lines tangential to the envelope.

This method fails to detect the onsets of many notes that are masked by simultaneously sounding notes. Occasional false onsets are also detected, such as those caused by amplitude modulation in the signal. However, this is no great problem for the tempo induction and beat tracking algorithms, which are designed to be robust to noise. It turns out that the onsets which are most difficult to detect are usually those which are least important rhythmically; whereas rhythmically important events tend to have an emphasis which makes them easy to detect.

Tempo Induction

The tempo induction algorithm uses the calculated onset times to compute clusters of inter-onset intervals (IOIs). An IOI is defined as the time interval between any pair of onsets, not necessarily successive. In most types of music,

Figure 2. Surfboard Method of Onset Detection, Showing the Audio Signal in Light Grey, the Smoothed Signal (Amplitude Envelope) in Black, and the Detected Onsets as Dashed Dark Grey Lines

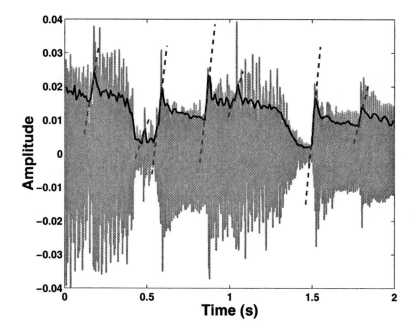

Figure 3. Clustering of Inter-Onset Intervals: Each Interval Between Any Pair of Events is Assigned to a Cluster (C1, C2, C3, C4 or C5)

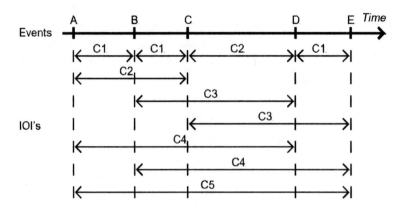

IOIs corresponding to the beat and simple integer multiples and fractions of the beat are most common. Due to fluctuations in timing and tempo, this correspondence is not precise, but by using a clustering algorithm, it is possible to find groups of similar IOIs which represent the various musical units (e.g., half notes, quarter notes, etc.).

This first stage of the tempo induction algorithm is represented in Figure 3, which shows the events along a time line (above) and the various IOIs (below) labelled with their corresponding cluster names (C1, C2, etc.). The next stage combines the information about the clusters by recognising approximate integer relationships between clusters. For example, in Figure 3, cluster C2 is twice the duration of C1, and C4 is twice the duration of C2. This information, along with the number of IOIs in each cluster, is used to weight the clusters, producing a ranked list of tempo hypotheses then passed to the beat tracking subsystem.

Beat Tracking

The most complex part of BeatRoot is the beat tracking subsystem, which uses a multiple agent architecture to find sequences of events which match the various tempo hypotheses and rates each sequence to determine the most likely sequence of beat times. The music is processed sequentially from beginning to end; and at any particular time point, the agents represent the various hypotheses about the rate and the timing of the beats up to that time and the predictions of the next beats.

Each agent is initialised with a tempo (rate) hypothesis from the tempo induction subsystem and an onset time. It begins with the first few onsets, which define the agent's first beat time. The agent then predicts further beats spaced according to the given tempo and the first beat, using tolerance windows to allow for deviations from perfectly metrical time (see Figure 4). Onsets that correspond with the inner window of predicted beat times are taken as actual beat times, stored by the agent and used to update its rate and phase. Onsets falling in the outer window are taken to be possible beat times, but the possibility that the onset is not on the beat is also considered. Any missing beats are then interpolated, and the agent provides an evaluation function which rates how well the predicted and the actual beat times correspond. The rating is based upon three factors: how evenly the beat times are spaced; how many predicted beats correspond to actual events; and the salience of the matched events, which is calculated from the signal amplitude at the time of the onset.

Various special situations can occur: an agent can fork into two agents if it detects that there are two possible beat sequences; two agents can merge if they agree on the rate and phase of the beat; and an agent can be terminated if it finds no events corresponding to its beat predictions (it has lost track of the beat). At the end of processing, the agent with the highest score outputs its sequence of beats as the solution to the beat-tracking problem.

Implementation

The system described above has been implemented with a graphical user interface, which provides: playback of the music with the beat times marked by clicks; a graphical display of the signal and the beats; and editing functions for correction of errors or selection of alternate metrical levels. The audio data can be displayed as a waveform and/or a spectrogram, and the beats are shown as vertical lines on the display (Figure 5).

Figure 4. Tolerance Windows of a Beat Tracking Agent After Events A and B Have Been Determined to Correspond to Beats

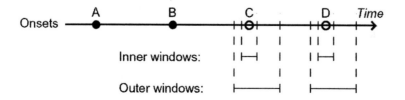

Figure 5. Screen Shot of BeatRoot Processing the First Five Seconds of a Mozart Piano Sonata, Showing the Inter-Beat Intervals in ms (Top), Calculated Beat Times (Long Vertical Lines), Spectrogram (Centre), WaveForm (Below) Marked With Detected Onsets (Short Vertical Lines) and the Control Panel (Bottom)

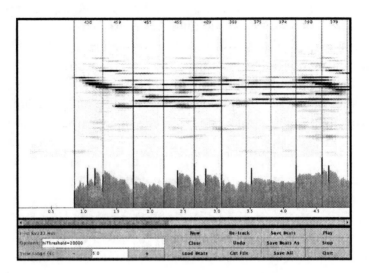

The main part of BeatRoot is written in C++ for the Linux operating system, comprising about 10,000 lines of code. The user interface is about 1000 lines of Java code. Although it would be desirable to have a cross-platform implementation (e.g., pure Java), this was not possible at the time the project was commenced (1997), as the JavaSound API had not been implemented and the audio analysis would have made the software too slow. Neither of these problems are significant now, so a pure Java version is in future plans. BeatRoot is open source software (under the GNU Public License) and is available from http://www.oefai.at/~simon/beatroot.

Testing and Applications

The lack of a standard corpus for testing beat tracking creates difficulty for making an objective evaluation of the system. The automatic beat tracking algorithm has been tested on several sets of data: a set of 13 complete piano sonatas, a large collection of solo piano performances of two Beatles songs, and a small set of pop songs. In each case, the system found an average of more than 90% of the beats (Dixon, 2001a) comparing favourably to another state of the art tempo tracker (Dixon, 2001b). Tempo induction results were almost always correct; so the errors were usually related to the phase of the beat, such as choosing beat onsets halfway between the correct beat times. Interested readers are referred to the sound examples at http://www.oefai.at/~simon.

As a fundamental part of music cognition, beat tracking has practical uses in performance analysis, perceptual modelling, audio content analysis (such as for music transcription and music information retrieval systems), and the synchronisation of musical performance with computers or other devices. Currently, BeatRoot is being used in a large scale study of interpretation of piano performance (Widmer, 2002) to extract symbolic data from audio CDs for automatic analysis.

JTRANSCRIBER

The goal of an automatic music transcription system is to create, from an audio recording, some form of symbolic notation (usually common music notation) representing the piece that was played. For classical music, this should be the same as the score from which the performer played the piece. There are several reasons why this goal can never be fully reached, not the least of which is that there is no one-to-one correspondence between scores and performances. That is, a score can be performed in different ways, and a single performance can be notated in various ways. Further, due to masking, not everything that occurs in a performance will be perceivable or measurable. Recent attempts at transcription report note detection rates around 90% for solo piano music (Marolt, 2001; Klapuri, 1998; Dixon, 2000a), which is sufficient to be somewhat useful to musicians.

A full transcription system is normally conceptualised in two stages: the signal processing stage, in which the pitch and timing of all notes is detected, producing a symbolic representation (often in MIDI format); and the notation stage, in which the symbolic data is interpreted in musical terms and presented as a score. This second stage involves tasks such as finding the key signature and time signature, following tempo changes, quantising the onset and offset times of the notes, choosing suitable enharmonic spellings for notes, assigning notes to voices in polyphonic passages, and finally laying out the musical symbols on the page. In this section, we focus only on the first stage of the problem: detecting the pitch and the timing of all notes or, in more concrete terms, converting audio data to MIDI.

Figure 6. Data Processing Steps in JTranscriber

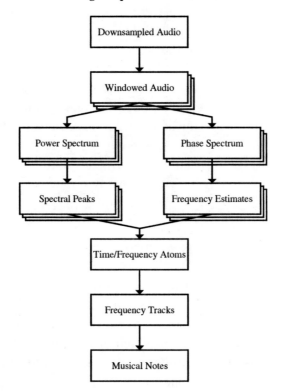

System Architecture

The data is processed according to Figure 6—the audio data is averaged to a single channel and downsampled to increase processing speed. A short time Fourier transform (STFT) is used to create a time-frequency image of the signal, with the user selecting the type, size, and spacing of the windows. Using a technique developed for the phase vocoder (Flanagan & Golden, 1966), which was later generalised as time-frequency reassignment (Kodera, Gendrin, & de Villedary, 1978), a more accurate estimate of the sinusoidal energy in each frequency bin can be calculated from the rate of change of phase in each bin. This is performed by computing a second Fourier transform with the same data windowed by a slightly different window function (the phase vocoder uses the same window shape shifted by one sample). When the nominal bin frequency corresponds to the frequency calculated as the rate of change of phase, this indicates a sinusoidal component (see Figure 7). This method helps to solve the problem of the main lobe of low frequency

Figure 7.   Rate of Change of Phase (Vertical Axis) Against FFT Frequency Bin (Horizontal Axis), with the Magnitude Spectrum Plotted Below to Show the Correlation Between Magnitude Peaks and Areas of Fixed Phase Change Across Frequency Bins

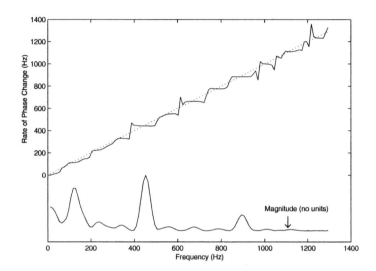

sinusoids being wider than a semitone in frequency, making it difficult to resolve the sinusoids accurately (see Figure 8).

The next steps are to calculate the peaks in the magnitude spectrum and to combine the frequency estimates to give a set of time-frequency atoms, which represent packets of energy localised in time and in frequency. These are then combined with atoms from neighbouring frames (time slices) to create a set of frequency tracks, representing the partials of musical notes. Any atom which has no neighbours is deleted, under the assumption that it is an artifact or part of the transient at the beginning of a note. The final step is to combine the frequency tracks by finding the most likely set of fundamental frequencies that would give rise to the observed tracks. Each track is assigned to a note; and the pitch, onset time, duration, and amplitude of the note are estimated from its constituent partials.

Implementation

An example of the output is displayed in Figure 8, showing a spectrogram representation of the signal using a logarithmic frequency scale labelled with the corresponding musical note names with the transcribed notes superim-

Figure 8. Transcription of the Opening 10s of the Second Movement of Mozart's Piano Sonata K.332 (The transcribed notes are superimposed over the spectrogram of the audio signal (see text). It is not possible to distinguish fundamental frequencies from harmonics of notes merely by viewing the spectrogram.)

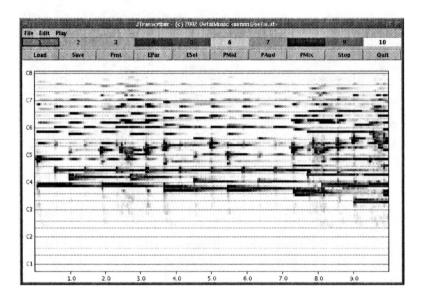

posed over the spectrogram in piano-roll notation. (The piano-roll notation is coloured and partially transparent; whereas the spectrogram is black and white, which makes the data easily distinguishable on the screen. In the grey-scale diagram the coloured notes are difficult to see; here they are surrounded by a solid frame to help identify them.) An interactive editing system allows the user to correct any errors made by the automatic transcription system, to assign notes to different voices (different colours), and to insert high level musical structure information. It is also possible to listen to the original and to the reconstructed signals (separately or simultaneously) for comparison.

An earlier version of the transcription system was written in C++; the current version, however, is being implemented entirely in Java, using the JavaSound API. Although the Java version is slower, this is not a major problem: the system runs at better than real time speed (i.e., a three-minute song takes less than three minutes to process on a 2GHz Linux PC). The advantages of using Java are shorter development time and portability, since the libraries used are platform independent.

Testing

The system was tested on a large database of solo piano music consisting of professional performances of 13 Mozart piano sonatas, or approximately 100,000 notes (Dixon, 2000a). These pieces were performed on a computer-monitored grand piano (Bösendorfer, SE290) and were converted to MIDI format. At the time of the experiment audio recordings of the original performances were not available, so a high quality synthesizer was used to create audio files using various instrument sounds.

The transcription system's accuracy was measured automatically by comparing its output to the original MIDI files. A simple formula combining the number of missed notes, falsely recognised notes, and played notes gave a percentage score on each instrument sound, which ranged from 69% to 82% for various different piano sounds. These figures show that approximately 10% to 15% of the notes were missed, and a similar number of the reported notes were false. (Some authors use a different metric, which would award the system 85% to 90% correct.)

The most typical errors made by the system are thresholding errors (discarding played notes because they are below the threshold set by the user, or including spurious notes which are above the given threshold) and octave errors (or more generally, where a harmonic of one tone is taken to be the fundamental of another, and vice versa). No detailed error analysis has been performed yet, nor has any fine tuning of the system been performed to improve on these results.

THE PERFORMANCE WORM

Skilled musicians communicate high level information such as musical structure and emotion when they shape the music by the continuous modulation of aspects such as tempo and loudness. That is, artists go beyond what is prescribed in the score, expressing their interpretations of the music and their individuality by varying certain musical parameters within acceptable limits. This is referred to as expressive music performance, and it is an important part of western art music, particularly classical music. Expressive performance is a poorly understood phenomenon, and there are no formal models which explain or characterise the similarities or differences in performance style. The Performance Worm (Dixon, Goebl, & Widmer, 2002) is a real-time system for tracking and visualising the tempo and the dynamics of a performance in an appealing graphical format, which provides insight into the expressive patterns applied by skilled artists. This representation also forms the basis for automatic recognition of performers' styles (Widmer, 2002).

The system takes input from the sound card (or from a file) and measures the dynamics and tempo, displaying them as a trajectory in a 2-dimensional performance space (Langner & Goebl, 2002). The measurement of dynamics is straightforward: it can be calculated directly as the RMS energy expressed in decibels, or by applying a standard psychoacoustic calculation (Zwicker & Fastl, 1999), the perceived loudness can be computed and expressed in sones. The difficulty lies in creating a tempo tracking system which is robust to timing perturbations yet responsive to changes in tempo. This is performed by an algorithm which tracks multiple tempo hypotheses using an online clustering algorithm for time intervals. We describe this algorithm and then the implementation and applications of the Performance Worm.

Real Time Tempo Tracking

The tempo tracking algorithm is an adaptation of the tempo induction subsystem of BeatRoot, modified to work in real time by using a fast online clustering algorithm for IOIs to find clusters of durations corresponding to metrical units. Onset detection is performed by the time domain surfboard algorithm from BeatRoot (see previous section), and IOIs are again used as the basis for calculating tempo hypotheses. The major difference is in the clustering algorithm, since it can only use the musical data up to the time of processing and must immediately output a tempo estimate for that time. Another difference from BeatRoot is that the Performance Worm permits interactive selection of the preferred metrical level.

The tempo induction algorithm proceeds in three steps after onset detection: clustering, grouping of related clusters, and smoothing. The clustering algorithm finds groups of IOIs of similar duration in the most recent eight seconds of music. Each IOI is weighted by the geometric mean of the amplitudes of the onsets bounding the interval. The weighted average IOI defines the tempo represented by the cluster, and the sum of the weights is calculated as the weight of the cluster.

In many styles of music, the time intervals are related by simple integer ratios, so it is expected that some of the IOI clusters also have this property. That is, the tempos of the different clusters are not independent, since they represent musical units such as half-notes and quarter-notes. To take advantage of this each cluster is then grouped with all related clusters (those whose tempo is a simple integer multiple or divisor of the cluster's tempo),

Figure 9. Screen Shot of a Weighted IOI Histogram and the Adjusted Cluster Centres (Shown as Vertical Bars with Height Representing Cluster Weight) for Part of the Song 'Blu-Bop' by Béla Fleck and the Flecktones (The horizontal axis is time in seconds, and the vertical axis is weight.)

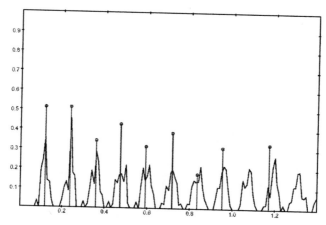

and its tempo is adjusted to bring the related groups closer to precise integer relationships.

The final step in tracking tempo is to perform smoothing so that local timing irregularities do not unduly influence the output. The 10 best tempo hypotheses are stored, and they are updated by the new tempo estimates using a first order recursive smoothing filter. The output of the tempo tracking algorithm is a set of ranked tempo estimates, as shown (before smoothing) in Figure 9, which is a screen shot of a window that can be viewed in real time as the program is running.

Implementation and Applications

The Performance Worm is implemented as a Java application (about 4,000 lines of code) and requires about a 400MHz processor on a Linux or Windows PC in order to run in real time. The graphical user interface provides buttons for scaling and translating the axes; selecting the metrical level; setting parameters; loading and saving files; and playing, pausing, and stopping the animation. A screen shot of the main window of the Worm is shown in Figure 10.

Apart from the real time visualisation of performance data the Worm can also load data from other programs, such as the more accurate beat-tracking data produced by BeatRoot. This function enables the accurate comparison of different performers playing the same piece in order to

Figure 10. Screen Shot of the Performance Worm Showing the Trajectory to Bar 30 of Rachmaninov's Prelude op.23 no.6 Played by Vladimir Ashkenazy (The horizontal axis shows tempo in beats per minute, and the vertical axis shows loudness in sones.)

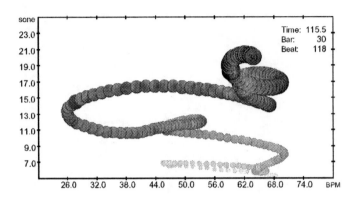

characterise the individual interpretive styles of the performers. Current investigations include the use of AI pattern matching algorithms to attempt to learn to recognise performers by the typical trajectories that their playing produces.

FUTURE WORK

A truism of signal analysis is that there is a trade-off between generality and accuracy. That is, the accuracy can be improved by restricting the class of signals to be analysed. It is both the strength and the weakness of the systems presented in this chapter that they are based on very general assumptions (for example, that music has a somewhat regular beat; and that notes are quasi-periodic, having sinusoidal components at approximate integer multiples of some fundamental frequency). In fact if these assumptions do not hold, it is even difficult to say what a beat-tracking or transcription system should do.

Many other restrictions could be applied to the input data regarding instrumentation, pitch range, or degree of polyphony, for example; and the systems could be altered to take advantage of these restrictions and produce a more accurate analysis. This has, in fact, been the approach of many earlier systems, which started from restrictive assumptions and left open the possibility of working toward a more general system. The problem with this approach is that it is rarely clear whether simple methods can be scaled up to solve more complex problems. On the other hand, fine tuning a general system by modules specialised for particular instruments or styles of music seems to hold a lot more promise.

Since the current systems are used primarily for performance research, it is reasonable to consider the incorporation of high-level knowledge of the instruments or the musical scores into the systems. By supplying a beat-tracking or performance analysis system with the score of the music, most ambiguities are resolved, giving the possibility of a fully automatic and accurate analysis. Both dynamic programming and Bayesian approaches have proved successful in score following such as for automatic accompaniment (Raphael, 2001). It is likely that one of these approaches will be adequate for our purposes.

A transcription system would also benefit from models of the specific instruments used or the number of simultaneous notes or possible harmonies. There are many situations in which this is not desirable; as an alternative we proposed (Dixon, 1996) a dynamic-modeling approach, where the system fine-tunes itself according to the instruments which are playing at any time.

CONCLUSION

Although it is a young field, analysis of musical content in digital audio is developing quickly, building on the standard techniques already developed in areas such as signal processing and artificial intelligence. A brief review of musical content extraction from audio was presented, illustrated by three case studies of state-of-the-art-systems. These systems are essentially based on a single design philosophy: rather than prematurely restricting the scope of the system in order to produce a fully automated solution, the systems make a fair attempt to process real world data and then to give the user a helpful interface for examining and modifying the results and steering the system. In this way, we are building research tools which are useful to a community that is wider than just other practitioners of musical content analysis.

ACKNOWLEDGMENTS

This work was supported by the START programme (project Y99-INF) of the Austrian Federal Ministry of Education, Science, and Culture (BMBWK). The Austrian Research Institute for Artificial Intelligence also acknowledges the basic financial support of the BMBWK. Special thanks to the Bösendorfer Company, Vienna, for some of the performance data used in this work.

REFERENCES

Allen, P., & Dannenberg, R. (1990). Tracking musical beats in real time. *Proceedings of the International Computer Music Conference,* (140-143). San Francisco, CA: International Computer Music Association.

Cemgil, A., Kappen, B., Desain, P., & Honing, H. (2000). On tempo tracking: Tempogram representation and Kalman filtering. *Proceedings of the International Computer Music Conference,* (352-355). San Francisco, CA: International Computer Music Association.

Chafe, C., Jaffe, D., Kashima, K., Mont-Reynaud, B., & Smith, J. (1985). Techniques for note identification in polyphonic music. *Proceedings of the International Computer Music Conference.* San Francisco, CA: International Computer Music Association, 399-405.

Desain, P. (1993). A connectionist and a traditional AI quantizer: Symbolic versus sub-symbolic models of rhythm perception. *Contemporary Music Review, 9,* 239-254.

Desain, P., & Honing, H. (1989). Quantization of musical time: A connectionist approach. *Computer Music Journal, 13*(3), 56-66.

Dixon, S. (1996). A dynamic modelling approach to music recognition. *Proceedings of the International Computer Music Conference,* (83-86). San Francisco, CA: International Computer Music Association.

Dixon, S. (2000a). Extraction of musical performance parameters from audio data. *Proceedings of the First IEEE Pacific-Rim Conference on Multimedia,* Sydney: University of Sydney (42-45).

Dixon, S. (2000b). On the computer recognition of solo piano music. *Mikropolyphonie, 6.*

Dixon, S. (2001a). Automatic extraction of tempo and beat from expressive performances. *Journal of New Music Research, 30*(1), 39-58.

Dixon, S. (2001b). An empirical comparison of tempo trackers. *Proceedings of the 8th Brazilian Symposium on Computer Music.* Brazilian Computing Society (832-840).

Dixon, S. (2001c). An interactive beat tracking and visualisation system. *Proceedings of the International Computer Music Conference,* (215-218). San Francisco, CA: International Computer Music Association.

Dixon, S., Goebl, W., & Widmer, G. (2002). Real time tracking and visualisation of musical expression. *Music and Artificial Intelligence: Second International Conference, ICMAI2002,* (58-68). Edinburgh, Scotland: Springer.

Eck, D. (2000). *Meter through synchrony: Processing rhythmical patterns with relaxation oscillators.* Doctoral dissertation, Indiana University, 2000.

Flanagan, J., & Golden, R. (1966). Phase vocoder. *Bell System Technical Journal, 45,* 1493-1509.

Goebl, W., & Dixon, S. (2001). Analysis of tempo classes in performances of Mozart sonatas. *Proceedings of VII International Symposium on Systematic and Comparative Musicology and III International Conference on Cognitive Musicology,* (65-76). Jyväskylä, Finland: University of Jyväskylä.

Goto, M., & Muraoka, Y. (1995). A real-time beat tracking system for audio signals. *Proceedings of the International Computer Music Conference,* (171-174). San Francisco, CA: International Computer Music Association.

Goto, M., & Muraoka, Y. (1999). Real-time beat tracking for drumless audio signals. *Speech Communication, 27*(3-4), 331-335.

ISO (2001). *Information Technology — Multimedia Content Description Interface — Part 4: Audio.* International Standards Organisation.

Kashino, K., Nakadai, K., Kinoshita, T., & Tanaka, H. (1995). Organization of hierarchical perceptual sounds: Music scene analysis with autonomous processing modules and a quantitative information integration mechanism. *Proceedings of the International Joint Conference on Artificial Intelligence.* Montreal, Canada: Morgan Kaufmann (158-164).

Klapuri, A. (1998). *Automatic transcription of music.* Master thesis, Tampere University of Technology, 1998.

Klapuri, A., Virtanen, T., & Holm, J.-M. (2000). Robust multipitch estimation for the analysis and manipulation of polyphonic musical signals. *Proceedings of the COST-G6 Conference on Digital Audio Effects.* Verona, Italy.

Kodera, K., Gendrin, R., & de Villedary, C. (1978). Analysis of time-varying signals with small BT values. *IEEE Transactions on Acoustics, Speech and Signal Processing, 26*(1), 64-76.

Langner, J., & Goebl, W. (2002). Representing expressive performance in tempo-loudness space. *Proceedings of the ESCOM 10th Anniversary Conference on Musical Creativity.* Liège, Belgium.

Large, E., & Kolen, J. (1994). Resonance and the perception of musical meter. *Connection Science, 6,* 177-208.

Longuet-Higgins, H. (1987). *Mental Processes.* Cambridge, MA: MIT.

Marolt, M. (1997). A music transcription system based on multiple-agents architecture. *Proceedings of Multimedia and Hypermedia Systems Conference MIPRO'97.* Opatija, Croatia.

Marolt, M. (1998). Feedforward neural networks for piano music transcription. *Proceedings of the XIIth Colloquium on Musical Informatics,* Gorizia, Italy: Associazione di Informatica Musicale Italiana (240-243).

Marolt, M. (2001). SONIC: Transcription of polyphonic piano music with neural networks. *Proceedings of the Workshop on Current Directions in Computer Music Research,* (217-224). Barcelona: Pompeu Fabra University.

Martin, K. (1996). A blackboard system for automatic transcription of simple polyphonic music. *Technical Report 385.* MIT: MIT Media Laboratory.

Mont-Reynaud, B. (1985). Problem-solving strategies in a music transcription system. *Proceedings of the International Joint Conference on Artificial Intelligence.* Los Angeles, CA: Morgan Kaufmann (916-919).

Moorer, J. (1975). *On the segmentation and analysis of continuous musical sound by digital computer.* Doctoral dissertation, Stanford University, 1975.

Piszczalski, M., & Galler, B. (1977). Automatic music transcription. *Computer Music Journal, 1*(4), 24-31.

Raphael, C. (2001). Synthesizing musical accompaniments with Bayesian belief networks. *Journal of New Music Research, 30*(1), 59-67.

Roads, C. (1996). *The Computer Music Tutorial.* Cambridge, MA: MIT Press.

Rosenthal, D. (1992). Emulation of human rhythm perception. *Computer Music Journal, 16*(1), 64-76.

Scheirer, E. (1995). *Extracting expressive performance information from recorded music.* Master thesis, MIT, 1995.

Scheirer, E. (1998). Tempo and beat analysis of acoustic musical signals. *Journal of the Acoustical Society of America, 103*(1), 588-601.

Schloss, W. (1985). *On the automatic transcription of percussive music:*

From acoustic signal to high level analysis. Doctoral dissertation, Stanford University, 1985.

Sterian, A. (1999). *Model-based segmentation of time-frequency images for musical transcription.* Doctoral dissertation, University of Michigan, 1999.

Watson, C. (1985). *The computer analysis of polyphonic music.* Doctoral dissertation, University of Sydney, 1985.

Widmer, G. (2002). In search of the Horowitz factor: Interim report on a musical discovery project. *Proceedings of the 5th International Conference on Discovery Science.* Berlin: Springer (13-32).

Zwicker, E., & Fastl, H. (1999). *Psychoacoustics: Facts and Models.* (2nd ed.) Berlin: Springer.

Chapter XII

Certain Aspects of Machine Vision in the Arts

Marc Böhlen
University at Buffalo, USA

ABSTRACT

This chapter attempts to consider the consequences of machine vision technologies for the role of the image in the visual arts. After a short introduction, the text gives a practical overview of image processing techniques that are relevant in surveillance, installation, and information art practice. Example work by practitioners in the field contextualizes these more technical descriptions and shows how computational approaches to digital imagery can radically expand the use of the image in the arts. A final note on possible future areas of investigation is included.

INTRODUCTION

The domain of the arts is wider today than is has ever been. The last decade has seen the appearance of activities in the arts previously reserved for science and engineering practices such as robotics, machine vision, data mining, and bioengineering. This chapter will discuss some conceptual, philosophical, and practical issues in machine vision as they apply to an extended art practice that blurs preconceived distinctions between engineering methods and artistic practice. This text is neither a treatise on machine vision[1] nor a history of automation of vision[2], nor concerned with issues of machine vision particular to human computer interaction[3]. This text is an attempt to place machine vision into a critical cultural context, and to show how machine vision allows for new forms of inquiries into imagery far beyond those of surveillance, and how machine vision used to extract information from image data changes the role of the image in the arts.

OVERVIEW

Our visual perception apparatus is so highly developed that we often equate what we see to a depiction of reality itself. Three color sensors, one each sensitive to the red, blue, and green spectra respectively, transduce together with intensity sensitive cells in the retina a curiously short interval of the electromagnetic spectrum into a data stream that our cerebral cortex discerns as objects in space. We have not always "seen" as we see today. Our visual apparatus evolved from less complex precursor sensory systems. Evidence that the human retina carries more than one copy of the middle wavelength sensitive cone ospin,[4] suggests that this development is not over. Tomorrow we may see things differently.

Early vision research began with investigations into amphibian visual perception[5]. Later research on the macaque monkey brain has shown that primate visual activity encompasses separate systems for visual perception and visual control[6]. In primates, vision is a dual system where one stream controls object recognition and another object-directed action[7]. While much of our understanding of primate vision comes from research on the level of neurobiology, much of what we know about human vision comes from physiological experimentation and case studies of pathologies. It is not clear how much of the low-level neurological findings in the macaque monkey and other primates actually apply to the human visual system. Nonetheless, there is evidence that this perception-action distinction is inherent in human vision as well[8].

Vision is more than sight. Much of the activity of the visual system has nothing to do with sight per se. The papillary light reflex and the visual control of posture[9] are examples of what is called reactive vision. Experience from everyday visual perception also confirms the assumption of two vision modalities in humans. The juggler can follow the trajectory of moving objects but cannot, and need not, remember particularities of these objects' appearances, while a few moments of viewing breathtaking scenery may be material for memories. Everyday experience further confirms a complex interweaving of these vision modalities. In the context of machine vision, gazing is a particularly interesting kind of seeing. It differs from watching, which is intentional and which anticipates, goal-oriented, an eventful action. Gazing is looking with no particular intention, a kind of removed surveying of events. The many forms of seeing are intimately linked to thinking; vision is meshed into the cognition process.

MACHINE VISION

A cultural paradigm shift occurred when automation reached into the realm of human perception. The automation of core involuntary perception processes we perform by biologic necessity turns the high regard attributed to sight since antiquity inside out.

Machine vision has many forms. X-ray, gamma ray, radar, sonar, and tomography are all methods of encoding spatial relationships by transducing atomic, electromagnetic, or sound energies. Radar and sonar, for example, map distance to an object by time of flight: the time it takes for a signal to be reflected from an object back to the point from which it was emitted. X ray, gamma ray, and radar are active where our sensory systems are blind and dumb. They are not limited to the bandwidth in which the human eye and ear operate.

Machine vision begins with capturing light energy and transducing light into electrical signals. All limitations and particularities of this initial sensing system modulate all processes following it. Computer vision generally deals with operations that follow image creation. Here, however, the terms will be used interchangeably. In this chapter, I focus on machine vision defined as the automation of vision processes that mimic the human visual system and operate in the same spectra as the human eye.

Parallel to the long term and possibly utopian end goal of strong artificial intelligence, the aim in machine vision is the full synthesis of human vision, the replacement of human seeing. Not surprisingly, the domains of machine vision and machine learning overlap and compliment each other. Machine vision systems today can robustly recognize faces and track automobiles. This success is a result of a marriage between findings in neurophysiology and computer science. It was David Marr's work[10] that laid the foundation for a computational approach to understanding vision. By grounding vision in the domain of mathematical information processing, Marr made available to vision research the general procedures of digital information applicable to any type of quanantized data. By abstracting the signal processing procedures from the locations in which they occur, the retina and brain, Marr laid the foundation for building artificial systems capable of synthesizing human vision-like perception. Marr's formulation takes into consideration the results from neurophysiology and maps vision primitives measured in amphibia[11] to primary operations. By Marr, such primitives combine to form the basis for higher and more evolved forms of seeing. Marr's approach begins with a 'primal sketch,' the most significant intensity changes in an image, followed by a '21/2 dimensional sketch' that delivers depth information, and a '3D representation' that includes object properties. The grand machine vision narrative Marr conceived has not fulfilled itself to date. Many high level visual processes and the link to thought and selective memory remain inaccessible to synthesis. Despite this, incremental but substantial progress has been made in solving particular problems in the automation of vision.

Interestingly, machine vision excels as some perception tasks while it fails at others humans perform effortlessly. Color constancy is an example in case. Color constancy describes the ability of the human visual apparatus to accommodate for changes in ambient lighting conditions when seeing color. To a human, a red apple always appears red, while machine vision systems cannot readily correct for color under varying ambient light. Because machine vision is very selective, it can miss much of the richness of visual information human beings enjoy through sight. In this regard, machine vision is a poor form of seeing, one that conveniently allows for certain types of precision but negates the existence of what it can not perceive.

CATEGORIES OF MACHINE VISION

There is no reason why artificial visual perception need be constructed along the example of human vision. However, the belief that our visual perception apparatus is a near-optimal solution to the problem of light capture and processing has lead vision research, from the first camera to current computer perception, to attempt to reconstruct key elements of human vision. Cameras are built to mimic the human eye. In the digital camera, the retina is typically replaced by a charge-coupled device that transduces the light energy impinging on the sensor into electrical signals. Quantization is necessary to map the continuous signal to discrete values. The result is a translation, a discrete map of the visual stimulus. One needs a useful data container to hold this information. One such suitable descriptor is the matrix, an ordered set of vectors. For the purpose of image manipulation, one can think of an image as a simple two-dimensional matrix, a table with rows and columns. Such an image matrix can be denoted as Im[i] [j], where Im is the image matrix, i the position of the row of a particular pixel and j, the column location of the same pixel. Each cell contains discrete information about the total image. Each of these ixj cells or pixels is encoded by n bits for color, intensity, and other properties. The density of the pixel arrangement defines the resolution of the image on the screen, the ratio of pixels per unit area. A 24bit per pixel color scheme, for example, reserves eight bits for each of the three colors red, blue, and green for all elements of the image matrix. By this scheme a simple color image is a multidimensional mathematical representation in which three dimensions or layers define color and two dimensions define location.

Matrices can be performed on by operations of linear algebra, such as subtraction, addition, multiplication, and division. Since images can be mapped as matrices, all operations defined on matrices can be applied to images. Of the many operations that linear algebra can perform on matrices, a subset is useful for image data.

The following section divides machine vision procedures into four main categories: fundamental operations on individual images, complex operations on individual images, fundamental operations on a sequence of images, and complex operations on a sequence of images. In each category some of the main ideas are discussed. The list is incomplete. It is only a subset of all known procedures, but can form a guideline for the uninitiated and a point of departure from which the interested reader may continue.

Fundamental Operations on an Individual Image

Fundamental operations on an individual image include geometric operations, color space operations and filtering.

Geometric operations include spatial transformations such as rotation, scaling, and translation of the image matrix. In all cases the approach is to multiply the original image matrix with the appropriate transformation matrix[12]. Rotation is achieved by multiplying the image matrix by a rotation matrix. The entries of the rotation matrix depend on the axis about which one rotates the object and the dimensionality of the space in which one rotates. For example, the rotation matrix that rotates an ellipse clockwise around its origin in the plane by the angle Θ, is the 3x3 matrix:

$R = [\cos(\Theta) \sin(\Theta) 0; -\sin(\Theta) \cos(\Theta) 0; 0\ 0\ 1]$.

Translation is similarly achieved by multiplying the image matrix by a translation matrix. In this example the matrix is:

$T = [1\ 0\ 0; 0\ 1\ 0; tx\ ty\ 1]$.

This results in a shift by tx in the x direction and ty in the y direction.

Color space operations alter the color components of an image; adding a constant to the R band of an RGB image results in a red shift. Some color operations require an image to be transferred into an alternate representation. An RGB image implicitly contains information about luminescence; as a property it is not directly available to linear operations. To change the luminescence of an RGB image, for example, it is necessary to map the image into the HSL (hue, saturation, luminescence) representation. This can be done through a multistep conversion algorithm[13]. Thereafter the brightness of an image can be altered directly by linear operations.

Filtering an image is achieved by convolution of the image matrix with a convolution kernel of appropriate size and weight. In the discrete case of a two dimensional convolution, the kernel itself is a matrix or mask, usually a few pixels wide. The convolution proper involves successive multiplication and summing of the convolution kernel with sections of the image, starting from the top left to the bottom right of the image. One can imagine the kernel as a small window sliding over the original image, operating on the respective overlapping area, only to be shifted in the next step. Smoothing or blurring is a typical convolution based filter. In order to smooth an image one convolves it with a particular mask that results in evening out the details. In such a mask, all entries are usually of the same value. Blurring is but a form of local averaging. The following 3x3 matrix could be used to smooth an image:

$B = [1/9\ 1/9\ 1/9; 1/9\ 1/9\ 1/9; 1/9\ 1/9\ 1/9]$

Convolution with this kernel can also be interpreted as a lowpass filter. It has the same effect as the removal of high frequency information and blurs the image. Different kernels have different effects when convolved with a given image. Image sharpening is the inverse of blurring. Here one chooses a mask in which the center values are much larger than those at the edge. A kernel that can be used to sharpen an image would be:

S = [-1 -1 -1; -1 9 -1; -1 -1 -1]

with a central value significantly larger (here nine times) than the others and opposite in sign.

Complex Operations on an Individual Image

The second category of operations comprises complex operations on an individual image. It contains, among others, methods of segmentation and pattern matching.

Segmentation is the process of distinguishing objects from the background in which they are set. Thresholding and edge detection are examples of segmentation operations.

Thresholding is the process of binning a large set of numbers into two or more categories based on a control or threshold value. Eight-bit grayscale images with values between 0 and 255 can be converted to binary black/white by thresholding all gray values into either white or black, depending upon whether they are more than or less than a given control value.

Edge detection is a problem of fundamental importance in image analysis. The human visual system is very sensitive to abrupt intensity changes and edges. Much effort has been placed into the synthesis of similar procedures in machine vision. Edges often characterize object boundaries. Synthetic edge detection makes use of this to delineate objects in the image matrix. This is a two-step process that comprises filtering and detection. Filtering is applied first to remove noise from the image. The detection component finds edges of objects in an image. Mathematically, this means finding local changes of intensity values in an image. In order to find such changes, one usually uses the first derivative or gradient of the image information as it assumes a local maximum at an edge. For an image $Im(x, y)$, where x and y are the row and column coordinates respectively, one typically considers the two directional derivatives or gradients. Local maxima of the gradient magnitude identify edges in $Im(x, y)$. These gradient matrices are formed by convolving the original image with appropriate kernels. One such kernel is the Sobel operator. The gradient in the x direction is created by convolving $Im(x, y)$ with:

Sx = [-1 0 1; -2 0 2; -1 0 1].

The gradient in the y direction is created by convolving Im(x, y) with:

Sy = [-1 -2 –1; 0 0 0; 1 2 1].

When the first derivative achieves a maximum, the second derivative is zero. For this reason, an alternative edge-detection strategy locates zeros of the second derivatives of Im(x,y). One well-known differential operator used in these so-called zero-crossing edge detectors is the Laplacian operator[14]. The results of a well-designed, robust edge detection algorithm yield visually pleasing results, at times with a similar sensitive delineation as a drawing by an accomplished draftsman.

Pattern matching requires objects and properties to be found first in a single image and then matched with similar findings in other images. Matchable properties include texture, color, geometric shape, and frequency components. The matching algorithm between images depends upon the properties to be compared. There is no universal, unique, and precise notion of similarity, particularly since similarity has both a quantitative and a qualitative aspect. Typically one contents oneself with a numeric representation of quantitative similarity. This is how one can imagine the process: Assume that representational features have been found in an image and that there are j features and i classes. The similarity S of the object with the i-th class is then given by:

$$S i = \Sigma(w j s j)$$

where w j is the weight for the j-th feature. The weight is selected based on the relative importance of the feature. The similarity value of the j-th feature is s j. The similarity S i is then the sum of all products of the weighted features times the corresponding similarity value.

The best similarity value is indicative of the feature of the image. Fitness or 'closeness' is usually translated into a distance measure. Least squares, correlation, and k nearest neighbor methods are commonly used to evaluate distance measures.

Fundamental Operations on Multiple Images

All of the methods discussed are described with regards to a single image. Applying such operations to a sequence of images allows one to find features that are not apparent in a single image. Some features become salient only when viewed in the context of other images.

The most important operation on sequential images is image differencing. It is a very simple procedure, computationally cheap and fast. This powerful method calculates the numeric difference between the matrix values of two images. For single band or binary images this gives a quick indication of change due to motion between two similar image frames[15]. Image differencing can be performed rapidly because subtraction as well as addition use few computation cycles, as opposed to multiplication- and division-based operations. Usually, sequential images are much more alike than different. In real time (30 frames/second) video streams, sequential images differ only slightly for many applications. The resultant difference information is much smaller, essential, and can be operated on much more efficiently. Because of these features, image differencing is the basis of motion segmentation and is often used as the basis for robust tracking algorithms. Tracking, in simple and complex forms, allows one to tally information over time, to log and to keep track of events. The diachronic nature of tracking gives a window into properties that single image analysis cannot reveal. With this, time becomes an image manipulation parameter.

Complex Operations on Multiple Images

In this category machine vision unfolds its full potential. For this text, the most important applications include object tracking and navigation. They are built to a large part upon the imaging primitives described earlier in this text.

Object tracking is the repeated finding of an object's location in sequential images. In tracking, an object must first be segmented from the background. Many methods can be applied to this end, but filtering and select feature detection are often part of it. From the result set the tracking algorithm must select a subset that fits a certain goal criteria such as geometric, texture, color properties, or feature factors. From this pruned result set, a tracking algorithm must then find the position of the sought objects in the image plane. This is often achieved by calculating the center of gravity of the result set. These procedures are then repeated for each image such that the goal object is continuously located in a steam of images. Applying such a tracking algorithm to a moving object results in a changing stream of x and y coordinates that indicate the path of the object across the image plane. To track an object over a field of view that is wider than the angle of the camera lens, the camera itself can be moved in sync with the object's projected path. Pan and tilt operations adjust for the motion of the target and are reactively based on feedback from the data stream of the moving object's position.

Navigation is a special kind of tracking. Usually one selects a few key features to extract and track from a video stream and uses this information in a feedback loop to control the heading of a vehicle. Speed is of essence is such procedures. Reaction time to change course must be accounted for in any navigation algorithm. Machine vision is generally susceptible to performance degradation under variable lighting conditions. In navigation, this can have dangerous consequences. For this reason, much care is given to adaptive processes that can dynamically adjust to change in ambient conditions, for example by varying color thresholds by neural networks[16].

Many more such derived operations on sequential images could be listed here. Many, such as optical flow from moving cameras and scene reconstruction in active vision are too involved to address in such a short survey[17]. Shape by motion detection, however, is interesting enough to mention. Shape by motion detection is an involved set of operations that reclaims from sequential images information on the shape of an object tracked and the relative motion of the camera. It requires prior knowledge in the form of estimations of shape and of motion. A two-stage approach is employed when applying shape from motion to video. In the first stage, two-dimensional point features are extracted and tracked though the image sequence. In the second stage, the resulting feature tracks are used to recover the camera's motion and the three-dimensional locations of the tracked points by minimizing the error between the tracked point locations and the image locations predicted by the shape and motion estimates[18].

All of these procedures operate on images that are captured from a single camera. It is also possible to apply them to image data from multiple cameras. In some cases, this delivers different information than is available from a single camera. Stereo vision, for example, employs two cameras in a fixed and calibrated configuration, just as our eyes are fixed in our eye sockets. With this, stereo can deliver distance information by measuring the disparity in simultaneous images from both cameras. Adding additional cameras adds further relevant information. Multiple view interpolation creates continuous scenes from single overlapping images.

BEYOND SURVEILLANCE

Earlier in this chapter, I singled out gazing from the many modes of human seeing. Actually, one can interpret machine vision as a kind of gazing. The machine vision camera must capture each image frame in totality before it can operate on it. There is no pre-selection of features and areas prior to image capture. The machine cannot see selectively. It is forced to see everything in its field of vision. Each entry into the image matrix must be filled before further operations can occur. Only after this will the numeric processing of the image data begin. This is in contrast to human vision that is more distributed and selective. The retina preprocesses image information and delivers to the cortex a subset and representation of the complete visual stimulus. As humans, we can voluntarily see selectively by focus of attention. That is the act of watching. But when humans gaze, they de-emphasize the early filtering, look with no imme-diate intention, and act very much as a machine must. Machine gazing and human gazing are similar in this regard. A gazing machine, however, is usually understood as a threatening machine since its resultant data is often recorded. The angst of surveillance is a construction of gazing and recording. If one removes the recording event from this process, surveillance becomes again a neutral gaze.

The next section describes work from practitioners who make use of machine vision in their work in a variety of ways. The focus is set not on conformance with standard procedures, but rather on understanding how artists interpret the results of machine vision processes as an expressive medium. In order to properly situate the use of machine vision in each of these pieces, short descriptions of the work beyond the topics of this text are included. As the reader progresses through the examples it will become clear how many of the above described procedures, and some not discussed here, become new methods of creating meaning and intention far beyond those of surveillance.

DAVID ROKEBY: SHOCK ABSORBER, 2001

Shock Absorber takes live feed from broadcast television and separates it into two parts in real time. One part contains all the movements, edits, and high frequency visual stimulation. Changes and movements are visible, but anything constant in the image is not seen. The other part contains everything that is left over after the movements and changes are removed. In this case, a cut becomes a slow cross-fade. Newscasters' bodies are solid, but their eyes and lips are blurred. Figure 1 shows an example of these two separated versions of a video feed.

This piece works from the insight that our brains build elaborate fictions as it constructs the images we see. Originally justified in the rational need for fast

Figure 1. Shock Absorber (courtesy David Rokeby)

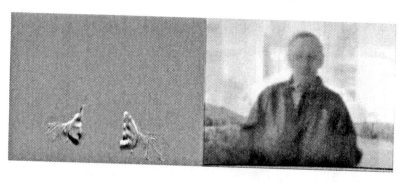

reaction and survival, seeing and social seeing have additional dimensions. For the artist, the television industry has developed a visual language that triggers the perceptual system in new ways. Changes and refinements are applied based on the feedback loop of the ratings mechanism. This work reacts directly to this new language and deconstructs its apparent cohesion it into two distinct readings, one nervous, agitated, and one barely moving and blurred into indistinction. This and related work leaves the content open. The artist describes this and related experiments as perceptual protheses. By this he means a work that the viewer looks through. Meaning is emergent with the realization of the altered perception process.

PAUL VANOUSE: THE RELATIVE VELOCITY INSCRIPTION ENGINE, 2002

The Relative Velocity Inscription Device (RVID) is a live scientific experiment using the DNA of a multiracial family of Jamaican descent. The experiment takes the form of an interactive, multimedia installation. The installation consists of a computer-regulated separation gel through which four family members' DNA samples slowly travel. Viewer interactions with an early eugenic publication within the installation allows access to historical precursors of this "race", while a touch-screen display details the results of this particular experiment.

The RVID is an assemblage of three different processes that have not previously been combined into a single apparatus in laboratory practice: Gel

Figure 2. Relative Velocity Inscription Device (courtesy Paul Vanouse)

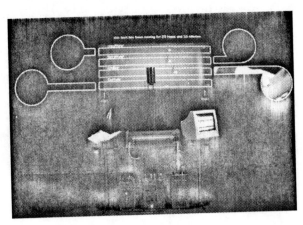

Electrophoresis, UV florescence imaging, and machine vision. Gel Electro-phoresis is a common laboratory procedure for both separating and sequencing DNA, which has been re-purposed in the RVID for racing DNA. Typically, a gel is "imaged" in a special, opaque cabinet that contains UV-light. The scientist then views the DNA bands through a camera (since the DNA glows orange when stained and bathed in UV-light, the camera blocks the harmful invisible UV-light from the eyes of the scientist.) The RVID is built from a combination of UV-emitting clear acrylic and UV-opaque clear acrylic to allow the UV light to make the DNA glow as the experiment runs, while protecting the viewer from the harmful UV-radiation.

The computer-controlled camera periodically grabs images of the glowing DNA, and machine-vision algorithms find each glowing sample. This last step is slightly difficult in the gallery context as background light levels change, the DNA florescence diminishes over time, and the coherence of a DNA band is reduced over long periods (two days) in the gel. The machine vision algorithm runs as follows: First, search the camera image for pixels containing the highest intensity orange values. Then, sort these pixels into groups of adjacent pixels. Then, evaluate which of these groups are brightest and have expected size and shape characteristics to determine the position of each DNA sample. It is through these steps that the software is able to determine the positions of samples at all points in the race and determine the winning sample at the end of each race. Here, machine vision is a neutral observer of a race of races.

STEVE MANN: DECONFERENCE, 2002

This exhibit attempts to demonstrate how we have become interdependent upon technological extensions of the mind and body, and hence, to some degree, have taken a first step to becoming cyborgs. The exhibit also attempts to show how authorities might view the cyborg being as a threat, therefore requiring that it be stripped of these extensions. The cyborg body, whether by way of a wearable computer, or by pens, pencils, portable data organizers, shoes, clothing, eyeglasses, and other personal effects, is potentially contaminated, and thus requires cleansing.

DECONference was conceived as a probe into society, to understand the culture and the technology of mass decontamination. In the exhibit, decontami-

Figure 3. Image of the Infrared Sensor Array (courtesy Steve Mann)

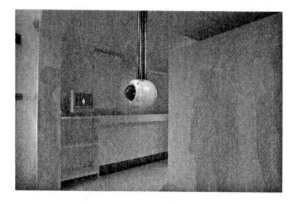

Figure 4. Screen Capture from the Body Scanner (courtesy Steve Mann)

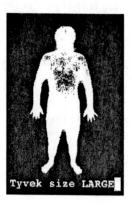

nation was deconstructed by literally building a futuristic mass decontamination facility, as might form the entrance to a space station or airport of the future, or as an entranceway into a high security government building or industrial facility such as a factory. In such a future world, an alleged need for cleanliness might also be used as justification for a mass decontrabanding (including a search of personal belongings).

Initially all persons entering a "clean facility" are assumed to be potentially contaminated. Since it is not known which if any of these persons are guaranteed to be free of contaminants, everyone must undergo decontamination. One of the many procedures contaminees are exposed to, includes automated prefab uniform measurement. This is achieved with a body scanner, comprised of an infrared sensor array and a DEC Alpha supercomputer. It calculates all body dimensions, and computes the optimal design for a uniform. This information can then be used to either custom-tailor a uniform, or to select from a fixed stock of pre-made uniforms. In this exhibit, the uniforms are all pre-made of white Tyvek.

The extracted body metrics of height, girth, and shoulder width reduce contaminees to a standardized metric and expose them to efficient control. This work employs computer vision, performance, and street theatre tactics to create a forced scenario of authoritarian population control. It is a warning sign. Security and control demand a price: freedom of mind and body.

MARC BÖHLEN: THE OPEN BIOMETRICS PROJECT, 2002

The Open Biometrics Project and its Keeper is an access granting machine and data management system that utilizes finger scanning and pattern matching techniques to challenge hard and fast classification of biometric data[19]. Of all biometric validation techniques, finger print classification is the most established and entrenched in law enforcement throughout the world. New imaging technologies replace the fingerprint with the digital finger scan, and use computational similarity measures to match one scan to another. The Keeper makes use of this technical knowledge and differs in its interpretation of it. The Keeper has a defined policy of data acquisition and retention, and a particular conception of biometric-based uniqueness.

The Keeper operates in different modes at different times. During normal business hours the Keeper acts as a functional and reliable gatekeeper to an area of restricted access. It employs the standard biometric validation scheme

Figure 5. CAD of the Keeper of the Open Biometrics Project (courtesy Marc Böhlen)

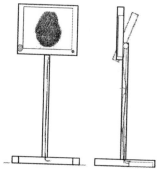

of data acquisition, feature extraction, feature comparison, and classification. The scanner can capture a high-resolution image of a fingerprint from a hand desiring access to a given room. The minutiae points, essential features traditionally understood to uniquely characterize each and every finger, are extracted from the image and certified by the system. The minutiae template is then compared with templates of finger scans previously accepted by the Keeper. As opposed to claiming clarity and ultimate authority, the result set of a finger scan from the Keeper is a list of probable results. By including the calculated likelihood together with the result proper, the machine acknowledges the probabilistic nature of data classification and prints this information as a probabilistic ID card (see Figure 6). At night, the Keeper gives the data

Figure 6. Probable Minutiae of Finger Scan, Certified by the Keeper (courtesy Marc Böhlen)

autonomy and group identities based on the results from the scan work. Rejected scans are of particular interest to the Keeper. But whatever investigations the machine may make at night, the data is discarded after 24 hours. Data deletion is programmatically inscribed into the system.

Machine vision is used in multiple ways: to capture finger scans, to extract characteristic minutiae points, and to manipulate the scan data. The feature extraction algorithm finds the same characteristic features a human fingerprint expert might find. But the goal of the Keeper is not efficiency. As biometric identification becomes commonplace, the Open Biometrics Project and its Keeper call for re-evaluating the limits of automated decision making. The Keeper cracks open the normally closed and newly automated classification process and acts as an open-ended interpretation device of biometric data records. Here, machine vision techniques challenge hard and fast one-way classifications for which biometric-based validation may be misused.

MACHINE VISION AS A METHOD OF PERCEPTUAL INTERVENTION

A common denominator runs through the works described above. They all challenge the viewer to rethink what they see and to ponder the chain of seeing, thinking, believing and behaving. It is easier to understand this development from a more removed vantage point.

In the arts, the history of automated vision is long and complex. Visual representation is a core creative act, exemplified in ancient Greek history by the legendary Xeuxis, whose painted grapes are said to have appeared so realistic that birds flew by to eat them. The desire to encode reality created the need for tools and methods to facilitate the task. The craft of making brushes and preparing pigments, and the formulation of the perspectively-encoded third dimension that began almost 1,000 years ago with Alhazen and continued in the early Renaissance in Italy with Giotto, Alberti and Masaccio, have all contributed to the automation of vision by the machine.

The last 150 years saw radical additions to this endeavor. Photography, film, cybernetics, and military research redefined the distinction between mimesis and visual perception. Machine vision can be seen as yet another step in the desire to organize visual data: automation principles of the early 20th century carried into visual perception. In this context the image becomes data and information. Image creation becomes data processing and all data processing tools become potential image manipulation operations. Appreciation of automated vision in the arts is often limited to the compositing of visual information. By this I mean the composition of image elements and the filtering and manipulation of global image properties. The well-know image enhancement application Photoshop is an example of image-processing software that operates on this level. The Renaissance goal of pictorial representation of reality terminates in Photoshop-like image processing since any object can be seamlessly added or removed from an image. Pictorial veracity is no longer a given. But machine vision allows yet more forms of intervention into visual data. Images can be mined for meaning. Now, images can be queried for content in color, text, and object classification — hence recognition and extraction of meaning. For the first time in the history of pictorial representation and perception, semantics can be extracted from an image by a machine. The data mining of streaming images changes the role of the image in visual culture in a fundamental way. The depth of meaning extractable from images is still shallow compared to human visual intelligence capabilities. The redefinition of mimesis in pictorial representation due to automation and insights from neurobiology and computer science described above extend the discussion of visual representation into the domain of practical philosophy. The use of imaging techniques that see differently is a technical catalyst to thinking differently about seeing. Machine vision can be used as a tool to question the epistemology upon which habitual vision is based and functions thus as a method of practical philosophy or intervention into the unconscious processes of perception. This is a new type of inquiry in the arts. However, it is important to understand that machine vision is very limited. Precision is no substitute for interpretation and accuracy is not related to truth. The convenience of machine vision techniques is seductive.

WHAT LIES AHEAD

Here, only a glimpse of what we might expect in the near future.

The urge to see, to interpret, and to know everything will drive machine vision development in the future. It is not unreasonable to assume that one will soon be able to register and access everything a human being might see in his/her life through synthetic vision. Furthermore, we can expect very high (>500 frames/second) capture and processing speeds from large numbers of networked high definition cameras to redefine the notion of "real-time" image processing. Nothing will be left unseen. One can expect artists to react differently from scientists to these new possibilities.

Parallel to the increase in bandwidth we can expect significant developments in recognition and classification techniques. Researchers at the University of Sussex[20], for example, are investigating the possibility of predicting
crowd behavior based on observations from simple surveillance cameras.
Together with phenomenal data mining[21], which seeks to find phenomena that
give rise to relationships in datasets beyond the apparent relationships themselves, automated prediction may become a contested area of investigation for
machine vision artists.

And this is just the beginning.

ENDNOTES

[1]   There is an extensive bibliography on machine vision in general. The
interested reader can start at the Computer Vision Homepage of Carnegie
Mellon University: http://www-2.cs.cmu.edu/~cil/v-pubs.html or the
Compendium of Computer Vision at the School of Informatics of the
University of Edinburgh: http://www.dai.ed.ac.uk/CVonline/

[2]   Issues particular to computer graphics and automation of perspective are
discussed in Manovich's text (see bibliography)

[3]   Pentland and Cipolla (1998)

[4]   Rowe (1997)

[5]   Lettvin et al. (1959)

[6]   Ungerleider and Mishkin (1982)

[7]   Goodale and Humphrey (1998)

[8]   Goodale and Humphrey (1998)

[9]   Goodale and Humphrey (1998)

[10]   Marr (1982)

[11]   Lettvin et al. (1959)

[12]   Detailed descriptions of all the matrix operations mentioned here can be
found in Strang's text (see bibliography).

[13]   Foley and Dam (1982)

[14]   A discussion of the particularities of the Laplacian and other operators are
beyond the scope of this essay. For details see Jain, Kasturi and Schunck
(1995)

[15]   Negative numbers are clamped to zero

[16]   Chen (1998)

[17]   Faugeras et al. (1998)

[18]   Strelow et al. (2001)

[19]   KK is created with the help of Richard Pradenas, JT Rinker and Nicolas Canaple

[18]   Troscianko et al. (2001)

[20]   McCarthy (2000)

REFERENCES

Böhlen, M. (2002-2003). *Keeper of Keys.* International Symposium of Electronic Arts in Nagoya Japan, 2002, and the Symposium on Language and Encoding at the University of Buffalo, 2002.

Chen, S. (1998). *Learning-based vision and its application to autonomous indoor navigation.* Doctoral dissertation, Michigan State University, 1998.

Davies, E. (1990). *Machine Vision: Theory, Algorithms and Practicalities.* Academic Press.

Faugeras, O., Robert, L., Laveau, S., Csurka, G., Zeller, C., Gauclin, C., & Zoghlami, I. (1998). 3-d reconstruction of urban scenes from image sequences. *Computer Vision and Image Understanding, 69*(3), 292-309.

Foley, J., & van Dam, A. (1982). *Fundamentals of Interactive Computer Graphics.* Addison Wesley.

Goodale, M., & Humphrey, K. (1998). The objects of action and perception. *Cognition, 67,* 181-207.

Jain, R., Kasturi, R., & Schunck, B. (1995). *Machine Vision.* McGraw-Hill.

Lettvin, J.Y., Maturana, H.R., McCulloch, W.S., & Pitts, W.H. (1959). What the frog's eye tells the frog's brain. *Proceedings Inst. Radio. Eng 47* (1940-1951).

Mann, S. (2001). *Intelligent Image Processing.* John Wiley & Sons.

Mann, S. (2002). *DECONference.* Performance, September 2002 at the Decon Gallery, Toronto.

Manovich, L. (2001). Modern surveillance machines: Perspective, radar, 3-d computer graphics and computer vision. In T. Y. Levin (Ed.), *Rhetorics of Surveillance: From Bentham to Big Brother.* Karlsruhe: *ZKM/* Zentrum für Kunst und Medientechnologie and Cambridge, MA: *MIT.*

Marr, D. (1982). *Vision.* W.H. Freeman and Company.

McCarthy, J. (2000). *Phenomenal Data Mining: From Data to Phenomena.* Stanford University.

Pentland, A., & Cipolla, R. (1998). *Computer Vision for Human-Machine Interaction.* Cambridge University Press.

Rokeby, D. (2001). *Shock Absorber*. Justina M. Barnicke Gallery Toronto 2001 and the Art Gallery of Hamilton, Canada.

Rowe, M. (1997). *The evolution of color vision*. The Talk Origins Archive.

Shapiro, L., & Stockman, G. (n.d.). *Computer Vision*. NY: Prentice-Hall.

Strang, G. (1986). *Introduction to Applied Mathematics*. Wellesley-Cambridge Press.

Strelow, D., Mishler, J., Singh, S., & Herman, H. (2001). *Extending Shape-From-Motion to Noncentral Omnidirectional Cameras*. Pittsburgh, PA: Carnegie-Mellon.

Troscianko, T., Holmes, A., Stillman, J., Mirmehdi, M., & Wright, D. (2001). Will they have a fight? *European Conference on Visual Perception. Perception, 30*, 72-72. Pion Ltd.

Vanouse, P. (2002). *The Relative Velocity Inscription Engine*. Henry Gallery Seattle, and International Symposium of Electronic Arts in Nagoya Japan, 2002.

About the Authors

John DiMarco is a teacher, trainer, consultant, and graphic artist who has 10 years experience in digital art, design, marketing, and graphic communications. Professor DiMarco is an assistant professor of Digital Art and Design & Interactive Multimedia at the C.W. Post Campus of Long Island University (USA) and has taught at Nassau Community College and SUNY Old Westbury. He strives to educate new and experienced artists and teachers on how to teach computer graphics and multimedia. Using personal experiences and five years of on-the-job research, Professor DiMarco has developed a systematic approach to teaching computer graphics and multimedia. In addition, he writes coursework, teaches, lectures, solves problems, and provides cross platform expertise on issues involving prepress, printing, multimedia, training, and marketing communications. Professor DiMarco has a wide range of experience teaching college level graphic art and multimedia within community college, a state university, a private institution, and graduate and undergraduate programs. John has trained art directors and managers for organizations including: Estee Lauder, SONY Music, Ademco, PriceWaterhouseCoopers, Heartbeat of The City (a TV show in LA), SUNY Farmingdale, Yellow Book, SUNY Old Westbury, Long Island University, Integrated Business Systems, Old Bethpage/Plainview Schools, and Cablevision. Professor DiMarco holds a Multi-Discipline Master's Degree in Digital Art & Design and Marketing from Long Island University - C.W. Post, a Bachelor's Degree in Communication/Public Relations from the University at Buffalo, and an Associates Degree in Business Administration from SUNY Farmingdale. He is currently working on curriculum development and instructional design projects in the digital imaging systems division of the Sales Training Group at Canon, USA

* * *

Robert Barone's PhD was conferred in September of 1996 by the State University of New York at Buffalo Department of Electrical Engineering. His dissertation, *Quasi-Factorization of Floquet's Characteristic Equation in the Case of Reflection Symmetry*, is a theorem and a proof. Upon graduation he instructed community college and then simultaneously worked in wireless communications, designing antenna-combining systems. He left the industry for full-time teaching and is, at the time of this writing, a member of the Computer Information Systems Department at Buffalo State College. His varied interests include jazz, wave phenomena, and Internet technologies.

Marc Böhlen makes machines that reconfigure expectations toward automation processes. After graduating from the Robotics Institute at Carnegie Mellon, he was on the faculty at the University of California and the Center for Research and Computing in the Arts, both in San Diego, and is currently a faculty member at the University of Buffalo in the Department of Media Study (USA). He has presented papers and exhibited artwork nationally and internationally including at the New York Digital Salon, the Andy Warhol Museum, the American Association for Artificial Intelligence (AAAI), the Association for Computing Machinery (ACM), and the Institute for Electrical and Electronics Engineers (IEEE). Recent work has been featured at the iMAGES International Film Festival Toronto 2002, ISEA2002 in Nagoya, the APEX Gallery in New York, Version3.0 at the Art Institute of Chicago 2003, and the International Garden Festival of Grand-Métis, Reford Gardens Québec 2003.

Marion Cottingham completed her BSc in Computer Science at the University of Glasgow (1981). She developed a strong interest in computer graphics during her honors year. She continued working in the graphics area while employed as a programmer for an oil company. She returned to Glasgow in 1983 and began research into ray tracing and CAD systems. Her doctoral thesis is on how to generate acceptably realistic CAD images efficiently. Marion emigrated to Australia in 1986, taking up a lectureship at Monash University. She joined UWA in mid-1989. Marion is the author of eight books on topics including visual basic for developers.

Ben Howell Davis is principal consultant, Davis International Associates (www.digitalcontinuity.com), a digital asset solutions provider focused on strategic planning for long-term digital continuity. Formerly, he was senior scientist and strategic director for Media and Entertainment, Razorfish, Inc. (2000); manager of Communications, Getty Information Institute; and manager of Electronic Publications, Getty Trust Publication Services, Los Angeles, CA. Davis came to the Getty Center in 1995 from the Massachusetts Institute of Technology were he was a research associate, manager of the AthenaMuse Software Consortium at the Center for Educational Computing Initiatives (MIT/CECI), and manager of the Project Athena Visual Computing Group, which developed distributed multimedia technology. He was also an instructor at the MIT Media Lab, a fellow at the MIT Center for Advanced Visual Studies, and a lecturer in the MIT Visual Arts Program. His publications include art and technology reviews for *Scientific American Magazine*; *Time and Bits: Managing Digital Continuity* (available on Amazon.com), Getty Publications; and *When Everything Learns*, Razorfish Publications (available as a PDF at http://www.digitaleverything.com/ wheneverythinglearns2.pdf).

Simon Dixon studied Computer Science (first class honors and university medal, 1989) at the University of Sydney (Australia), and continued his studies there with a PhD (1994) in the area of Artificial Intelligence (belief revision). During his undergraduate studies he also obtained the AMusA and LMusA in classical guitar. He then worked as a lecturer in Computer Science at Flinders University of South Australia, during which time he started research on computer music. In 1999, he moved to Vienna to work on the project "Computer-Based Music Research: Artificial Intelligence Models of Musical Expression" at the Austrian Research Institute for Artificial Intelligence.

Linda Emme has a BS and MFA in Photo-Illustration, Motion Graphics, and New Media. University of Wisconsin, Art Center College of Design; California Institute of the Arts. Digital imaging, photo-illustration, and motion graphics. Her clients include Warner, Forsythe Marcelli Johnson, Amgen, KCET, CNN, UCLA, Disney, iNSCAPE, Interactive Arts, La Salsa, Converse, Pacific Communications, Allergan, and many others. She has been on the faculty of the Art Center College of Design since 1990 and also taught at the American Film Institute. She worked with fractal guru Ken Musgrave at Yale on visual communication in computer graphics and studied with Marguerite Wildenhain, the first woman potter trained at the Bauhaus. Her awards include an Emmy Award for "The Great War" and ACCD Faculty Enrichment Award.

Jianping Fan received an MS degree in Theoretical Physics from Northwestern University, China, in 1994, and the PhD degree in Optical Storage and Computer Science from the Shanghai Institute of Optics and Fine Mechanics, Chinese Academy of Sciences, China, in 1997. From 1998 to 1999, he was

JSPS researcher at the Department of Information Systems Engineering, Osaka University, Osaka, Japan. From 1999-2001, he was a visiting scholar at the Department of Computer Science, Purdue University, West Lafayette, IN, USA. He is now an assistant professor with the Department of Computer Science, University of North Carolina at Charlotte (USA). His research interests include adaptive video coding, video analysis, video indexing, error correction codes, and nonlinear systems.

Kevin H. Jones has degrees from Virginia Commonwealth University, the University of Texas at Austin, and Yale University. Kevin works as a designer and artist blurring the distinction between these two fields. In his studio work, he has been focusing on interactive installations that investigate our understanding of the physical world and its laws. Kens has exhibited throughout the US, Europe, and Asia; and his work has been featured in *ID Magazine*, *idea Magazine* (Japan) and *The New York Times*. Kevin is currently an assistant professor of Digital Design at the University of Oregon (USA).

Helen Purchase is senior lecturer in the Computing Science Department at the University of Glasgow, where she is a member of the Glasgow Interaction Systems research group. Her PhD research was conducted at the University of Cambridge in the area of Intelligent Tutoring Systems. Helen's current research interests include information visualization, empirical studies of human comprehension of graph layouts, and the effective application of graph-layout algorithms to software engineering diagrams. The research reported in her chapter was conducted while she was at the School of Information Technology and Electrical Engineering, University of Queensland.

Mark Snyder, EdD, is an associate professor in the Graphic Communications Department at Clemson University, South Carolina (USA). Dr. Snyder teaches prepress, flexographic printing, lithographic printing, screen printing, color management, and professional courses. He earned a Bachelor of Science from Millersville University of Pennsylvania, a Master of Arts from Eastern Michigan University, and an Educational Doctorate in Vocational and Technical Education from Virginia Polytechnic Institute and State University.

Karl Steiner is an assistant professor of Computer Science at the University of North Texas (USA). He has both a research and professional background in human-computer interaction, with particular interests in intelligent interfaces, virtual environments, and narrative. Dr. Steiner received his PhD in Computer

Science from the University of Illinois at Chicago. In addition to supervising research-oriented efforts, Dr. Steiner has also consulted on many industry projects. His design work has been recognized with a number of industry awards, and he has been a frequent speaker at local and national design-oriented events.

Jing Xiao is a professor of Computer Science, the University of North Carolina at Charlotte (USA). She received her PhD in Computer, Information, and Control Engineering at the University of Michigan, Ann Arbor, Michigan (1990). Her research interests cover intelligent systems, in general, and span robotics, computer vision, and artificial intelligence. They also include spatial/geometric reasoning, planning, and computation in robotics; physical simulation and haptics; learning and classification. Dr. Xiao also works in optimization with evolutionary computation and other heuristic methods.

Xingquan Zhu received his MS in Communication and Electronic Systems from Xidian University, Xian, China (1998), and a PhD in Computer Science from Fudan University, Shanghai, China (2001). He is currently a researcher at the Department of Computer Science, Purdue University, West Lafayette (USA). Before he joined Purdue, he previously spent four months with Microsoft Research, Beijing, China, where he was working on relevance feedback for image indexing and retrieval. His research interests include data mining, information retrieval, multimedia processing, video database, and multimedia systems.

Index

NEW from Idea Group Publishing

- **The Enterprise Resource Planning Decade: Lessons Learned and Issues for the Future**, Frederic Adam and David Sammon/ ISBN:1-59140-188-7; eISBN 1-59140-189-5, © 2004
- **Electronic Commerce in Small to Medium-Sized Enterprises**, Nabeel A. Y. Al-Qirim/ ISBN: 1-59140-146-1; eISBN 1-59140-147-X, © 2004
- **e-Business, e-Government & Small and Medium-Size Enterprises: Opportunities & Challenges**, Brian J. Corbitt & Nabeel A. Y. Al-Qirim/ ISBN: 1-59140-202-6; eISBN 1-59140-203-4, © 2004
- **Multimedia Systems and Content-Based Image Retrieval**, Sagarmay Deb ISBN: 1-59140-156-9; eISBN 1-59140-157-7, © 2004
- **Computer Graphics and Multimedia: Applications, Problems and Solutions**, John DiMarco/ ISBN: 1-59140-196-86; eISBN 1-59140-197-6, © 2004
- **Social and Economic Transformation in the Digital Era**, Georgios Doukidis, Nikolaos Mylonopoulos & Nancy Pouloudi/ ISBN: 1-59140-158-5; eISBN 1-59140-159-3, © 2004
- **Information Security Policies and Actions in Modern Integrated Systems**, Mariagrazia Fugini & Carlo Bellettini/ ISBN: 1-59140-186-0; eISBN 1-59140-187-9, © 2004
- **Digital Government: Principles and Best Practices**, Alexei Pavlichev & G. David Garson/ISBN: 1-59140-122-4; eISBN 1-59140-123-2, © 2004
- **Virtual and Collaborative Teams: Process, Technologies and Practice**, Susan H. Godar & Sharmila Pixy Ferris/ ISBN: 1-59140-204-2; eISBN 1-59140-205-0, © 2004
- **Intelligent Enterprises of the 21st Century**, Jatinder Gupta & Sushil Sharma/ ISBN: 1-59140-160-7; eISBN 1-59140-161-5, © 2004
- **Creating Knowledge Based Organizations**, Jatinder Gupta & Sushil Sharma/ ISBN: 1-59140-162-3; eISBN 1-59140-163-1, © 2004
- **Knowledge Networks: Innovation through Communities of Practice**, Paul Hildreth & Chris Kimble/ISBN: 1-59140-200-X; eISBN 1-59140-201-8, © 2004
- **Going Virtual: Distributed Communities of Practice**, Paul Hildreth/ISBN: 1-59140-164-X; eISBN 1-59140-165-8, © 2004
- **Trust in Knowledge Management and Systems in Organizations**, Maija-Leena Huotari & Mirja Iivonen/ ISBN: 1-59140-126-7; eISBN 1-59140-127-5, © 2004
- **Strategies for Managing IS/IT Personnel**, Magid Igbaria & Conrad Shayo/ISBN: 1-59140-128-3; eISBN 1-59140-129-1, © 2004
- **Beyond Knowledge Management**, Brian Lehaney, Steve Clarke, Elayne Coakes & Gillian Jack/ ISBN: 1-59140-180-1; eISBN 1-59140-181-X, © 2004
- **eTransformation in Governance: New Directions in Government and Politics**, Matti Mälkiä, Ari Veikko Anttiroiko & Reijo Savolainen/ISBN: 1-59140-130-5; eISBN 1-59140-131-3, © 2004
- **Intelligent Agents for Data Mining and Information Retrieval**, Masoud Mohammadian/ISBN: 1-59140-194-1; eISBN 1-59140-195-X, © 2004
- **Using Community Informatics to Transform Regions**, Stewart Marshall, Wal Taylor & Xinghuo Yu/ISBN: 1-59140-132-1; eISBN 1-59140-133-X, © 2004
- **Wireless Communications and Mobile Commerce**, Nan Si Shi/ ISBN: 1-59140-184-4; eISBN 1-59140-185-2, © 2004
- **Organizational Data Mining: Leveraging Enterprise Data Resources for Optimal Performance**, Hamid R. Nemati & Christopher D. Barko/ ISBN: 1-59140-134-8; eISBN 1-59140-135-6, © 2004
- **Virtual Teams: Projects, Protocols and Processes**, David J. Pauleen/ISBN: 1-59140-166-6; eISBN 1-59140-167-4, © 2004
- **Business Intelligence in the Digital Economy: Opportunities, Limitations and Risks**, Mahesh Raisinghani/ ISBN: 1-59140-206-9; eISBN 1-59140-207-7, © 2004
- **E-Business Innovation and Change Management**, Mohini Singh & Di Waddell/ISBN: 1-59140-138-0; eISBN 1-59140-139-9, © 2004
- **Responsible Management of Information Systems**, Bernd Stahl/ISBN: 1-59140-172-0; eISBN 1-59140-173-9, © 2004
- **Web Information Systems**, David Taniar/ISBN: 1-59140-208-5; eISBN 1-59140-209-3, © 2004
- **Strategies for Information Technology Governance**, Wim van Grembergen/ISBN: 1-59140-140-2; eISBN 1-59140-141-0, © 2004
- **Information and Communication Technology for Competitive Intelligence**, Dirk Vriens/ISBN: 1-59140-142-9; eISBN 1-59140-143-7, © 2004
- **The Handbook of Information Systems Research**, Michael E. Whitman & Amy B. Woszczynski/ISBN: 1-59140-144-5; eISBN 1-59140-145-3, © 2004
- **Neural Networks in Business Forecasting**, G. Peter Zhang/ISBN: 1-59140-176-3; eISBN 1-59140-177-1, © 2004